COP LIVING ON THE EDGE

Jon "Scott" Haroldsen

ISBN 978-1-956010-72-5 (paperback)
ISBN 978-1-956010-73-2 (hardcover)
ISBN 978-1-956010-74-9 (digital)

Copyright © 2021 by Jon "Scott" Haroldsen

All rights reserved. No part of this publication may be reproduced, distributed, or transmitted in any form or by any means, including photocopying, recording, or other electronic or mechanical methods without the prior written permission of the publisher. For permission requests, solicit the publisher via the address below.

Rushmore Press LLC
1 800 460 9188
www.rushmorepress.com

Printed in the United States of America

NON-DISCLAIMER

ALTHOUGH I HAD NUMEROUS NEAR-DEATH experiences as a Denver police officer, after leaving the department, I had quite a few more. Several times, I was actually dead. I worked in construction, where I had several close calls! Even when I was a scoutmaster for years, I had several near-death experiences; one of which was on the Grand Teton Mountain.

I am now 74 years old, but most of the time, I feel like I'm in my mid-50s. When I started writing this composition, I never pictured making it into a book, but several people who read the first chapter said it's a real page-turner, and they couldn't wait to read more stories! All of the stories in this book are true, and some of them are almost unimaginable.

Although the title is "Cop Living on the Edge," after leaving the police department, I still have been living on the edge.

TRAINING BUREAU STAFF

DIRECTOR OF TRAINING
AND EDUCATION
Captain L. Disbracoff

COMMANDING OFFICER
Lieut. P. J. O'Hayre

ASST. COMMANDING OFFICER
Sgt. J. L. O'Shea

TRAINING OFFICERS
Tech. D. A. Carr
Tech. G. L. Gosage
Tech. A. M. Hutchison
Det. C. L. Lombard
Det. N. L. Walton

SECRETARY
Betty Abbott

REFRESHMENTS
Courtesy of Denver Police Protective Association

DENVER POLICE DEPARTMENT

POLICE RECRUIT CLASS
72 — 2

COMMENCEMENT EXERCISES

November 17, 1972 — 2:00 P. M.

Junior Police Building
2105 Decatur Street

CERTIFICATES PRESENTED TO

Francis Amitrano
Robbi N. Arnold
Robert C. Bickhard
Ronald L. Blair
Raeburn D. Bontz
Philip H. Booker
Ralph R. Bravo
Joe R. Brown
Daniel F. Cameron, Jr.
David W. Dixon
George A. Everitt
Joseph A. Garcia
Eugene E. Gold
Jon S. Haroldsen
Freddie A. Herrera
Carole C. Hogue
George H. Johnson
Alfred E. Koger
Miriam S. Lupfer
James E. Malone
Alexander P. Martinez

Charles A. Martinez
Douglas R. Mauler
James C. Nuanes
Robert A. Ortiz
Thomas M. Ortiz
Paul E. Owens, Jr.
Jay S. Pieratt
Richard J. Polak
Michael H. Pytlinski
Evelyn L. Rehberg
Steven Reyes
Stephen A. Robbins
Daniel D. Rubin
Roger L. Sealy
Steven C. Shott
Welles E. Tonjes
Ronald P. Torres
Frederick R. Walsh
Myron R. Wasinger
William A. Westerdahl
Richard D. Whetstone

PROGRAM

Detective N. L. Walton, Presiding

PLEDGE OF ALLEGIANCE ------- Pat. Daniel Rubin

CLASS SPOKESMAN ----------- Pat. Jon Haroldsen

PRESENTATION OF CERTIFICATES

RECEPTION FOLLOWING

GUESTS

Honorable William H. McNichols, Mayor
Dan Cronin, Manager of Safety
Honorable City Councilmen
Art G. Dill, Chief of Police
Rev. Raymond N. Jones, Catholic Chaplain
Dr. William H. Mackintosh, Protestant Chaplain
Rev. William H. Magill, Chaplain
Civil Service Commissioners:
Jesse Manzanares, Houston "Hoot" Gibson, Ted Bach

BOOK I

COP LIVING ON THE EDGE

1

GUN IN MY FACE

Getting the kids ready for church was always a real challenge. My wife and I would look all over the house to find their shoes, and even matching socks were hard to find. Since I worked every Sunday, I had my police uniform put away in a safe place. I got them all dressed before I put on my outfit with my gun, mace, handcuffs, and nightstick. I felt very safe and confident with my wife and kids in tow when we arrived at church. I always had my uniform dry cleaned with the pants and shirt pressed and looking brand new. I would polish my boots, my leather Sam Brown gun belt, my brass buckle, and of course, my badge. There never was one day that I didn't look forward to going to work. I thrived on the action in such a crime-filled city. My wife used to feel a little uncomfortable with me in my police uniform and me having a gun in the chapel. She finally got used to it and was happy that I loved my job.

It was a beautiful fall Sunday when we went to church. Once a month, we were asked to fast two meals and take the money that we would've spent on the food and give it to help the poor and the needy. It was always hard for me to go twenty-four hours without eating. Fixing breakfast for the kids made it even harder. This particular time, I decided I would fast and just knew that the Lord would bless me for my effort. I left church early and said goodbye to my wife and kids and headed to the district station. I've always had this unusual thing I do when I'm driving somewhere. I pray out loud. I remember saying I felt that the Heavenly Father was going to bless me this day to keep me safe. Then I said out loud, "And maybe he'll help me make a good arrest!" I remember that when I said that, I thought it did not seem like the right thing to say in a prayer.

I got to the district station and lined up for a roll call. Because they were short of officers, the sergeant asked me, "Officer Haroldsen, would you mind working solo?" I usually was accompanied by a training officer, but I was excited that I was going to be able to work by myself. Because I was going to be solo, I could go wherever I wanted to and cover whatever calls came out on the radio.

Once I got in the police car, I headed out to my assigned area. I was a little disappointed because the areas I was assigned to work in had a low crime rate. I had been driving only for ten or fifteen minutes and was hoping for a little excitement when I saw a car run a stop sign right in front of my police car. The driver of the car looked right at me and sped down the road with me close behind him. I turned on the overhead lights and siren, and at first, he started to accelerate, but after going about three blocks, he slowed down, made a right turn, and stopped right in front of a big Catholic church.

Up to this point, my training officer would advise me of all the right steps that I should take. I forgot to call in the license plate and description of the car and the location where I was making the stop. I was walking up to his car when I heard a voice say softly, "Look out; this guy could hurt you!"

I turned around to see who had said it and there was no one there. I remember thinking I needed to pay attention and not be distracted by anything. I took a couple more steps towards the car and heard the same words, "Look out; this guy could hurt you!"

Once again, I looked behind me, and there was no one there. I looked in the backseat of the car as I approached the driver and saw kids' toys and several colorful buckets with toys on top, and some of them had lids. Some zipped closed bags appeared in the backseat and looked like they were stuffed with toys. Even the back window ledge was covered with toys. I thought to myself, *This looks like a family man, and maybe, I won't write him a ticket.* I had my hand on my gun when I approached the driver's door. The window was down about five or six inches, and the driver had both hands on the steering wheel with his driver's license between two fingers. He handed me his driver's license through the open window without saying a word. Just as I was turning to go back to the police car to run an ID check, I turned back to the driver and said, "Willey Walter Cordoba, have you been arrested before?"

He replied, "Yeah!"

I asked him, "What for?"

He said back to me, "You name it!"

I said, "No, you name it!"

He rattled off a list of numerous felonies and then added, "I just got out of jail on bond for stabbing a man twenty-one times in the chest in Longmont, Colorado!" He didn't say that he was just arrested for stabbing a man, but he just admitted to me that he had stabbed a man.

I immediately said, "Mr. Cordoba, step out of the car this very instant!" He didn't reply or even look at me. As I reached down to open the door, he quickly slammed down the lock.

I then reached through the open window to unlock the door, and he ran the power window up and almost caught my arm.

It was a beautiful sunny fall day with leaves falling from the trees onto the car and the road. The sun was shining very brightly on his window, and I had a hard time seeing what he was doing in the car. However, I did see him bring his hands off the steering wheel down between his legs, and he brought up a pearled-handled automatic and aimed it right at my head. I quickly drew my 357 and pointed it at his head against the window. I saw his finger pull the trigger, but the gun misfired! Just as I was pulling the trigger on my revolver, I felt something pulling on my pant leg. I looked down and saw a boy about eight years old looking up at me, and he said, "Mr. policeman, are you going to shoot that man?"

I had the thought flash through my head that I was going to fire my gun, and it was going to ricochet off the window and kill this boy! I then turned and started to run back to my police car to call for help. It was not until at that point that I realized there were hundreds of people surrounding the vehicle and were watching my every action. The people had just come out of the church.

Reaching the door of my cruiser in a panic, I threw it open, grabbed the mic, and called the dispatcher! With a very emotional loud voice, I said, "A man with a gun just tried to kill me, and I need backup immediately!"

I then saw Mr. Cordoba carefully taking off his jacket and putting it in his car, leaving the door open, and walking back to my police car with his hands in the air! I quickly threw the mic down on the seat and started to get out of the car when I heard the dispatcher ask for my location. I quickly grabbed the mic and told the dispatcher I didn't know where I was, but there was a large Catholic church on the corner. The dispatcher started to ask me more questions, but I had to get out of the car because Mr. Cordoba was standing right outside the door with his hands in the air. I threw the mic down and jumped out of the car and got Mr. Cordoba spread eagle on my police car. I did everything right as I was trained in the police academy. I had my one leg in front of his leg, so if he tried to move, I could quickly get him to fall onto the car. I had him pulled way out from the car so that if he moved, I could slam his head down against the car and get him handcuffed.

His muscles were all tensed up, and he was big and powerful, and I had my gun in the middle of his back, and I was just getting ready to handcuff him when I heard a voice say, "Put your gun away!"

I had a flashback to my FBI training course, where I learned that most police officers are killed by their own weapons. I carefully switched the barrel of my gun with my finger and holstered my weapon. As I reached down to get my handcuffs, I heard a voice say, "Button your gun holster!" Without hesitation, I snapped my holster close.

As I brought the handcuffs up towards his wrist, he somehow instantly pushed himself off the police car and pushed me off balance, kicking me in the chest with such power it sent me flying backward.

The fight was on, and before I knew it, we were next to his car, and he got up on my shoulders, riding me piggyback; he pulled me towards the open door and grabbed his jacket. I knew that he was going after his gun! I used every bit of strength I had, knowing that I could easily be killed because of his almost superhuman strength, and he now had a gun. Although I managed to get him off my back, he grabbed my gun and started trying to pull it out of the holster. He was pulling so hard with such force to my Sam Brown belt that he was lifting me into the air. In a flash of movement, he slammed me down on my back on the road and began to pummel me with his fists. When I landed on the asphalt road, it knocked the wind out of me, and I could hardly breathe.

I then heard the most beautiful sound in the world—the siren of a backup police cruiser coming to my aid. I saw the officer jump out of his car, and as he was running towards me, his boot came off, and he was hopping along, trying to pull it on his foot. I remember thinking I am about to be killed here, and you're worried about your stupid boot! When the backup officer arrived, that gave a boost to my adrenaline. I somehow managed to flip over and slam Mr. Cordoba down on the pavement and started to pound on him. The backup officer came up to me and said, "Stop! Everybody is watching!"

I then realized that I had forgotten about the hundreds of people that were around watching. This was not a fight like you might see on television, where two people are punching each other like boxers. We were grabbing each other, trying to rip the other person apart. Cordoba was trying to break my neck and crush my ribs, and I was trying to gouge out his eyes.

After a real struggle, even though the backup officer was a big guy, we finally got the handcuffs on Mr. Cordoba. An older lady stepped from the crowd towards us and reached down and picked up a pair of broken glasses that Mr. Cordoba had been wearing. She shoved them in the face of my backup officer. She yelled at him, "Do you know what it's like not to be able to see because your glasses are broken?"

We both looked at each other and her and were both bewildered. He then reached down and grabbed the gun that was sticking out underneath the jacket and shoved it up in her face and said, "No, I don't know what it's like not to be able to see because I don't wear glasses. But I sure as blank know what it's like to get shot with one of these!" He then ripped his shirt open, sending the buttons flying, and thrust his stomach out, revealing a massive scar from gunshot wounds to his belly.

We grabbed Cordoba and lifted him into my police cruiser. My partner then drove the green Mercury down the road, and we stopped a couple of blocks away to look in the car. Mr. Cordoba gave us verbal permission to search his vehicle. The buckets and bags in the backseat were packed full of drugs, all packaged and ready to sell. We took Cordoba into the narcotics bureau for booking. When I brought all the drugs into the narcotics detectives, they were very impressed with the haul. They nicknamed me "Supercop Haroldsen."

They said it in a way that was kind of sarcastic and tauntingly funny. The life-changing lesson I learned from this life-threatening experience was always to pay attention to the whisperings of the spirit because Supercop Haroldsen is way more super when he listens to the spirit.

Cops: 1. Bad guy: 0.

CORDOVA, William Walter
5-10 150lbs. Hzl. Brn.
1591 Hooker St.
DOB 2-18-53 DPD #175222

Numerous arrests for Agg.
Rob. and Theft.
Is an active member of the
Crusade for Justice.

DENVER POLICE DEPARTMENT
COMMENDATORY LETTER

From: _____Vice/Drug Control_____ Date March 30, 1974
_____Division - District - Bureau_____

Recognition is hereby given to ___Officer Jon Haroldson___ ,serial number___72-33___ ,

who is presently assigned to ___District One___ ,

for the following described activity: _On December 2, 1973 Officer Haroldson, working_

solo, stopped one William W. Cordova for driving through a stop sign

at 44th and Vrain St. Officer Haroldson, upon approaching Cordova's

car, observed a small revolver between Cordova's legs. Cordova refused

to exit the car and Haroldson radioed for help. At this time Cordova

exited his vehicle and a struggle ensued as Cordova attempted to re-

enter same. Covering Officers arrived to assist Haroldson and

Cordova was arrested. A search of his person divulged, not only the

revolver, but two baggies of marijuana. A search of the vehicle

divulged a diaper bag in the rear containing twenty-three baggies of

marijuana. This arrest led to the confiscation of 300 grams marijuana

and filing of Felony Possession of Narcotics for Sale against Cordova.

Officer Haroldson is to be commended for his alertness and devotion

to duty in a situation that placed great hazard to his well being.

Submitted By: J. E. McCormick, Sergeant 50-40

Approval of Command Officer: C. J. Kennedy, Captain
Vice/Drug Control Bureau

DISTRIBUTION:

Original - Recipient Officer
  Copy - Officer's Personnel File
  Copy - Commendations Board

Form 139A (4/70) DPD

2

RAMBO-LIKE STOP

MOST POLICE OFFICERS ARE OUTSTANDING people. When I was on probation in my first year, I was assigned to work with the training officer that seemed to be mad at the whole world. He was driving the car on the first half of our night shift when a motorcycle went by, and he made a quick U-turn, sped up, and turned on the overhead lights and siren.

When I asked him the reason for the stop, he said, "Didn't you see that long-haired scumbag?" The man we stopped was wearing an army coat with an American flag on one shoulder. We approached the very soft-spoken man, and he answered every question very respectfully with "yes, sir!" or "no, sir!"

He had very recently gotten out of the military, where he had served two years in Vietnam. My partner was very arrogant, disrespectful, and plain mean. The guy could not have responded nicer without getting mad at all. Even when he started getting poked and pushed in the chest, he just backed up and took it. Trying very hard to avoid him forcing this guy into a fight, I asked my partner, "What did he do wrong?"

He replied, "Just look at this guy! So he just got out of the military—who gives a blank! He can't go riding around on his motorcycle showing off his military uniform like this!" He took out his nightstick and started ramming it into the guy's chest. The soldier didn't make any defensive moves until my partner hit him in the throat with his nightstick. The soldier knocked the nightstick away from his throat when my partner went berserk and started pounding on him. He yelled at me to help him put the handcuffs on the man. The only reason I helped was that I was a rookie on probation. I knew if I didn't help him, I would be facing the possibility of being fired.

The guy never did a single thing to warrant being arrested. I wanted to tell the sergeant what happened, but I was told in the police academy never to be judgmental of our training officers. The night it happened reminded me of the movie "Rambo" wherein the character was arrested only because of the way he looked. I could not believe that I actually saw almost the same thing happen in real life.

It came as no surprise when I found out later that this training officer was arrested for numerous assaults on law-abiding citizens. He was also arrested and charged with several aggravated rapes. He would pick up a young woman for whatever reason, take them down a dark alley, and park the car so the passenger's door could not be opened. He would rape them and threaten their lives if they ever reported what had happened. I am thankful I can't remember the cop's name, but hopefully, he is still in prison.

Good cops: 1. Bad cop: 0.

3

CAR 54, WHERE ARE YOU?

WORKING A CAR IN DOWNTOWN Denver was always a challenge, especially when getting a call with all the bad traffic. A call came out of an auto accident with possible injuries, so we turned on our red light and siren. We were arriving at the scene when a traffic car came and said they would handle it. My wife convinced me that everything happens for a reason. We had driven only a couple of blocks from the accident when a man came running over to our car, very excited. He was very animated, making gestures with his hands, saying quite loudly, "A 2-11, a 2-11!"

I quickly rolled down my window and asked him what the heck was going on. He repeated the same thing, saying over and over again, "A 2-11, a 2-11!"

I tried to get him calmed down to ask what he meant by a 2-11. He stopped and tried to catch his breath and pointed behind him, saying, "A 2-11, right there!"

As I was trying to make out what he was pointing at, it suddenly dawned on me what a 2-11 was. There was a police show on television called "Car 54, Where Are You." Remembering back to the show that a 2-11 was a stick-up in progress. I said to the guy, "You mean a stick-up in progress?"

He said, "That's what I've been trying to tell you guys!" I asked him where the stick-up was occurring, and he almost screamed as he turned around and pointed at the Shasta Hotel and said, "Right there! Are you guys blind?"

At that very moment, a car blocking our view pulled away, and we could see a guy with a gun aimed at the head of the night clerk. He was reaching into the cash register and taking out the money. My partner reached down for the radio inserted in the unit just as I picked up the hand mic to call for backup. The police cars at that time had a portable radio that you could take out of the insert part in the dashboard, or you could use the mic with the cord. If you removed the radio out of the insert in the dashboard, then the hand mic would not work. I realized then that we would not have any backup coming, so we would have to handle it. My partner was already entering the door as I ran around the police car. Having just gotten out of the police academy, drawing my gun did not come naturally.

Seeing my partner with his revolver pressed against the head of the stick-up, I thought, *Oh, that's a good idea!* and whipped my gun out. I felt like I was with Clint Eastwood when I heard my partner shout, "One false move, and I'll blow your head off!"

My heart was pounding, and I was so excited I could hardly breathe. We arrested the guy so quickly that we didn't even have any reason to call for backup. While we were taking him to jail to be booked, I felt disappointed that I didn't get to be part of a "high-five, way to go, super arrest" camaraderie with the backup officers. It did feel better, though, a few days later, when I got an official police commendation for an outstanding arrest. With all the commotion going on taking down this stick-up suspect, we did not have the opportunity to thank the man yelling 2-11. It never occurred to me that watching a stupid cop show on television could help bring down an armed robber.

Cops: 1. Bad guy: 0. (I would like to send out a thank you to that guy who pointed out the 2-11.)

DENVER POLICE DEPARTMENT

OFFICIAL COMMENDATION

TO: Office of the Chief of Police

Date June 13, 1973

FROM: Robbery Detail
Division – District – Bureau

I wish to commend Officer Jon S. Haroldsen , Serial No. 72-033 ,
who is presently assigned to District One, Patrol Division
for the following:

- [X] Class Two Award
- [ ] Class Three Award
- [ ] Class Four Award

WHEREAS it is realized that the great bulk of police work is done routinely by good policemen, let it be known that the above-named officer displayed initiative and alertness decidedly in excess of the norm in this particular instance.

Fact Situation: Officer Haroldsen and his partner, Officer Richardson, reacted immediately to the beckoning of a citizen in the 400 block of 15th St. on June 8, 1973, 10:30PM, which resulted in the apprehension of a suspect, Gilbert Rael, DPD#210564, in the act of committing an armed robbery of the Shasta Hotel. Their immediate response, made possible the apprehension of the suspect, recovery of the weapon and the money. This response probably prevented any serious injury to both the victim and the suspect. These Officers performed in the highest tradition of the Department.

Commending Officer   Det. J.R.Laurita   61-27

Command Officer's Approval

Read and Approved
Division Chief

Chief of Police

DISTRIBUTION:
    Original and one copy to Commendations Board

(Separate set for each officer mentioned)
– DO NOT FOLD –

DPD 139 (Rev. 6/70)

4

INNOCENT DIES

I HAD JUST GOT OUT of the six months in Denver Police Academy and was assigned to a training officer who was a very likable guy. Unlike some of the other training officers, he wanted to let me drive so that I would have the full feel of being a policeman. Since his primary assignment was in the traffic division, he had me set up a radar gun on a busy road. I was so anxious to write my first ticket. I was a little over rambunctious. The speed limit on the highway was 35 mph, and every time I would get somebody going like 40, I'd say, "Can we stop him?"

He told me that we wanted to get somebody going at least 10 miles over the speed limit, and it wouldn't take very long. After being set up for about 30 minutes, my radar gun showed a car going just under 60 miles an hour. Without even asking him, I reached down, turned on my siren and overhead lights, pulled out into the traffic, and almost caused an unfortunate accident. Just because you're in a police car and have your emergency equipment lit up doesn't mean that you don't need to give people time to either brake or get past the area where you're pulling out onto the road. Luckily, no one hit me, and I didn't hit anyone else. I took out after the speeder. The closer I got to the car, the faster it was going and was weaving all over the road, so I knew I had a drunk driver on my hands. Because he would not stop, I got thinking that maybe I was chasing a bank robber or somebody on the Wanted list. Suddenly, without warning, the car stopped right in the middle of traffic. I bailed out of the car and started to pull my gun out when my partner said, "Hang back and let me handle this."

Not wanting to miss anything, I stayed right behind my training officer to back him up since I was sure this was a felon we had stopped. Much to my amazement and disappointment, this so-called felon was a kid about 12 years old who was shaking and scared to death. His older brother told him that he could carefully drive the car out of the driveway out onto the street and park it. When he had it where his brother told him to park it, instead of hitting the brake, he mashed the gas pedal to the floor and took off not knowing how to control this runaway car. While my partner was asking him about what happened, the little boy started to cry, which made me feel foolish.

A couple of months later, when I was working the night shift around two o'clock in the morning in a residential neighborhood, we saw a very suspicious car driving very slowly like they were casing a place to rob it. We pulled the car over and approached it very cautiously, sensing that things did not seem right in this neighborhood at that hour in the morning. I immediately recognized them as the Velardei brothers. They were ex-cons who had committed about every crime imaginable. I had a run-in with Lee Velardei earlier that year when I arrested him for burglary, carrying a concealed weapon, and illegal use of narcotics. When I attempted to stop him last time, it ended in a chase when we finally apprehended him. My partner and I sensed that something really bad was about to go down, but we couldn't quite figure out what it was. We searched the suspects and their car but found no probable cause to arrest them. We separated them to try to see if that would divulge some part of a plan but came up with nothing. None of them had much to say. They all said pretty much the same thing—that they were driving around hanging out. We wrote up contact cards to alert the stick-up and burglary detectives of who we had encountered, what they were driving, where they were at, and what time of day it was. Their past MO did not fit them, pulling a burglary in this kind of neighborhood. We knew that pulling stick-ups of businesses was more their thing. There were no businesses in that area, so we finally had to let them go.

Often, since that next morning, I so wished that I would've figured out what they were planning. What I did not know was there was a large grocery store only four blocks away. The next morning, they went in with shotguns and handguns and were in the act of robbing the store. The store manager somehow managed to push a silent alarm before they grabbed him. Several marked police units got to the front of the store along with the sergeant before the gang of robbers were ready to exit the store. The officers all had there had guns drawn using their police cars as shields. While they were waiting for the bad guys to leave the store, a newly hired recently returned army veteran was working in the store. He had special forces training and managed to wrestle a shotgun away from one of the bad guys and knocked him down. Probably figuring he would have a better chance of getting the stick-ups as they left the building, he walked back out the front door, wearing a white apron with a shotgun in his hands. He was not aware of any police out in front since he had his back to all the cars and police officers. The sergeant yelled at him to drop the gun and turn around with his hands in the air. Since he did not know who had yelled at him, he instinctively turned around with the shotgun near his waist. He could've very well thought there were more stick-ups outside getting the drop on him.

Because the shotgun was aimed out in front of him as he turned around, one of the officers fired at his head and instantly killed him. It was a sad day for everyone because of the death of a war hero who was in the act of stopping a well-planned armed robbery. We could only hope and pray that these terrible criminals will be locked up forever. Better yet, the felony murder law should have them executed since they were committing a felony that ended in the death of an innocent store employee.

When I graduated from Brigham Young University in Provo, Utah, there was a full-page ad in the newspaper, stating that if you had a bachelor's degree, the LAPD could hire you after going through an oral board and no written test. I had always wanted to be a police officer, so I scrounged together all the money I could and drove to Los Angeles for the oral board. There were, I believe, five police personnel seated at the table when I walked into the room to start my oral examination. I felt very confident about my quick responses to the numerous questions thrown my way. One question was, "If you were on duty in your uniform and a man came at you with some club as a weapon, what would be your response?"

I told the board members that for the past several years, I had studied karate and judo and was an instructor in both martial arts during my college years. I told them that I had a black belt and had trained vigorously and could easily disarm someone with a knife, a club, or even a gun. I further told them that numerous times I would assign six or seven martial arts students to try to land any blow to my body. In addition to that, I explained how many times I gave a starter pistol to a class member with them holding it aimed at me, and then the rest of the students would be judges to determine if I disarmed the person with the gun quickly enough to have not been shot. Not once did anyone come close to having the gun aimed at me when the trigger was pulled. I then explained to them that I could disarm someone coming at me with any club and get them subdued and handcuffed. As soon as I finished talking, they said I was dismissed, having flunked the oral board.

Since I had driven so far, thinking I would have a job for sure, I waited around till the end of the oral board meeting to ask why I did not pass the oral board. I was told that the correct answer was that you should shoot the person coming at you five times, making sure they're dead, and leave one round in your gun just in case. I was speechless at the reply and couldn't believe what they said the correct answer was. Not too surprisingly, a few weeks after this, the Rodney King beating was on the news. The police action comes down from the top, and, at that time, the top of the LAPD was a bunch of morons. Shortly after that, when I was hired as a police officer in

Denver, I was happy and so grateful that I was not working in the LAPD force.

To add to my distress at that time, I ran out of gas on the way from LA to Provo, Utah. I wrote a little something on a piece of cardboard that said, "Out of gas, can you help?" I was on the interstate, and the cars just zoomed past me for a couple of hours when, finally, a pick-up came to a quick stop behind me. A guy came running up with a red gas can and set it down right by me and told me to have a good day, and then he jumped back in his truck and started to leave.

As he began to pass by me, I yelled at him, "Wait a minute I want to give you the gas can back and pay you for the gas!"

I'll never forget his response when he said, "That is a Pass-Along gas can. Fill it up, and give it to the next person out of gas, and don't break the chain!"

I could hardly believe my ears and yelled, "Thank you!" as loud as I could. Just as I finished pouring the gas into my tank, I noticed the writing on the outside of the can in black letters that said *Pass-Along Gas Can!* Later, when I filled the can, I drove around with it in my car. I could hardly wait to find someone else out of gas. A couple of months later, I saw a guy on the side of the road, and I ran up to him all smiles and said, "Are you out of gas?"

He probably thought I was crazy when I seemed to be so happy about it. When he said he was out of gas, I said, "Great!" and ran up to my car, got out the gas can, and gave it to him, telling him to pass along the container and not to break the chain!

Cops: 4. Bad guys: 0. (Good Samaritans: 3 and counting.)

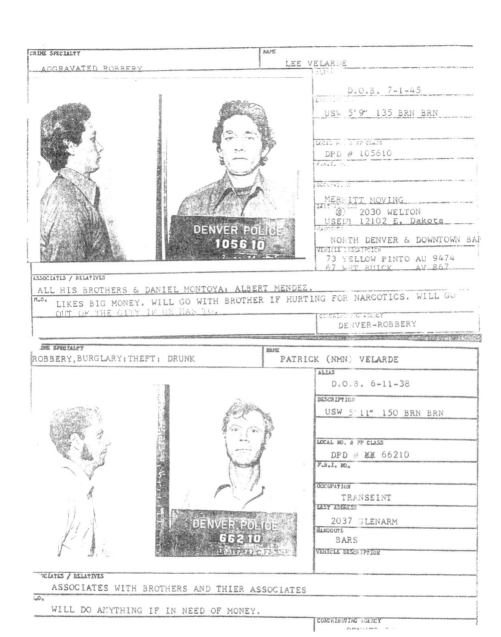

CRIME SPECIALTY	NAME
AGGRAVATED ROBBERY	LEE VELARDE

ALIAS

D.O.B. 7-1-45

DESCRIPTION
USW 5'9" 135 BRN BRN

LOCAL NO. & FP CLASS
DPD # 105610
F.B.I. NO.

OCCUPATION
MERRITT MOVING
LAST ADDRESS 2030 WELTON
USED 12102 E. Dakota
HANGOUTS
NORTH DENVER & DOWNTOWN BARS
VEHICLE DESCRIPTION
73 YELLOW PINTO AU 9474
67 WHT BUICK AV 867

ASSOCIATES / RELATIVES
ALL HIS BROTHERS & DANIEL MONTOYA; ALBERT MENDEZ,
M.O.
LIKES BIG MONEY. WILL GO WITH BROTHER IF HURTING FOR NARCOTICS. WILL GO
OUT OF THE CITY IF HE HAS TO.

CONTRIBUTING AGENCY
DENVER-ROBBERY

CRIME SPECIALTY	NAME
ROBBERY, BURGLARY; THEFT; DRUNK	PATRICK (NMN) VELARDE

ALIAS

D.O.B. 6-11-38

DESCRIPTION
USW 5'11" 150 BRN BRN

LOCAL NO. & FP CLASS
DPD # MM 66210
F.B.I. NO.

OCCUPATION
TRANSEINT
LAST ADDRESS
2037 GLENARM
HANGOUTS
BARS
VEHICLE DESCRIPTION

ASSOCIATES / RELATIVES
ASSOCIATES WITH BROTHERS AND THIER ASSOCIATES
M.O.
WILL DO ANYTHING IF IN NEED OF MONEY.

CONTRIBUTING AGENCY
DENVER

CRIME SPECIALTY	NAME
AGGRAVATED ROBBERY, BURGLARY, ETC.	EUGENE "GENE" VELARDE

ALIAS
D.O.B. 6-29-41

DESCRIPTION
CAUC. 5'8" 160" BRN BRN

LOCAL NO. & FP CLASS
62734

F.B.I. NO.

OCCUPATION

LAST ADDRESS
3233 W. 21st Ave

HANGOUTS
NORTH DENVER BARS

VEHICLE DESCRIPTION
1966 CHEVY 4DR GREEN AD735
1966 BUICK 2DR BLUE BB7384

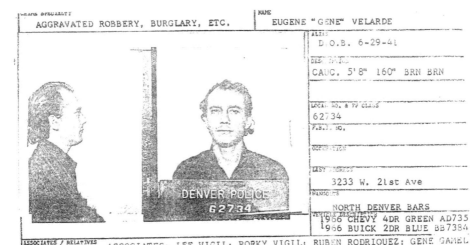

ASSOCIATES / RELATIVES
ASSOCIATES: LEE VIGIL; PORKY VIGIL; RUBEN RODRIQUEZ; GENE GAMEL
BROTHERS: RICHARD VELARDE; LEE VELARDE; PATRICK VELARDE; DANIEL VELARDE.

M.O.
THIS PARTY IS VERY SELDOM CAUGHT IN A CRIME DUE TO THE FACT HE PLANS AND
FURNISHES THE ITEMS TO BE USED IN THE OFFENSE THEN STANDS BACK UNTIL
THE JOB IS COMPLETED BY OTHERS THEN DIVIDES THE PROFITS
HAS BEEN ARRESTED IN OTHER CITIES IN COLORADO.   DENVER-ROBBERY

CRIME SPECIALTY	NAME
Aggravated Robbery; Burglary; Narcotics	RICHARD R. "BUTCH" VELARDE

ALIAS
D.O.B. 11-28-47

DESCRIPTION
USW 5'11" 165 Brn Brn

LOCAL NO. & FP CLASS
DPD #109615

F.B.I. NO.

OCCUPATION
Merritt Moving

LAST ADDRESS
3233 W. 21st Ave.
2540 W. Dunkeld

HANGOUTS
NORTH DENVER BARS

VEHICLE DESCRIPTION
SAME AS BROTHER "GENE"

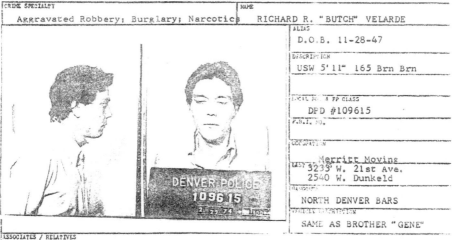

ASSOCIATES / RELATIVES
ASSOCIATES: GARY LEE SCOTT; RUBEN J. "DEACON" RODRIQUEZ AND BROTHERS

M.O.
PARTY WILL GO IN ON JOBS WHERE HIS BROTHER WON'T. LIKES GUNS. WAS ON PAROLE
IN WASHINGTON BUT IS IN DENVER NOW. HAS BEEN ARRESTED
IN OTHER CITIES IN COLORADO.   DENVER-ROBBERY

5

RUSSIAN ROULETTE

The Denver police academy training officers told us that we most likely would go 20 years without ever arresting a bank robber. My partner and I were responding to a bank robbery in progress when my wise senior partner said, how often when we go to a bank robbery in progress are the bank robbers still in the bank? I responded well, and it's never happened that I can remember. He said you're right, so in this case, instead of going straight to the bank, we are going to slowly drive around the area a few blocks from it and see what we can come up with. After only a few minutes of driving in the residential area a few blocks from the bank, we saw a guy matching the description of one of the two bank robbers. My partner wisely drove right next to the guy walking down the sidewalk, going the same speed as he was. Not once did the suspect ever turn and look at the police car. You think about it. If a vehicle was driving along slowly next to you in the street, your natural reaction would be to look and see what was going on. If a police cruiser was driving next to anyone walking down the road, they could easily see it out of their peripheral vision. The fact it was a police car would, of course, make anyone curious enough to turn and look.

    We both immediately knew that we had the right person, and my partner hit the brakes, and the guy took off running full blast down the sidewalk. I jumped out and started to chase him. After running past a couple of houses, I saw him pulling a 45 automatic out of the front of his waistband, and I immediately drew my gun. He ran around the house, and I carefully approached the corner of the house, thinking he could very well be waiting for me with that gun. Just as I peered around the corner of the house, I saw him throw the gun into a dumpster. He continued running and climbed over a chain-link fence. I vaulted the fence and tackled him about halfway across the backyard of the house. After a brief struggle, I got him handcuffed just as my partner came running around the house. We loaded him into the police car and headed for the station to book him. My partner, nicknamed "Mad Dog" Burton, said you take over driving. Mad Dog then climbed into the backseat sitting right next to the suspect. He told me to drive very slowly as I headed to the station. I ran an ID check on our suspect, Richard Sanchex, and he came back wanted as an escapee from Illinois. He told Sanchex that since two people had robbed the bank, he wanted to know where the other guy was. Sanchex did not respond. Mad Dog then pulled out his .357 magnum and started to remove the shells. He left one in the chamber and spun the cylinder and closed it. He said, "do you know how to play Russian roulette?" Once again, there was no response. He held the gun up to Sanchex's head and told him he had to the count of three to tell us where his partner in crime was. At the count of three, he pulled the trigger with a loud click. At that point, I had no idea that he knew where the live round was, and there was no danger of the gun going off for another four clicks. At the second count of three, as the gun went click once more, Sanchex blurted out, "It was all my cousin's idea!" He then yelled, "He lives right up there on the left!" as he pointed at the house.

Within a few seconds of knocking on the door, his cousin answered it with a very bewildered look on his face. "How did you find me so fast?" I told him that his response just now will be valuable evidence at his trial.

We read him his rights as we handcuffed him and took him to the police car. When we opened the door to place him in the backseat, and he saw his cousin and screamed, I'm going to kill you. We kept the two apart while we took them into the robbery detectives. Their arrest cleared up four other armed robberies.

Cops: 2. Bad guys: 0.

DENVER POLICE DEPARTMENT

OFFICIAL COMMENDATION

TO: Office of the Chief of Police

Date December 20, 1973

FROM: Detective Bureau - Robbery Detail
Division – District – Bureau

I wish to commend Officer   J. S. Haroldsen   , Serial No.   72-33   ,

who is presently assigned to   District 1

for the following

- [x] Class Two Award
- [ ] Class Three Award
- [ ] Class Four Award

WHEREAS it is realized that the great bulk of police work is done routinely by good policemen, let it be known that the above-named officer displayed initiative and alertness decidedly in excess of the norm in this particular instance.

Fact Situation: Recently we had numerous armed robberies on West Colfax off of Kalamath. A description was broadcasted on a possible suspect. This officer, along with Officer C. D. Burton, covering in the area, chased down and arrested a juvenile escapee from Illinois by the name of Richard Sanchez. As a result of this arrest information was developed on Richard's brother, Freddie Sanchez, an adult. Investigation further disclosed that Freddie Sanchez was involved in a finance company robbery and an attempt robbery at a store on Santa Fe Drive, in which these officers attained an identification and within hours arrested Freddie Sanchez. Without these officers assistance and fast work in the arrest of the juvenile, who was unknown to this department, my investigation would have been hindered, however, as the result of their comprehensive attention to duty, four cases were cleared on these parties, two of which were filed on the adult, Freddie Sanchez.

Commending Officer _____
Det. J. C. Tyus   65-04

Command Officer's Approval _____

Read and Approved _____
T E Rowe
_____ Division Chief
Arthur G. Dill
Chief of Police

DISTRIBUTION
Original and one copy to Commendations Board

(Separate set for each officer mentioned)

– DO NOT FOLD –

DPD 139 (Rev. 6/70)

DENVER POLICE DEPARTMENT

OFFICIAL COMMENDATION

TO: Office of the Chief of Police

Date November 20, 1973

FROM: PATROL - DISTRICT ONE
Division — District — Bureau

I wish to commend Officer Scott Haroldsen , Serial No. 72-33
who is presently assigned to District One - Detail Two
for the following:

[X] Class Two Award
[ ] Class Three Award
[ ] Class Four Award

WHEREAS it is realized that the great bulk of police work is done routinely by good policemen, let it be known that the above-named officer displayed initiative and alertness decidedly in excess of the norm in this particular instance.

Fact Situation: Outstanding police action in the arrest of Richard A. Sanchez for Aggravated Robbery at 1201 Santa Fe and 1010 West Colfax Avenue.

Commending Officer Lieutenant L.J. Britton, #56-25

Command Officer's Approval Capt. L.C. Lik...

Read and Approved Paul A. Montaya
Division Chief

Arthur G. Dill
Chief of Police

DISTRIBUTION
Original and one copy to Commendations Board

(Separate set for each officer mentioned)
– DO NOT FOLD –

DPD 159 (Rev. 6/70)

6

GANG FIGHT

DURING OUR TRAINING IN THE police academy, Friday nights, we got to ride with two veteran officers so we could see how the pros do things. A call came over the radio that there was a big gang fight at a local high school. We were pretty close to the school, and made it there in a matter of a few minutes. I was quite surprised when the officer driving turned his lights off and pulled up onto a ridge about a hundred feet above the outdoor basketball court where the fight was about to start. How could we ever be effective that far away, trying to stop a big gang fight? Since we were told in the police academy to keep our mouths shut and not try to give veteran officers any of our rookie advice, I wisely didn't say a word. Just as the two groups moved forward to start the fight with chains swinging, clubs in their hands, some with knives, and even had some guns, what happened next really shocked me. The officer riding shotgun turned on the overhead lights, briefly hit the siren, turned on the PA system, and said in a very commanding voice, "When you guys are done trying to kill each other, if any of you need an ambulance, just let us know; we'll be up here watching."

With that said, both officers pointed their spotlights down on the crowd. The would-be gangbangers took off like they were running away from a bomb ready to explode. One of the officers sensing the incredulous look on my face explained, by handling the call in this manner, no police officers were injured, and no ambulance drivers, doctors, or nurses had to mess with these scumbags! He then added besides that there weren't any cars to cover us, and the idea is for every officer to return home safely to their families, not to get hauled off to the mortuary. At the end of the shift, thoughts were racing through my mind, but I finally concluded what they said did make sense.

7

HIDE AND SEEK

VERY OFTEN, WHEN WE WOULD receive a call from a business that the burglar alarm was going off, it would turn out to be a false alarm. Since we often were dispatched to many false alarms, it was easy to let your guard down. One night, we received a call from the Denver Mattress Company, which had a silent alarm going off. Upon arriving at the building, the dispatcher told us that each door inside was wired to go off if the door was opened. My partner and I first determined there was only one entrance or exit to the whole building. We called for a backup car to watch the door while we searched the building. Just as we entered the building to start our search, the dispatcher called and said that one of the doors going up the stairwell at the other end of the building had just been opened. At this point, we felt sure that the burglar was still in the building. We immediately ran to the stairwell where the door had been opened and continued searching. The dispatcher called us again and said the door on the second-floor stairwell had just been opened.

We then were positive that we had at least one or more suspects trapped in the building. Because the building was so big and was four stories high, we called for additional backup officers to help in the search. Not more than about thirty seconds later, the dispatcher called again and said a door on the third floor in a different stairwell at the other end of the building had just been opened. There were thousands of mattresses stacked on each floor of the warehouse.

28

Coming up with a plan of attack to do a well-coordinated search would be absolutely the only way we'd catch our burglars. We knew there had to be more than one since the door alarms were so far apart when they went off. I called all the responding officers in the building and those just arriving to meet me in the front entrance to develop a proper search. With seven officers searching inside and one posted at the door, I felt confident we could quickly catch these bad guys.

Starting on the first floor with three officers in each of the two stairwells, we started working our way up floor by floor. There was a 2x4 wall with chicken wire on it, dividing the warehouse into two areas. Each stack of the mattresses went all the way to the ceiling, which was about ten feet high. With the first floor cleared, we started moving up to the second floor when the dispatcher told us that a door on the fourth floor had just tripped an alarm. We were all pretty stoked, knowing for sure we had these guys trapped up on the fourth floor. Changing our plan of going up one level at a time, it seemed best to go straight up to the fourth floor where we knew they had to be. We all converged at the end stairwell where the door was reported being opened and ran up to the fourth floor. We all searched carefully through all the mattresses and came up empty-handed. We were taking a quick breather and talking about where on earth these guys could be when the dispatcher said a door had just opened at the other end of the building in the stairwell at level four. We all ran down to the third floor in the same stairwell because we couldn't get through the wire mesh, which divided the warehouse floor in the middle.

We played this game of cat and mouse for several hours. Some of the officers wanted to leave because they felt like there was no way we were ever going to catch these guys. It was getting close to the end of our shift, and I wanted to stay until I could arrest these guys. At that exact moment of thought, we heard some feet scrambling down the stairwell and caught a glimpse of one of the burglars. That gave us new hope, so we all ran down the stairs after him. I called the dispatcher to ask if any door alarms had gone off on the second floor. The dispatcher responded that no door alarms were going off. I then knew we had them trapped on the second floor. Upon closer inspection, we realized that there was a gap between two stacks of mattresses, which led to the wire mesh partition. The burglars had cut an opening in the wire mesh so that they could go back and forth so they could access either stairwell.

I called the sergeant to request overtime so that we could continue the search. He said my partner and I could remain to guard the door and could fill in the oncoming shift to what had taken place for the past several hours. My partner and I took up our post at the door, waiting for the oncoming shift change. Only a few minutes after all the other officers had left, the dispatcher came on with a report of some more door alarms going off. The second-floor door just opened, followed by the third-floor door, and finally, the fourth-floor door indicated movement.

The next shift of officers finally showed up, and I filled them in on the situation. Since we were unable to catch the burglars, I thought the best thing to do would be to call for a canine unit. Only one canine unit was available, so we were still very relieved when they showed up. The officer with the dog was not too happy since we had traipsed all over the warehouse, making it difficult for the dog to pick up a scent. I suggested that we station officers at each door on all four levels and have the canine unit go up to the rooftop, which we had not searched, and work their way down. We all took our positions and waited for the dog and his trainer to start on the roof.

What happened next was both alarming, horrifying, and just plain sad. Police dogs are trained when they are released to go up to the highest point and then continue their search going down level by level. When the trainer released his police dog on the roof, the dog instinctively ran around part of the roof, which was totally dark, and the dog jumped up on what it thought was another level, but it was a parapet wall. The dog fell four stories through the air landing a few feet away from the officer posted at the door. The horrific impact of that large police dog hitting the cement almost caused the officer to have a heart attack. It both scared him and made him sick. Because it was so dark for a few seconds, he thought that an officer had been pushed off the roof. I was so upset at this point I was almost in a rage to catch our burglars. My sergeant came by and told me to go home immediately, and the new shift just coming on duty would catch these guys.

I found out at roll call the next day that two burglars were caught hiding in between the stacked mattresses.

Police: 2. Bad guy: 0. (I never thought a funeral for a dog could be so sad. The one good thing that happened was the judge really threw the book at these two guys.)

8

SKYLIGHT BURGLAR

We received a call to respond to a local restaurant on a burglary. We checked the doors for any signs of forced entry and found them all intact. There was a large wooden cutting block in the kitchen with a skylight over it. The large butcher block was also used as an area for food preparation and had food and plates and pots and pans on it. I noticed what appeared to be a wallet right in the middle of the table. The restaurant owner said it was not his, so I picked it up and looked inside. We quickly determined the wallet didn't belong to any of the employees. As soon as we got all the information for the burglary, we went to the address on the driver's license that was in the wallet.

The person who answered the door was the same person whose picture was on the drivers' license. Before we said a single word, the suspect responded, "How did you find me this fast?"

I answered him, saying, "Your comment will be of great help to the prosecuting attorney on this burglary."

He then repeated the same question, wondering, "How in the world did you find me so fast?"

When I held up his wallet, he made another dumb comment. "That's my wallet. What are you doing with it?"

I asked him what his wallet was doing on a butcher block. He thought the question over for a minute and finally responded. "I've never been to that restaurant before!"

I said to him, "How did you know that your wallet was in a restaurant?" He looked at me, dumbfounded and speechless. I told him that the only thing we said was we found his wallet on the butcher block. He then made another stupid comment that was going to be very useful in a courtroom. He said he had no idea how someone could get through the skylight on a roof. At that point, my partner and I could not hold back our laughter. I then added, "We never mentioned a thing about a skylight!"

I then got a call from the burglary detectives who had found his fingerprints inside the vending machines that have been pried open. I asked the suspect if he had been working in the past for any vending machine companies. Of course, I knew his response before he ever gave it to me, which was, "I have never worked for any vending machine company!"

We then had the pleasure of arresting him for burglary with an airtight case all ready for the district attorney.

Cops: 1. Dumb bad guy: 0.

Some might say crime does pay! But to most of the dumb criminals out there, the answer is crime does not pay!

9

DAGGER IN HEAD

Money was getting tight with our fourth little one, and as a Denver Police officer, my pay was not quite enough. I knew I could not work in a bar since I did not have the required years on the job yet. I thought, *What the heck. I need the money.* One night, at roll call, I heard an officer saying he needed to get somebody to fill in his off-duty job at a bar. I told him I was interested and wanted to know how much it paid. He said it was $10 bucks an hour, which, at that time, was like $50 an hour now. I asked him if it was a mellow bar because I sure didn't want to have any problems that could get me in trouble. At the time of talking to him, I meant trouble with the department rules, not with somebody in the bar. He told me that this was just a bunch of old Indians that would be drinking, and there wouldn't be any trouble.

I had a rare Saturday night off work and couldn't imagine making $80 in eight hours, wow! He said my job would be to sit inside the bar area, which was shaped like a box. I would sit inside the area with the bartender keeping an eye on things. There were barstools on all four sides, and there was a small door to get in and out the same height as the bar.

I went to work at six o'clock in the evening and would be getting off at two in the morning. The first couple of hours went without any problems at all. Around half-past eight that night, some of the people seated back in the booths started getting rather rowdy and noisy, but

I ignored them. By nine o'clock, things were getting a little out of control. Some of the drunk Indians started yelling things like, "You, stupid dirty rotten lousy cop."

Others quickly caught on, and I was called every bad name you can ever imagine. I expressed my concerns to the bartender, who only answered, "You got to get tough with these people!"

Things were going from bad to worse, and by ten o'clock, I was getting worried. So I could get their attention, I yelled for everyone to quiet things down. This only added fuel to the already burning fire. Most of the commotion was coming from the table booths way in the back of the bar. This time, I yelled louder to hold things down back there, or they would have to leave. Just as I said that, I saw a large Indian woman stand up with a dagger in her hand, and she stabbed a white man several times in the head. She left the knife in his head, and blood spurted all over as his head hit the table with a loud thump. I leaped over the bar and headed back to the table booths to arrest her. Almost like it was planned ahead, the people slid out of their benches into the walkway and blocked my path. I thought about drawing my gun, but there were too many fists flying and hands grabbing at me. I quickly turned and jumped back over the bar into the center, where at least I felt a little cushion of safety. I told the bartender to call for help immediately, or we both could be dead.

Within a few seconds, a whole bunch of Indians came right up to the bar and started yelling obscenities at me. Since I had taught judo and karate in college, I thought the best thing to do was to startle them. I thought of firing my gun, but I decided they would probably end up taking it from me, and I would be shot dead. I decided another option would be better. I jumped up on the bar and screamed the loudest karate yell "hi-ya!" probably ever done. Thinking I had stunned everyone looking at me, I screamed again as loud as I could as I jumped out, landing on a group of Indians closest to the bar. I took several down to the floor with my momentum.

As I started to stand up, I was quickly swarmed with more people than I could count. The only thing that saved me from being shot or beaten to death was how there were so many people on top of me that nobody could get in a good solid punch. Someone was pulling frantically on my gun, but thankfully, I had snapped my holster closed. My special holster made it almost impossible to unlock my gun unless you know exactly where to push. Then, some of the less drunken Indians finally decided the best way to get to me was to get everyone off. That way, I'm sure they figured they would have a clean shot at beating me to death.

The sound of sirens and screeching tires in the parking lot gave me a huge shot of adrenaline, which I took advantage of. I took in a deep breath and made my third loudest scream, followed by some karate moves that landed squarely on three or four attackers. Very seldom when an officer is calling for help do the officers arrive in time. Most often, when they go charging into a bar or some other place, the attackers have backed off or gotten away, or the officers are down for good. In this case, as they came charging through the door, their drawn nightsticks had many targets to hit. Because they knew the reputation of this violent bar, there were more officers in the room now than I could've imagined. Many arrests were made, but I never found a drunk Indian woman who had killed the guy right in front of my eyes. What was even crazier is that we never found his body. Corpus delicti, nobody—therefore, no one could be charged with murder. The arrests were made, and the people were hauled off to jail. Two terrific officers stayed until two in the morning when the bar was to be closed to make sure that I was safe.

I felt like I had been run over by a Mack truck! I went out to the parking lot, got in my Volkswagen bug, and started for home. When I got to the first traffic signal, I was dumbfounded when I looked to my left and saw a car full of Indians. One of them had a gun aimed out the window right at me. I quickly drew my weapon and was ready to fire when their car went squealing through the intersection with the tires smoking. They were going so fast that they quickly disappeared from my line of sight. Thinking they were long gone, I continued driving toward home.

A few blocks later, they came screaming from the side street aimed right at my car. My Volkswagen barely had enough power to get me out of the way. I was now driving with my gun in one hand and watching the rearview mirror as they came barreling up to me. They never got in a position that could grant me a clean shot. I didn't see them coming alongside me, and when I reached out the window to take a shot, they went past me, going way faster than I could. I slowed way down, hoping I could add a lot of distance between them. I noticed a car lot on my right, and I immediately pulled in, drove in the middle between two cars, and killed the lights and engine. I was in a real panic and was trying to slow down my breathing just as a very bright spotlight came on my car, and a loudspeaker blasted very loud. "Get that car out of here at once. I've got a shotgun up here, and I won't hesitate to use it!"

The last thing in the world I needed was to have a bright spotlight on my car so that the Indian gang would easily find me. I left my lights off as I drove out of the parking lot as fast as my little car would go. I drove onto a side street, taking a long route to get home, hoping I would not run into those crazy bloodthirsty drunk Indians. I had the pedal to the metal when I heard a beautiful sound of a siren and red lights flashing behind me. The officers got up to my car, and we're a little surprised to see an officer in uniform that looked like he had been badly beaten. I told them I just wanted to get home. They were going to escort me, but they got a hot call, and I said I'll be okay. I pulled into our garage and quickly shut the door and went into the house, still in a panic. I told my wife what had happened, and I told her I would like to call right now and resign from the police department. She wisely told me let's get a good night's sleep and see how you feel in the morning. The events of that night terrified me, made me furious, scared me to death, and made me want to kill somebody. I didn't think I could ever get over it so quickly.

However, with a night's sleep and a new day, I was ready to go back to work. One week later, I was asked to go with the missionaries to a family they referred to as a golden contact. They said this family was so excited to learn about the church and the life of the Savior. We drove in my car since they were on bicycles and arrived at the house. We walked up on the porch, and a missionary rang the doorbell. The door opened, and to my utter amazement as I drew my gun, standing behind the screen door was the very Indian who had tried to pull my revolver out of my holster. If I hadn't been with those missionaries, I think I might've been crazy enough to shoot him. I pulled the missionary aside for a second, and I said, "We have to leave this very second because that man tried to kill me last week!"

One more good arrest and I finally could put the Indian bar incident behind me. Now that I think of it, there was a little more to the story. The next day at roll call, I ran into the officer who offered me the off-duty job at the bar. I was rather angry when I gave him a blow-by-blow description of my horrible night. He shrugged it off and told me, "There was only one thing you had to do. The first time anyone of those Indians said a derogatory thing aimed at you, you jump over the bar and crack their head wide open with your nightstick and call an ambulance. You then yell at the other stupid Indian and say, 'Does anyone else want their head split open?'" He told me that if I would've done that, I would've had a nice quiet evening in the bar.

I found out a few days later that Russell Means and Dennis Banks used that bar as their Denver headquarters for AIM (American Indian Movement). AIM is a very violent militant organization that took over Alcatraz prison and occupied it from 1969 to 1971 in San Francisco Bay. They have had numerous encounters with US Marshals, Cops Sixteen.

Bad guys: 0. (To be real honest, bad guys almost got one! Me!)

10

MAFIA HIT

Before I knew very much about organized crime in Denver, my partner and I one day decided to have lunch in the Italian restaurant Gaetano's. A lot of restaurants in the Denver area give police officers half-price deals because they like the presence of uniformed officers in their establishments. We were pretty sure that Gaetano's would also offer the half-price off. My partner and I went out of service and entered the restaurant, all set for a great half-price Italian meal. We were a little surprised when we went inside that there was no one else in the restaurant except a maitre d'. He escorted us to a table and told us that the men in blue were always welcome at Gaetano's. He also said that the meal would be free, of course, for all Denver police officers. He suggested pasta with meatballs and sausage, which we ordered. When he took our order to the kitchen, one of the two swinging double-hinged doors stayed open. I had a clear view into the kitchen area and saw a long table with several men seated around it. I immediately recognized two of the men as the top mafia bosses for the Smaldon family. One man, I recognized from the organized crime book as Eugenie Checker Smaldon, the top boss. I then realized that we were eating in a restaurant where the mafia headquarters was located.

The food was so unbelievably good that we couldn't pull ourselves away from the table until we finished eating. I asked the maitre d' for a check, and he said, "Remember, men, the boys in blue are always free and welcome here."

I insisted on paying, but he would not let me. I even tried leaving a large tip that I thought would cover the meals, but he wouldn't take it. I left a tip on the table, and when I wasn't looking, he picked it up and came over to shake my hand, leaving the money in my palm.

When we called the dispatcher, going back into service, we heard the sergeant say he would meet us at the district station immediately. We could tell by the look on his face when we walked into his office that we were in big trouble. He said to me, "Officer Haroldsen, I thought you were supposed to know all the information in the organized crime book! Why on earth would you ever think of going to have dinner at Gaetano's Restaurant?"

"He said he was guessing that a free meal was too tempting to turn down." I quickly responded that we had no idea that it was the organized crime headquarters. I started to explain to him that I tried to pay for the meal, but they wouldn't accept it.

He interrupted me, shouting, "You two guys have to be stupid to have ever entered that disgusting place!" He said he should suspend us for two weeks without pay. I think, because of our shocked and sad-looking faces, he decided to give us a break. Instead of suspension, he said we were now going to be working the day shift. He knew we loved the action of working the night shift. At least the day shift was better than two weeks without pay.

A few days later, on a beautiful warm sunny summer day, we got a lucky turn of events. We were driving past Gaetano's Restaurant when we noticed the parking lot was full of big black Cadillacs and Lincoln's. We were going to sit a little way back and discreetly write down the license plate numbers. The distance was too far to be able to make out the plates, so I drove into the parking lot, took a clipboard, and started writing down all the car information. There were cars from Chicago, New York, Kansas City, and Los Angeles. Thanks to the car dealer's logos below the license plates, we knew which cities they were from.

When I had about half of the car's information written down, I saw the restaurant door opening and Eugenie Checker Smaldon walking towards us. He leaned down through my open window so he could see my name tag and ask us what we were doing here. I had turned my clipboard over so he couldn't see the information I had written down. I guessed he knew exactly what we were doing, so I turned over the clipboard. Clearing my throat, and in a voice as tough as I could muster, I told him I was writing down all of the plate numbers and car descriptions for the organized crime unit. He leaned in more so he could put his face right in front of me. He said with his teeth clinch, "Officer Haroldsen, I am going to put a hit out on you, and it's only going to cost me twenty or thirty thousand dollars."

Even though I was shocked and honestly terrified, I responded by saying, "Mr. Eugenie Checker Smaldon, knowing that you are the head of the Denver Mafia gives me a great idea. I have over two thousand friends that carry guns and will gladly put a bullet in your head, and it won't cost me a dime!"

He glared disgustingly at me for a good thirty seconds before standing up and going back into the restaurant. My partner was laughing hysterically and said, "That was the world's greatest comeback!"

I had done my very best to talk in a very stern and tough voice. I continued writing down all the vehicle information even though I was shaking so badly that I couldn't read some of my writing.

However, just a few days later, I got a call from the organized crime unit commending my partner and me for outstanding work. They said that the information was most valuable, knowing what top mafia bosses were up to in Denver. I asked how serious I should take the threat of a hit put out on me. They advised me to be extra careful and make sure I was not being followed. For the next two or three months, I was always looking over my shoulder and had my hand on my gun.

Cops: 50. Bad guys: 0.

CONFIDENTIAL
ORGANIZED CRIME

REPORT BY THE ORGANIZED CRIME UNIT
OFFICE OF THE DISTRICT ATTORNEY
DENVER, COLORADO

JULY 1, 1970	O.C.U.

Smaldone and Joe "The Ram" Salardino indicted by the grand jury to assult to murder and assault n.

For The Information of Commissioned Law Enforcement Officers and Prosecutors Only

000016   To _J. HAROLDSEN_
10/21/7×   From _B PRICE_

Information was developed which indicated that on the evening
of the shooting Joseph P. Nuoci, Michael E. Pauldino, Robert
E. Woolverton and Antonio Ciccarelli met with Joe "The Ram"
Salardino, DPD 23154 and Eugene "Checkers" Smaldone, DPD 76794,
in the back room of the Ice Cream Store. This meeting was held
to discuss money owed by Joseph Nuoci to "Checkers" Smaldone,
DPD 76794, as a result of a loansharking operation run by Smaldone.
During this meeting apparently Joe "The Ram" Salardino and "Checkers"
Smaldone attacked Joseph Nuoci and "Checkers" shot the victim with
a 38 caliber revolver.

On April 27, 1970, the Grand Jury, Second Judicial District,
returned a True Bill indicting Eugene "Checkers" Smaldone and
Joe "The Ram" Salardino, with assault to murder, assault with a
deadly weapon and conspiracy.

On April 28, 1970,
members of the Organ-
ized Crime Unit executed
arrest warrants and
search warrants at the
homes of each of the
the indicted gangsters.

Eugene "Checkers"   Joe "The Ram"
Smaldone   Salardino

At the residence of Eugene "Checkers" Smaldone, 3314 W.
37th Avenue, the officers seized suspected bookmaking records.

- 38 -

11

ODD COUPLE

WHEN I GRADUATED FROM THE police academy, I was anxious to hear what my assignment would be. Some officers are assigned to traffic duty (which I didn't want) while others are assigned to patrol (which I wanted). Some of the rough-looking characters would sometimes be assigned to do undercover work. I was elated when I found out that I was assigned to patrol in District One, where I lived.

When I became known as Supercop Haroldsen, some of the officers gave me a hard time, especially the ones in the traffic division. A particular officer named Dale Canino and I hit it off wrong and had something akin to hatred for each other. What made it even worse was that Canino was a traffic officer, and as far as I was concerned, he knew very little of police work since he only had to write tickets. We always had very unpleasant things to say to each other right after roll call.

One night, I had an interview with one of our church leaders to determine if I was worthy to go to the temple. I answered all the questions—I didn't drink alcohol; I didn't smoke cigarettes; I was faithful to my wife in every way. At the end of the interview, when everything went well, I got one more unexpected question. He asked if I had any bad feelings towards anyone. I answered no but added, "Well, I can't stand one dumb traffic officer whose name is Dale Canino."

My church leader then gave me a challenge that left me speechless with my mouth hanging wide open. He said, "I couldn't sign your recommendation to attend the temple until you make good friends with this Officer Canino."

I told him there was no way I could do that because we were real enemies and hated each other. He assured me it was the right thing to do, and things would work out great.

I thought about what he said for several days, and finally, one night, I worked up enough courage to approach Canino. I apologized to him for the way I had been treating him, asked him for forgiveness, and said I wanted to be his friend. He was speechless for a minute or two before he finally reached out, shook my hand, and said, "I'm sorry myself for the way I've talked about you."

Although we had our little talk far away from the sergeant's office and the roll call room, we both got a big surprise when the sergeant gave out car assignments. He called out, loud and clear, "Officer Haroldsen and Officer Canino will be in car 108."

All the other officers at roll call knew of our bad relationship, and all of them started laughing quite loudly. The sergeant yelled, "That will be enough. Get into your cars, and get to work right now!"

Over the next few weeks, we got to be good friends and found out we had a lot of the same standards and goals in life. When I went to my church leader to get my temple recommendation signed, I was delighted to tell him what great spiritual wisdom he had telling me to make friends with Canino.

We were patrolling our assigned area together when we saw a car parked around the corner from a house and saw a man place a television in the trunk of his car. We stopped, questioned him, and quickly discovered that he did not know the address of the house where he said he lived. Since he had told us he was taking a television out of his house to take it in to fix it, we knew he was lying. We placed him under arrest, and when we searched him, we found a large switchblade knife in his front right pocket. My partner kept an eye on him while I checked the house for signs of forced entry. The front door had been pried open, and I noticed some wires along one of the walls had been cut off. He then told us that it wasn't his house; it was his sister's place, and she is the one that told him to get the television. I went through a stack of mail on the table and located the name of the owner and her phone number at work. I called her and quickly determined that she did not have a brother, and there was no one she had given permission to enter her home.

A further search of the open trunk revealed stereo equipment that had the back of the cords cut off and other merchandise he had stolen from the house. We placed the suspect under arrest and advised him of his rights as we handcuffed him, and we took him to the station. Officer Canino and I became a well-oiled machine when it came to our police work.

DENVER POLICE DEPARTMENT
COMMENDATORY LETTER

From: Burglary / Theft   Date November 14, 1973
Division - District - Bureau

Recognition is hereby given to S. Haroldson ,serial number 72-33 ,

who is presently assigned to District 1 ,

for the following described activity: That on the afternoon of 11-12-73 while on

routine patrol, Officers Canino and Haroldson apprehended one John

Ortiz Jr., DPD #157110 while in the act of committing a residential

burglary at the residence of William J. Younce located at 5091 Zuni St.

With this alert action, full recovery made of property this party had

removed from the above residence. A filing was completed and the

suspect Ortiz is presently awaiting trial for Burglary and Theft

felony's.

Submitted By: R. E. Burns
a. d. De Pinto

Approval of Command Officer: Capt RF Mickelluy 52-1

DISTRIBUTION:

Original - Recipient Officer
Copy - Officer's Personnel File
Copy - Commendations Board

Form 139A (4/70) DPD

DENVER POLICE DEPARTMENT
INTER-DEPARTMENT
CORRESPONDENCE

TO **Burglary Detail**

DATE 11-12-73

FROM officers, Haroldsen 72-33, Canino 71-39

SUBJECT **arrest of John Ortiz Jr.(2-20-51) DPD#157110**

While on routine patrol in the 2400 blk. of W. 51st ave, officers observed the suspect walking toward a parked 67 Lincoln,BF2798. The suspect was carrying a stero and two speakers. The suspect placed the items on the trunk lid of the car. The suspect was only about 30 feet from the police car where officers were watching him. The suspect never even looked at the car or the officers until they walked up to him. Officers asked the suspect for an I.D., and asked him where the stero came from. The suspect stated he was helping a mailman move from the second house down from the corner. Officer Haroldsen patted him down for weapons and found a 4" knife in his right back pocket. The party was then placed under arrest for CCW, handcuffed, and placed in the police car. Officer Haroldsen then started toward the corner house to see the mailman. The suspect then told Off. Canino to stop him, "I took the stuff from the first house there. The suspect was then advised of his rights by Canino. Off. Haroldsen was told of the statement of the suspect, and Haroldsen then searched 5091 Zuni St. for evidence of the crime. The front window of this house was broken and the front door of the house was open. Officer Canino called for a cover car, at which time Car 113, Scat 11, Scat 14, Scat 5, And X-12 covered. Baker-4 was also called for pictures and prints. Det. Burns, X-12, responded and advised officers what was needed by him.

The suspect had a color t.v. present in the back seat of his vehicle which he stated he took from the house. The suspect had a cut present on his left wrist with blood present.

Investigation of the house showed pry marks on the front door, the north front window and the south front window. Entry was made by the north bedroom window, by breaking the glass. The suspect crawled through this window cutting his wrist, and leaving blood on a white envelope inside the bedroom. Glass was present both outside the house and inside the house with prints on it, believed to be the suspects. Empty shelves were present inside the house in the southeast livingroom, where the stolen items were being kept by the owner. The owner responded to the scene from work and confirmed that the items found in the possesion of the suspect were taken from his house, 5091 Zuni St.

The suspect was taken to HQ and he was advised of his rights formally by Det. Burns, and gave a statement to Det. Burns admitting to his guilt. All itms were tagged and placed in the storage of the custodians office.

12

BOMB IN MAIL

RARELY ARE BOMB THREATS REAL, but they still have to be thoroughly checked out. One of the police officers that were in the police academy with me received a suspicious-looking large envelope. She didn't recognize the return address and wisely called the bomb squad. My partner and I were called to the scene.

Unlike the bomb squad trucks you see on television, the vehicle used to detonate the bomb is very different. It consists of a heavy-duty frame with huge rubber tires and a large steel cylinder five or six feet in diameter and about five or six feet tall. Suspended in the middle of the cylinder is a very durable heavy-duty netting. The bomb is placed on the mesh, and when detonated, the blast goes in both directions up and down. The heavy-duty cylinder is entirely open at both ends, so it does not contain the bomb, but directs the blast in such a way that nothing in the area is damaged. The bomb trailer is designed to go up in the air from the blast hitting the ground, so nothing under the cylinder is damaged. If a bomb were placed in a reinforced steel truck as you see on television, it would be like creating an enormous grenade-like device. The more tightly contained bomb causes the explosion to turn the steel into flying fragments.

When we arrived at the scene, the bomb squad was carrying the device into the bomb trailer. They carefully set the device on the suspended mesh and got back from the cylinder, ready to detonate. We were all amazed at the enormous blast that occurred. The trailer went two or three feet in the air, and the blast shook everything in the area but caused no damage. The area under the cylinder was blackened by the explosion, but there was no damage to the road.

Everyone told Officer Hogue how wise she was calling the bomb squad. The bomb was made in such a way that if the device was pulled out of the large envelope, there was a spring trigger device that would've hit the C-4 explosive and blown the officer and her home to bits. Because of that scary occurrence, all Denver Police Officers were alerted to call the bomb squad if they received any suspicious-looking package as described by the bomb squad.

A few days after this bomb incident, I was at home when I heard a loud knock at the door and went to see who was there. The only thing on my front porch was a brown grocery bag with the top folded down several times. My first reaction was to call the bomb squad. I thought of how foolish I would look if it were not a bomb, but I had no idea what it could be. I had my family go out in the backyard and told them to stay there until I said differently. I took a broom and very carefully started to open the top of the sack. It took me several minutes to accomplish that task, while all the time, I thought I could be blown to bits. I could not get the bag open enough to see what was in it, so I very slowly and reluctantly bent over and opened the sack with my hands. I kept my face and head twisted back away from it just in case there was an explosion. I knew deep down inside that if it was a bomb, I was so close I would be obliterated. I finally got the sack opened enough to see what was in it. To my utter amazement, there was a gallon of ice cream with a note attached to it. The note read, "You all have a wonderful family home evening, and we hope this dessert makes it even better signed by the family home evening Phantom!"

To say that I was relieved and happy would be a gross understatement. I looked up and down the street, hoping to see who had left such a treat for us. Since I didn't see anyone, I called the family in the house and told them we were going to have a great family night together and celebrate with all the ice cream we could eat. Our church group had started a tradition that was named "The Family Home Evening Phantom!" Church members would take treats to the different member's homes and leave them on the porch to add to their weekly family night activity. A few days later, at church, Mike and Nadine Doyle told me that they were the ones who put the ice cream on our porch. Mike asked me what on earth I was doing with the broom with that grocery sack on the porch. He told me his kids said I must have thought there was a big snake inside the bag. He said that his wife and children were watching with great interest, but could not figure out why I was acting like I was afraid of the grocery bag. When I explained to him about the recent bombing, and that we were advised to call the bomb squad if we received any suspicious packages, he then quickly understood why I was acting so weird. We both had a good laugh over the whole incident, and when he told his family, they were rolling on the floor with laughter.

The very next night shift I was working started with a Denver police officer's motorcycle shop being bombed. We responded to the call, red light and siren going as fast as we safely could. When we got to the awful scene, I started to get out of the car, and I could hardly move and felt like I was going to die any minute. I called my sergeant and told him that I was deathly sick and didn't know what was wrong, but I could not continue working the shift. He told me that he was sorry, but we had too many hot calls, and everyone was too busy, and we are shorthanded, and I'd have to tough it out. My whole life, I have never felt so awful, and my partner kindly told me to sit there in the car, and he would cover our calls.

Typically, on a busy night like we were having, the time just flies by. But this night seemed to drag on for so many hours; it didn't seem real. When our shift ended, and we returned to the station, I could barely walk to my car and had a hard time driving home. As bad luck would have it, my wife was leaving the next day driving a U-Haul to move her mother to Provo, Utah. I had the next three days off, and I was going to drive the truck myself, but I felt way too sick to do anything. My wife questioned me, saying, "Surely, you could feel good enough to drive and not make me drive that big old truck."

I felt guilty making her drive the truck, but there was no way that I could. She left me at home with our three young children as she drove that big truck out of the driveway and down the road. Just minutes after she left, I collapsed on the living room floor, not quite unconscious. With the greatest effort and in great pain, I dragged myself to the car and drove one block to her family doctor, leaving our oldest daughter in charge of the kids. It only took a few minutes before the doctor determined that he was positive that I had hepatitis C, and I would be dead if I didn't get to the hospital immediately. I told him I had little children at home, and I would figure out something and left his office. This time, when I went into the house, I collapsed on the floor. My oldest daughter, Cherish, called a close friend and a good neighbor and told her the situation. Within two or three minutes, Sandy Taylor came to the house, and with the help of our kids and her, they dragged me out to her station wagon and loaded me in it before heading for the hospital.

My two-week stay in the hospital was a total blur in my mind. I found out later that the doctor who met me when I was taken into the hospital told my friend Sandy Taylor that if she had waited another hour, I would've been dead. My wife was contacted and said that I might not make it, and she should return immediately. As more bad luck would have it, there was a gas shortage at the time, and you could wait up to two hours at a gas station to fill up. She had to wait in line for hours to get gas to make it to the hospital. My wife later told me that my skin was so yellow, and I had no signs of life that it scared her to death.

Thanks to my sergeant who searched through all of my arrest records and found that a guy I had arrested had hepatitis and, therefore, it was considered a job-related injury/illness. My mother, who was related to the apostle Harold B. Lee, pleaded with him to send a blessing to me so that I would not die and would recover from my life-threatening illness. Within two or three days after receiving that blessing, I felt healthy and was ready to go back to work.

I was assigned the desk at the downtown Denver police headquarters for a couple of weeks to recover fully. The second day on the job, I was amazed when the man came in and said he was turning himself in for a first-degree murder that he had committed. The sergeant on duty said he had never seen someone working the desk make a felony arrest of a person wanted for murder. Even though that was not the only felony arrest I made working the desk, I was very relieved when I finally was able to go back on the street.

Cops: 7. Bad guys: a big 0. (Thanks to the loving Heavenly Father for his blessing and saving my life!)

13

DEA AGENTS RIPPED OFF

ON AUGUST 25, 1973, TEN minutes before seven o'clock in the evening, while I was working the desk at the downtown Denver police station, Earl D. Branche walked up to the counter and started two tell me about a terrible day he was having. He appeared to be very high on some drugs, and I could barely understand what he was saying. He told me that for the last couple of months, he thought he was losing his mind, so he started to take LSD and several other types of drugs. He rattled on and mentioned something about gasoline and the fire he started. He said he wanted to talk to the guys in the arson squad. When I called the detective bureau, they advised me to have him go to the fire department. I sent him there, knowing they would get him in touch with the arson detectives. A few minutes later, he came back up to the desk and said to me, "I don't think you understood me. I am high on pills, and I poured gasoline all over my apartment and lit it on fire!"

I hurried around the counter and handcuffed him and placed him under arrest for investigation of arson and advised him of his rights. Detective Ferguson of the bomb squad came over and had him write out a statement and sign it. I walked him to the elevator, where he was taken up to the top floor where the jail is.

I was working off duty in a store that had been hit hard with shoplifters. I saw a guy enter the store and started walking around, looking very suspicious. I was not able to watch his hands every minute as he walked throughout the whole store. He finally stepped up to the counter to pay for just one small item, which didn't make sense for how long he had been in the store. He was wearing a very bulky loose jacket that had several big bulges around his waist. I identified myself as a police officer, showing him my badge and ID, and started to pat him down for possible weapons and stolen merchandise. He pushed my hands away and told me that I did not have a search warrant. I advised him if he didn't hold still and let me search him, he would be arrested for interference. He finally held still and allowed me to search him. After discovering several items he had hidden under his jacket, I asked him for his identification. He stated that he didn't have any, but I found some in his wallet. I walked over to the phone to run an ID check on him, and he ran out of the store. I yelled at him to stop where he was, or he would end up going to jail not only for shoplifting but for resisting arrest. I asked him if he'd ever been arrested before and he said he had not. The ID check came back that he had a long record for theft, including shoplifting. I told him he was under arrest for giving false information to a police officer and for shoplifting. I told him to put his hands behind his back, so I could handcuff him, and he pushed me away. I grabbed his arms and started to put the handcuffs on him when he resisted even harder. I finally slammed his body down against the counter, and when his head hit, he finally relaxed so I could handcuff him. I had car 117 come, pick him up, and take him to jail. The store cashier watched the whole incident and said that I had never used excessive force. The store manager thanked me for doing a great job and preventing more merchandise from being stolen.

On June 16, 1975, two undercover officers—one a DEA agent and the other a Denver police drug detective—were making a purchase of a large number of drugs from a very well-known drug dealer. The two undercover officers were in the backseat of the dealer's car when the drug dealer turned around in his front seat and aimed his gun at the officers, ripping them off of the money and the drugs. As soon as we heard about it, we started to make inquiries to try to locate the suspect, Charlie Lange. We called the DEA office and talked to Julie Williamson and offered our total assistance. Shortly after, she contacted us via the police radio and told us that a confidential informant had an address on Mr. Lange. We went to the address 320 Osceola. We contacted Scat 21 officers Baldwin and Reed, Scat 7 Detective Brenning, and car 109 officers Abell and Pierson. Lange was not at the house, but his girlfriend Mrs. Lindsey stated that he had been at her residence earlier in the day. While talking to her, we noticed a cab arriving in front of the house, and a passenger got out of the car. He informed us that Lange was staying at the Ramada Inn at 3737 Quebec, room 345, and was armed with this .38 caliber revolver. We took the informant with us to the Ramada to make sure he was giving us the straight scoop.

We had car 217 with officers Larsen and Cramer as a backup. We handcuffed the informant to the headrest in the car and entered the Ramada. We obtained the key from the clerk and went to the door of room 345. As soon as we got the steel door unlocked, we slammed it open and rushed into the room with our guns drawn. The suspect had been standing naked behind the door with the gun in his hand when the door slammed into him, and he fell on the floor. He had heard us out in the hallway and thought he could get the drop on us when we came through the door. We took the gun away from him, and some of us started to search the room while he was being handcuffed.

The 38 Smith & Wesson revolver had been taken in a burglary in Lakewood, Colorado. We found a hundred-dollar bill behind the light fixture, and the serial number matched the money taken when he ripped off the undercover agents. We had officers Baldwin and Reed take him to the jail. Lange was advised of his rights and was asked where the other money was located. He told us a guy named Hugh, who lived on W. Gill Pl., had the rest of the stolen money. He said he could point out the house.

When we went back to our police car, the informant was gone, along with the headrest and handcuffs. He was taken to the house, which turned out to be 3424 West Gill Pl. I obtained a search warrant for the home, and with the assistance of detectives Brennan, Reed, and Baldwin, we executed the search warrant at half-past four in the morning. DEA agent Dave Taketa assisted us with the search and supplied us with the serial numbers of the hundred-dollar bills. We contacted Hugh S. Heeley, who had eight of the hundred-dollar bills stolen from the undercover officers. We found another eight of the hundred-dollar bills stolen from the officers under the mattress. The money and the gun were taken to the custodian's office and checked in. We talked to the landlord who told us that Heatley had rented the basement apartment and has only been there for two days. She also said that she had seen Lange earlier in the day but only for a few minutes coming out of the basement apartment. They were charged with aggravated robbery and assault to a federal officer, as well as a parole violation. Lange was also charged for an earlier DUI and an outstanding warrant for failure to appear.

Cops: 4. Bad guys: 0.

INTER-DEPARTMENT
CORRESPONDENCE

TO Captain Kennedy, Narcotics and Vice Bureau, and the Drug
Enforcement Administration

DATE 4-16-1975

FROM Sgt. David L. Michaud 67-31, Scat Unit, 572-1446

SUBJECT Arrest of Charles Lang, wanted Aggravated Robbery, and Assault to a
Federal Officer

On this date, I became aware of the robbery of the Federal Officer, Dave Taketa, and Denver
Police Detective Stan Baker, and the outstanding warrant for Charles Lang, DPD number 16007
Myself and Officer Scott Haroldson made several inquires into the matter, including calling
D.E.A. I talked to Julie Williamson in that office, and offered our assistance. At approx
11:00 P.M. on this date, Ms. Williamson contacted me via the police radio, and I learned th
their office had received information from a confidential informant stating that Lang might
possibly be found at the address of 320 Osceola with one Valerie Lindsey. I contacted Scat
21, Officers Baldwin and Reed, and Scat 7, Detective Brenning, and car 409, Officers Abell
and Pierson, and we went to this address on an attempt pick-up for Lang. He was not locate
at the house, however, Miss Lindsey stated that he had been at her residence earlier in the
day. While in the house, we noticed a cab arriving in front of this residence, and as the
passenger got out of the cab, we contacted him. We questioned this party regarding any knc
ledge he might have on Lang, and learned from him that Lang was presently staying at the
Ramada Inn, 3757 Quebec, room 345, and that he was armed with a .38 calibre revolver. Myse
and the above officers then proceeded to that location, and contacted car 217, Officers
Larsen and Cramer. We obtained a key from the clerk, and we were able to arrest Lang in th
room. At the time of his arrest, he had in his possession a loaded .38 calibre Smith and
Wesson revolver, serial R 77498. It was subsequently learned that this gun was taken in
a burglary in Lakewood, Colorado, their case number 75-24910. Also found in the room behi:
a light fixture was a $100.00 bill bearing serial J 00827084A. I directed Officers Reed an
Baldwin to take custody of the gun and the $100.00 bill and place these items in the Custo
ian's office. These two officers also transported Lang to City Jail. Lang was verbally a
vised of his rights in the room, and I inquired of him the whereabouts of the rest of the
stolen money. He stated that it was with a "guy named Hugh" on West Gill Place. He also
stated that he would point out this address to us. I directed Officers Reed and Baldwin
to do this. I then obtained a search warrant for this location which was 3424 W. Gill Pla
and with the assistance of Detective Brenning, Officers Haroldson, Reed and Baldwin, executed the warrant at approx. 4:30 A.M. We contacted one Hugh R. Heatley, 1-27-1946, who h
several rooms in the basement of this house. We recovered from his billfold eight of the
$100.00 bills listed as stolen from the officers. We also found under several mattress' eight
more of the $100.00 bills listed as stolen. Agent Dave Taketa also assisted with this sea
and he supplied the serial numbers for the stolen money. $1500.00 of this money was from
the DEA, and $100.00 was from the Denver Police Narcotics and Vice Bureau fund. The money
was taken to the custodian's office, and checked in, and the $1500.00 belonging to DEA was
then released to Agent Taketa. The remaining $100.00 bill is in the custodian's office as
evidence. Heatley was taken to City Jail, charged with Investigation, Theft by Receiving
Stolen Goods. The house at 3424 W. Gill is occupied by one Barbara Stein's, 936-4456. W
talked to her, and learned that Heatley had been living in her basement for approx. two da
She added that she saw Lang at her residence today; however, only for several minutes. E:
closed find the Affidavit for Search, the Search Warrant, arrest slipps for Lang and Heat:
and an advisement form for Lang, as well as copies of the three pick-up for Lang. One is
the Aggravated Robbery and Assault to a Federal Officer, second a Parole Violation pick-u
from Glenwood Springs, Colorado, and third a warrant Failure to Appear, for DUI, Summit
County Sheriff's Office.

☐ ORDER IN   ☒ JAIL, BOND REQUIRED   ☐ HOLD FOR HEALTH

☐ JAIL, BOND NOT REQUIRED (AFTER I.D. PROCESSING AND WHEN SOBER)

COMPLAINT

3 - 53Q33

DENVER COUNTY COURT

GENERAL SESSIONS SUMMONS AND COMPLAINT

IN THE COUNTY COURT IN AND FOR THE CITY AND COUNTY OF DENVER AND STATE OF COLORADO
THE CITY AND COUNTY OF DENVER, PLANTIFF, V.

ID. NO.

NAME _Branch_ _Earl_ _F._ DEFENDANT

ADDRESS _808 E. 19th Ave A2_ EMPL. BY _College Inn_ Date of Birth _9/12/31_

YOU ARE HEREBY ORDERED TO APPEAR BEFORE THIS COURT AT THE TIME AND PLACE SHOWN BELOW TO ANSWER THE CHARGE(S) OF VIOLATION(S) OF THE REVISED MUNICIPAL CODE OF THE CITY AND COUNTY OF DENVER AS INDICATED BELOW, AGAINST THE PEACE AND DIGNITY OF THE PEOPLE, AND WHICH OCCURRED IN THE CITY AND COUNTY OF DENVER AT OR NEAR

Location of Offense _808 E. 18th Ave_ On Or About (Date) _8/25_ , 1973, Time ___ M.

Court appearance at 8:30 A.M. on the ___ day of ___ , 1973 ; Courtroom "J", City and County Bldg., 1440 Cherokee St., Denver, Colorado

✓	SEC. NO.	RELATING TO	✓	SEC. NO.	RELATING TO	✓	SEC. NO.	RELATING TO	✓	SEC. NO.	RELATING TO
	821.1	GAMBLING		823.8	INDECENT ACT		824.2	UNLAWFUL ACTS IN OR ABOUT SCHOOLS, COLLEGES OR UNIVERSITIES		846.3	FIRING OR DISCHARGING A WEAPON
	821.2	KEEPING A GAMBLING HOUSE		823.9	FILTHY LANGUAGE		828.1	USE OR OFFER OF FALSE IDENTIFICATION		847.1	INTERFERENCE
	822.2-1	UNDER THE INFLUENCE OF ALCOHOL IN A PUBLIC PLACE		823.11	UNLAWFUL REGISTRATION (HOTEL)		842.1	DISTURBANCE		837.1	RESISTANCE
				823.13	OPR SEX(S) OCCUPYING SAME ROOM UNLAWFULLY		842.6	UNLAWFUL USE OF TELEPHONE		850.1	DESTRUCTION OF CITY PROPERTY
	822.2-2	UNDER THE INFLUENCE OF ALCOHOL IN A PRIVATE PLACE		824.1-2	CONDUCTING SELF IN LEWD, WANTON OR LASCIVIOUS MANNER		846.1 (a)	CONCEALED WEAPON		850.2	DESTRUCTION OF PRIVATE PROPERTY
	823.5-1	PROSTITUTION		824.1 -11A	PROSTITUTE LOITER VS STROLLING, ACCOSTING OR SOLICITING		846.1 (b)	FLOURISHING A WEAPON			
	823.5-1	LEWD ACT					836.1 (b)	UNLAWFUL CARRYING OF WEAPONS			

OTHER VIOLATIONS (DESCRIBE)

INV. oF ARSON

COMPLAINANT ___

COMPLAINANT _(signature)_ SER NO _7233_

SUBSCRIBED AND SWORN TO BEFORE ME DATE ___ 1973
ELLIOT A. DRAINE, CHIEF CLERK

COMPLAINANT ___ SER NO ___
THE ABOVE COMPLAINANT KNOWS OR BELIEVES AND SO ALLEGES THAT THE ABOVE NAMED DEFENDANT VIOLATED THE ABOVE SECTIONS OF THE REVISED MUNICIPAL CODE OF THE CITY AND COUNTY OF DENVER

BY ___ DEPUTY CLERK
DATE SERVED ___ 1973, TIME ___ BY ___

ADVISEMENT FORM

Name _EARL E. BRANCH_   Birthdate _9-12-31_

Date _8-25-73_ Time _7:00 PM_ Location _13TH & Champa (Police B_

You have a right to remain silent.

Anything you say can be used as evidence against you in court.

You have a right to talk to a lawyer before questioning and have him present during questioning.

If you cannot afford a lawyer, one will be appointed for you before questioning.

Do you understand each of these rights I have read to you?

Answer _yes_

Signature of the Person Advised _Earl E. Branch_

Knowing my rights and knowing what I am doing, I now wish to voluntarily talk to you.

Signature of the Person Advised X _Earl E. Branch_

Witnessed by _Charles R. Ferguson_ _64-9_

Signature of the Advising Officer _Jon Scott Harolden_ _72-33_

OPD 369 (6/67)

14

KIDNAPPED BABY

I WAS WORKING THE DAY shift on a beautiful sunny summer day when I spotted a stolen Corvette in a low-income project. The car was legally parked, the engine was running, and no one was in the car. Your typical stolen vehicle is parked in a crazy way, and no one is ever around, and that's the end of the story. However, in this case, the situation made it very clear that someone would be eventually coming out to use it. Further investigation revealed the car had been taken at a burglary from a Chevrolet dealer. When my sergeant heard the information over the radio to the dispatcher, he brought me an unmarked police car and a pair of binoculars, and he told me to sit on the vehicle until it was moving.

Because we did not want a high-speed chase to ensue, I advised officers in the area of the situation so that they could immediately respond and block the car in when it was starting to move. I told all of them to stay a bit away so that we wouldn't tip off the thief.

I sat in the car for about thirty minutes when another car pulled in and blocked my view. Just as I got into position, I looked up and saw a guy go over and open the car door. I immediately called for backup and said, "Hurry up; we don't want a highspeed chase!"

A few seconds after I asked for backup, that guy turned around and walked back up the stairs into an apartment. Since, at this point, I could not make an arrest, I quickly called all the cars off. Several of them made comments like, "Make up your mind, Haroldsen!" and "Do you want us there or not?"

I responded with, "The suspect is not in the car, and I'll call you when he's getting ready to move."

It was a very hot day, and the heated black asphalt made it very hard to watch the car with all the heat waves rising and blurring my vision. I put the binoculars down for a minute or two for my eyes to quit watering. When I looked back through them, the suspect was already in the car and was about to pull out. I grabbed the mic and called for help. Some of the officers asked, "Do you really need us this time, or is this another false alarm?"

I told them all in a somewhat anxious voice, a little hyper too, "Get here now he's getting ready to go."

Even though the officers coming to back me up were giving me a hard time, they showed up in a matter of not more than a minute or two, and we had the Corvette boxed in. I was the only officer directly behind the suspect as he started to pull out. All of the converging officers, including myself, had their guns drawn, and I yelled at the driver to get out with his hands up.

To my astonishment, he got out of the car holding a tiny little baby in a bundle in his arms. Since I could clearly see that the only thing in his hands was a baby, I told all the officers to put their guns away. I started to slowly approach him when he suddenly threw the baby into the car with such force that I heard a powerful impact as the baby hit the passenger door. He jumped back into the Corvette, pulled up on the sidewalk, and drove past all the jammed-up police cars. I was the only one in a position that allowed me to follow him. The high-speed chase that the sergeant did not want just started.

The dispatcher called me and said to terminate the chase. My sergeant interrupted him and said, "This suspect is wanted for burglary, auto theft, and possible kidnapping; therefore, the chase must continue!"

Luckily, I have been given an unmarked car with a large interceptor police engine that really could fly. Although the Corvette was faster on the straightaway, the driver did not know how to make turns without slowing down. I was the number one top driver in the police academy high-speed pursuit driving course. Every time he made a turn, I quickly caught up with him. His car drifted on one turn he took too fast because he was trying to get away from me. The back end of the Corvette hit a telephone pole and sent fiberglass flying in the air, but he kept going.

Unlike in the movies where chases go smooth and fast and look easy, that was not the case in real-time. Every time my car became airborne when it finally landed, the dirt came up off the floor and dashboard into my eyes. More than once, when I was making sharp turns, the cord from the mic got wrapped around the steering wheel. There were even times when I would tell the dispatcher and other officers trying to catch up with me, and I was heading south on a road that ran east and west. During a chase, you are supposed to remain calm and not have any emotion in your voice. Well, I broke all those rules, and at times, I would almost scream into the mic saying things like, "He just ran a red light at over 130 miles an hour!"

The high-speed chase lasted about twelve minutes, although it seemed like an hour. Towards the end of the pursuit, I came up a steep roadway where there was a red light and four lanes of traffic going perpendicular to that light. The Corvette became airborne and crossed the four lanes of traffic without hitting a car and continued. As I got to the red light at the intersection I heard on the radio, the words "command one!" from the chief of police. I came screeching to a stop at the red light as command one asked, "What is the location of the chase?"

Was I extremely grateful that I had not driven through four lanes of traffic and got in a horrific accident right in front of the chief of police? Yes! Of course, I was. A couple of seconds later, the light turned green, and I screamed through the intersection, trying to catch up with the Corvette.

By this time, there was a helicopter in the air, and he advised me that he was directly above. The last place where he saw the Corvette was an alley that he directed me to. He said it disappeared while the chopper had to make a turn to avoid a radio tower. I drove down the alley and checked all the garage doors. Some of them were unlocked and were empty, and some of them were locked and had no windows.

To this day, I'm not sure if the chief of police who looked at me at the intersection knew that I was the officer in pursuit. I was too busy driving to respond to his question regarding the location of the chase.

I went back to the house where the possible kidnapping had taken place. I found out from the mother of the baby a possible location where the baby could've been taken. She did confirm that her baby had been kidnapped. I got my sergeant's permission to take some backup officers to Littleton, Colorado to the address I was given. We got to the house and saw the Corvette parked sideways in the driveway with black skid marks everywhere. We knocked on the door, and as soon as it was open a couple of inches, we all hit it so hard that it flattened the suspect behind the door where he was holding a gun. We questioned him concerning the burglary, the kidnapping, and the high-speed chase, which would be considered a felony in itself.

He told us that he went down an alley and drove the car in an open garage and locked the door. We found the kidnapped baby asleep on one of the beds and had no injuries.

I found out later that the owner of the Corvette also owned the largest furniture store in Denver. I got a call from him a couple of days later, and he said, "Because you got my Corvette back, even though there was some fiberglass damage on the back, come on into my store, and you can pick any television, stereo, or any furniture— free of charge."

Since he had taken his Corvette into the dealership to have the fuel injection system super tuned for racing, he was amazed that I was able to keep up in the chase. I wisely declined his offer of free merchandise. Not more than a couple of weeks later, I was taking a lie detector test. One of the questions I was asked is have you ever taken a gift or gratuity while on duty. I was so happy that I could answer the question honestly with a *no*.

Police: 1. Bad guys: 0.

15

MACHETE

On July 21, 1974, right after celebrating our eighth wedding anniversary, I was working with a rookie right out of the police academy. He said he was happy to be working with the police officer that had such an excellent reputation for big-time arrests. He razzed me about the name Supercop Haroldsen. Less than an hour into our eight-hour shift, I spotted a car going by; I knew the driver to be a wanted felon. Making a quick U-turn and hitting the overhead lights and siren, I chased after the car. My partner wanted to know who we were chasing after. I told him because the driver was wanted for numerous felonies.

For a couple of minutes, he sped up like he was trying to elude us, but since I was right on his tail, he finally pulled over. I took the driver's side of the car. We stopped, and I told my partner to be very careful because this was one dangerous man. With my gun in hand, I cautiously approached the driver's side door and immediately saw the driver, Willey Rezabe, reaching for a huge machete on the dashboard. As I cocked my .357 magnum, I told Rezabe he would be dead in his tracks if he didn't freeze. I told him to put both of his hands on the steering wheel very slowly. His right hand hesitated at the steering wheel and started to reach again for the machete. I informed him that I had my gun worked on by the Denver Police range master, so it had a hair-trigger. That comment finally got his attention, and he held perfectly still. He slowly exited the vehicle, and I got him handcuffed. I did a meticulous search but found no weapons or drugs on him. Sitting on the backseat in plain view were several boxes and containers of easily identifiable drugs. Some of the packages were clearly labeled precisely the way they are in a pharmacy or a hospital.

The NCIC check I had the dispatcher run came back with Rezabe wanted for burglary and armed robbery of a pharmacy and hospital, and felony menacing. The passenger in the car, Larry, was also searched and arrested and handcuffed. A search, after the arrest, revealed substantial amounts of narcotics that had been taken from a hospital pharmacy during an armed robbery.

Several months later, when I was out of town, I was requested to fly back to Denver to testify against Rezabe. During a change of planes in the Salt Lake City Airport, I heard my name announced over the PA system. The Denver district attorney's office told me that I did not need to come to testify because Rezabe had pleaded guilty to the charges. I was only disappointed because I was getting my plane fare paid for by the city of Denver.

Cops:2. Bad guys: 0. (Denver General Hospital and the pharmacy: very happy to have the drugs returned to them.)

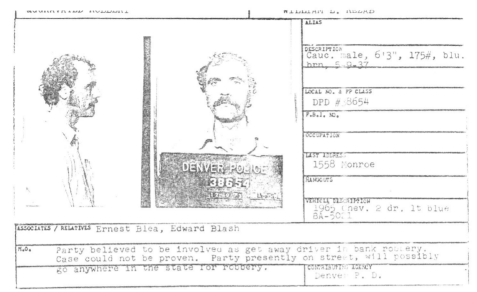

AGGRAVATED ROBBERY	WILLIAM L. REZAB
	ALIAS
	DESCRIPTION Cauc. male, 6'3", 175#, blu. brn, 5-9-37
	LOCAL NO. & FP CLASS DPD #38654
	F.B.I. NO.
	OCCUPATION
	LAST ADDRESS 1558 Monroe
	HANGOUTS
	VEHICLE DESCRIPTION 1965 Chev. 2 dr. lt blue 8A-5021
ASSOCIATES/RELATIVES Ernest Blea, Edward Blash	
M.O. Party believed to be involved as get away driver in bank robbery. Case could not be proven. Party presently on street, will possibly go anywhere in the state for robbery.	COMMISSIONING AGENCY Denver P. D.

O-

REZAB, Wm. LeRoy, DPD 38654, DOB 5-9-37, USW, 6'3", 175, blue eyes brn. hair, 1558 Monroe St. DANGEROUS, USE CAUTION.

DENVER POLICE DEPARTMENT

OFFICIAL COMMENDATION

TO: Office of the Chief of Police

Date ___July 23, 1974___

FROM: ___Vice/Drug Control Bureau___
Division — District — Bureau

I wish to commend Officer ___J. C. Haroldsen___, Serial No. ___72-33___,

who is presently assigned to ___District One___

for the following:

[X] Class Two Award
☐ Class Three Award
☐ Class Four Award

WHEREAS it is realized that the great bulk of police work is done routinely by good policemen, let it be known that the above-named officer displayed initiative and alertness decidedly in excess of the norm in this particular instance.

Fact Situation: ___On July 21, 1974 Officers Haroldsen and Reed observed a wanted___ party driving a car at 18th and Federal Boulevard. This party was stopped and identified as William Rezab wanted for burglary, felony menacing, and possible stick up. This party was to be considered armed and dangerous. Also arrested with Rezab was Larry Learned who was a passenger. A search, subsequent to the arrest, revealed a large amount of narcotics in the vehicle. These narcotics are suspected to be from recent drug store and hospital stick ups in the area.
These officers are to be commended for the arrests of these two dangerous parties, and the recovery of such a large amount of narcotics. These arrests should clear several burglary and stick up cases.

Commending Officer _____
D. Simmons, Sergeant

Command Officer's Approval _____
J. J. Kennedy, Captain

Read and Approved _____
Division Chief
T. E. Rowe

_____
Chief of Police
Arthur G. Dill

DISTRIBUTION:
Original and one copy to Commendations Board

(Separate set for each officer mentioned)

— DO NOT FOLD —

DPD 139 (Rev. 6/70)

2 Arrested In 'Wanted' Case Probe

Two men were arrested Sunday for investigation of illegal possession and use of narcotics and for investigation of aggravated robbery when a policeman recognized one of them as wanted from the June 17 police bulletin.

Patrolmen Jon Haroldsen and W. T. Reed identified the suspects as William Rezab, 37, of 1558 Monroe St., and Larry Learned, 22, of 1111 Galena St.

They said they were patrolling at W. 18th Ave. and Federal Blvd. when Haroldsen recognized Rezab, who was driving south, as wanted from the old bulletin.

They stopped the car at W. 16th Ave. and Federal Blvd., saw a hunting knife on the dashboard and a sack containing hypodermic needles and vials on the seat and arrested Rezab and the other occupant, Learned, they reported.

The officers said suspected morphine was in the vials. Other suspected drugs also were confiscated from the car, they reported.

30—Rocky Mountain News

Police jail pair for check into drug possession

7-22-74

Two men were arrested for investigation of narcotics and robbery charges Sunday after they were spotted on a routine traffic violation and found to have $10,000 worth of suspected narcotics in their car, police said.

In City Jail were William Rezab, 37, who listed his address as 1558 Monroe St., and Larry Learned, 21, of 1111 Galena St., Aurora, police said.

Patrolmen Tom Reed and Scott Haroldsen said they stopped the pair at W. 16th Avenue and Federal Boulevard when they saw the vehicle's brake lights were out.

They said they spotted the suspected narcotics inside both the front and rear seats of the car.

They said the suspected drugs were later inventoried as 100 vials of morphine, 19 bags of suspected heroin, 64 vials of suspected Demerol, several hundred hypodermic needles and more than 600 assorted unknown pills.

Both men were being held for investigation of possession of narcotics, possession for sale, illegal use of narcotics and investigation of aggravated robbery.

16

A MOM TO BE SAVED

A CALL CAME OUT OVER the radio that a pregnant woman was being beaten in a low-income housing project. It was a very busy Saturday night with so many calls that there weren't sufficient cars to backup calls in dangerous areas. Because of the nature of the call, even without backup, we went red light and siren until we got close to the scene.

It was very dark since most of the lights on the apartment buildings were out. We saw a big guy at the door of the address where the call had originated from. Just as we approached him, the door opened, and we saw the victim of the assault. She was obviously seven or eight months pregnant and was bleeding severely from numerous cuts all over her body. We called for an ambulance and then started to place Mr. Samuel Siearra under arrest for assault. He pushed the victim back into the apartment so hard that she went flying in the air and slammed down hard on the tile floor. When we advised him of his rights and started to handcuff him, he turned into a wild man. Even though there were two of us, he was about six-four tall and about two hundred pounds of muscle. Every time we thought we had him subdued and ready to handcuff, he would slam one of us down onto the grass.

The situation got very precarious when several rough-looking characters gathered around us. We had already called for backup, but there were no cars available, so we knew we had to handle this horrific situation ourselves. I reached for my nightclub, but Siearra had already gotten it from me, along with our police hats and our radio, which were somewhere in the grass. Finally, our adrenaline kicked in, and we took charge of the situation. I pulled out my gun and stuck it in the back of Siearra's head and yelled that if he moved, he would be a dead man. Just as my partner got the handcuffs on him, the crowd of people started moving towards us in a threatening manner. Knowing that it wouldn't work just to start shooting people, I holstered my gun and started spraying my mace at the crowd.

The ambulance arrived, and we escorted the paramedics with the pregnant girl and Siearra back to the ambulance and our police car. We raced out of the parking lot in a hurry because the crowd was now starting to get ugly and throwing things at us. We arrived back at the district one station a little before the next shift was coming on duty. We placed Siearra in one of the lock-up cells and walked toward some desks in the roll call area. As we were sitting down to start our paperwork, several of the officers came over and said, "What the heck happened to you guys?"

Neither of us realized until that point how beat-up and bloody we were, and our uniforms were shredded. Another officer in the group said, "Whoever did this to you guys better be at Denver General Hospital now!"

My partner told them about the pregnant woman whom Sammy Siearra had beaten up, and that he was in a holding cell down the hall. The one officer's face turned bright red when we told him the girl was pregnant. He ran down the hall and grabbed Siearra, shoved him into the roll call room, and had him standing in the middle of the room. All the officers that were waiting to go on duty stopped talking, and all sat down on the chairs around the perimeter. They were cheering me on saying, "Put him in the hospital!"

They removed my handcuffs off of him, gave them to me, and said, "You know what you need to do!"

I was incredulous as I looked at this tough situation. One of the officers approached me and said, "Take off your gun belt and give me your badge!"

Very reluctantly, I did as the officer asked. The officers then yelled, "Get to it!"

One of the officers pushed me into the middle of the room, standing about 4 ft in front of Siearra. He made the mistake of smiling with the stupid grin on his face and said, "You don't really think you could take me unless, of course, your buddies are going to jump in!"

The one officer said, "This would only be between you and him!"

He then added, "Haroldsen is not a police officer now! You don't see a badge or gun, do you?"

I stood with my hands down at my sides, acting like I was not ready for whatever he was going to throw at me. He raised his fist and threw a couple of jabs at my face that I quickly ducked. He had no idea that I taught karate in college and knew a lot of tried-and-true moves. He then came at me with a big powerful roundhouse punch aimed at my face. My reaction was instant as I hit the inside of his wrist as he threw the punch, and I shattered the bones in his wrist. He dropped to his knees, screaming in pain, and two officers quickly escorted him back to his cell. All of the officers stood and yelled and clapped their hands, saying, "Way to go, Haroldsen. It sounded like you broke every bone in his wrist!"

The sergeant then walked into the room and announced the lineup for roll call. My partner and I walked out the door and headed home.

The next day, I got a call from the DA, telling me to get my partner and be in court at half-past nine in the morning. When we arrived in the courtroom, I was relieved when the DA asked some things about the arrest but said nothing about Siearra's broken wrist. Sammy Siearra walked into the courtroom with a cast on his arm, escorted by his defense attorney. They walked over to the defense attorney's table and sat down.

The judge walked in, heading to the bench when we were all asked to arise. He hit his gavel down, and the bailiff read out the case. "The City and County of Denver, Colorado versus Sammy Siearra."

The judge asked my partner and me to come forward please to address the court. The defense attorney said, "I object this is not part of the preceding!"

The judge told him to please sit down while he asked us some questions. To say that we were apprehensive and anxious at this point would be an enormous understatement. The judge asked if it was true that Mr. Siearra caused cuts and bruises on two officers and pretty much destroyed our uniforms. He also said, "Is it true that he beat up a pregnant woman who is now in the hospital and could have died if you two had not stopped him?"

We both responded that it was correct. The defense attorney jumped up and said, "You honor, this is not right!"

The judge told him to sit back down. The judge then asked us what it would cost to replace all of our damaged equipment and uniforms. I started to explain to the judge that some of our equipment and uniforms were covered by the Denver Police Department. The judge said he didn't care about that and wanted to know the dollar value that it would cost to replace everything. Once more, the defense attorney jumped up and objected. The judge, in a raised voice, told him to sit down and stay there. The judge then asked again how much money it would cost. I quickly did some numbers in my head and told him about two hundred dollars, maybe a little more. The judge asked if two hundred fifty dollars would cover everything. I said it would. The judge then requested Mr. Sammy Siearra to stand and ordered him to pay us both the said amount. Siearra said he didn't have that kind of money. The judge then told the bailiff to remove Mr. Siearra's wallet. At that point, the defense attorney jumped up and screamed, "Your Honor, this is wrong; you can't do this!"

The judge pounded down his gavel and yelled at the defense attorney, "Sit down and shut up!" The bailiff removed the wallet and pulled out five hundred-dollar bills.

Once again, the judge brought down the gavel and said, "Mr. Siearra, you're in contempt, and perjury charges will be filed immediately!"

The defense attorney looked like he was going to implode as he sat there, not saying a word. The two of us, Officer Haroldsen and Officer Bales, walked out of the courtroom, all smiles. It was all we could do to contain ourselves from shouting for joy and jumping up down over the great turn of events. We then understood why the judge was nicknamed "The Hanging Judge."

At roll call that night, the sergeant called out our names and told us to take one step forward. I thought we were going to be in trouble, but my fear quickly turned to pure joy when he announced that because of these two fine officers, a pregnant woman's life was saved and that there was going to be some icing on this beautiful cake. Our sergeant found out that Mr. Sammy Siearra was a well-known pool hustler who had taken thousands and thousands of dollars from hundreds of people as a pool hustler. The doctor told our sergeant that Siearra's pool hustling days were over, and his severely damaged wrist would never work again. A big cheer went up, and we both got a lot of high fives and pats on the back.

Cops: 2. Bad guys: 0. Bad defense attorney: 0.

17

OFFICER DOWN

About three years after becoming a Denver police officer, my Sergeant had me start working with officer Bill Smith. He was a fantastic partner in every way imaginable. The first several shifts I worked with him, the only thing I didn't like is he insisted on driving all the time. I very quickly understood the reason because he just always had a sense of where to be and what car to stop. He was so professional, so knowledgeable, and I felt so very safe working with him. Very quickly, we knew each other so well that when we would pull a car over, we didn't have to say a word because we just knew what each of us was going to do. For example, if we placed a party in the backseat of our police car, we knew for sure that one of us had searched him very thoroughly. We very literally always had each other's back in any circumstance.

In the middle of our night shift, I got a call to go into the district station about an important message. We went to the District One station where I had a message to call my mother as soon as possible. Back in those days, we didn't have a cell phone, so I called my mother to collect, which she, of course, accepted. She told me she was on the way to Denver to see us and that her train would arrive at the station very early Thursday morning. I didn't know how we could pick her up because I had to work and didn't have enough seniority to get the night off. I told her I'd figure out something and said goodbye. I went to my Sergeant's office and explained the situation to him, and he said I'm sorry, but seniority always takes precedent. I told my partner Officer Smith about my mom coming, and he said he wished he had the Wednesday night shift off and would trade me, but he had to work the same as me. We made a couple of outstanding arrests, including one guy who was wanted on the federal warrant for armed robbery. I searched the suspect and handcuffed him and put him in the backseat of the police car. My partner asked me if I did a meticulous search because this guy was always known to be carrying a gun, which I had not found. We pulled him out of the police car, and my partner had him spread his legs and tapped lightly up towards his groin area and felt a hard thump. He had a 38-revolver hanging from a string on his belt near his groan. The gun was loaded, and I was very impressed with Officer Smith's instinct about the hidden weapon. We advised him of his rights and headed to the District 1 station, where he was transferred to the jail downtown. The Sergeant called me into his office and told me to shut the door. He told me that he had been thinking of my request to have a Wednesday night shift off. A police officer who was in the police academy with me who had sued the police department for discrimination, and got hired as one of the first women not to have to do the physical agility test wanted to work that night shift. He said she was so set on working that shift. I could take the night off, and she would take my place working with my partner officer Bill Smith. He said he was happy it worked out and this way you'll be able to pick up your mother at the train depot. Being so relieved that things worked out this way, I gave him a big smile and shook his hand, telling him words could not express how thankful I was, and he was giving me the night off. I also told him that it might sound crazy, but I had a weird feeling that something horrible was going to happen to me if I work tomorrow night. He assured me everything was okay and told me to go home to my family. As I was driving home, I wanted to say to Officer Smith to be extra careful tomorrow night, but I knew that he would tell me you worry too much. My wife was pleased to hear that I was going to be able to pick my mother up at the train station tomorrow night.

Since we only had one car, if I would've had to work, we figured the only way to get her picked up would be with a taxi cab. The next day I did some cleaning around the house and some honeydew things. The day flew by, and the next thing I knew it was time to go to the train station. The train arrived right on time, and my mother was so happy to see me. With her baggage loaded in the car, we headed to our house, talking all the way. I had the radio turned down low but could still hear it while we were talking. I picked up on the words "Denver police officer killed!" and quickly turned up the volume. The radio newsman said that Officer William Smith was killed about two o'clock that morning as he walked into a bar on a routine call. I felt so overwhelmed by the news that I had to pull over to the side of the road as my mother tried to comfort me. Finally, pulling myself together, I was able to drive home, and my mother did an excellent job of changing the subject to my dad and her and what they've been doing. Thursday was a blur both at home and at work. This particular Thursday, I was anxious to go to work where I knew I would find out all the details of my partner being murdered.

Roll call thursday night was not like any other I had ever attended. Our Sergeant went through all the details leading up to my partner being killed. At about 2 AM, Officer Bill Smith and his new partner received a call of information from the bartender at Pier II 3730 FederalBlvd. I couldn't figure out why he was the first one to enter the bar because I knew he always drove the car. Our Sergeant then explained that his partner insisted on driving and told him if he didn't let her drive, he would be in big trouble. They never did figure why more specific information as to the seriousness of the incident wasn't called in.

Unknown to the dispatcher or Officer Smith and his partner, the bar was being robbed by two men just out of prison. One man was sitting on the barstool close to the door with a 357 aimed at the door in case someone came in. The other guy was going around robbing and torturing everyone in the bar. He was ramming pencils in the people's ears and burning them with hot coffee. Since Officer

Smith was riding shotgun, he was the first one to open the door to the bar. He was immediately shot right through the heart, and a second round went into the door jamb. My blood ran cold when I then realized that if the Sergeant had not let me have Wednesday night off to pick up my mother at the train station early Thursday morning, I would've been the one killed entering the bar. The guy who killed my partner didn't have any other rounds in his gun and ran out the door and turned to go down the alley. His partner called for help and said shots fired and an officer was down. Officer Smith would have lived had it not been for his bulletproof vest was very dirty and smelly, and his girlfriend had washed it, and it was hanging out on the line drying when he went to work. I didn't even have a bulletproof vest at this time. There was an off-duty officer across the street in a restaurant with his family when the shooting occurred. He instantly pulled out his 45-caliber automatic and yelled for his family to get down and fired through the window across four lanes of traffic and hit the suspect as he was running down the alley. Other officers arriving at the scene also shot the suspect as he ran down the alley. The suspect was only wounded and crawled in between two old buildings.

Numerous police officers were quickly on the scene, and it only took a few minutes to find the injured shooter. Officers called for an ambulance, and he was taken to the hospital.

Officer Smith's funeral was one of the saddest that I've ever attended. What made it even harder is that he was such a top professional best cop you could ever meet. To lose such a wonderful person was such a sad, gut-wrenching experience made even worse because of the circumstances of his death. Police officers came from all over the country and formed a long blue line that reached for miles on the highway. Many times since his senseless death, I have so wanted to sit in front of the parole board that released these two terrible men from prison. How could so-called professional parole board members be so easily conned by such horrible people and you know this happens all the time. These two creeps had just got out of prison when they went into that bar, acting like possessed animals. Officer William Smith had to buy his own bulletproof vest because the department would not do that. Had he been issued one, he most likely would've been wearing it at the time of the shooting and would have only suffered a broken rib or two. As the editor of the Police Protective Association newspaper, I led hundreds of men to meet with our Chief of Police Art Dill. Our group then headed to the capitol building to confront the governor. Hundreds of other officers joined us on the way to the capitol building. I told him that we were demanding every officer be issued bulletproof vests, hollow point ammo (which was used to kill Officer Smith), and shotguns in every car.

Cops: 2. Rotten bad guys: 1. (It is very reassuring to know that Officer Smith is in heaven and two rotten criminals are in hell or will be going there very shortly.)

OFFICER KILLED DURING STICK UP ATTEMPT

The PPA and members of the Denver Police Department express their sympathy to the family of Officer William Edwin Smith 70-71, 12-31-46, who came on the department June 16, 1970. Officer Smith was fatally shot as he walked into a bar on a routine call at 38th and Federal on January 23, 1975 at 2 a.m.

Nation Should Honor Pursuers of the Law

Officer William Smith is laid to rest.

OVER THE PAST 10 years, 3 officers have died from criminal action. Of these, 613 have d from handguns. For no particular reason that presents it-, Sunday nights are the most gerous nights, and the hours ween 10 p.m. and 2 a.m. are most dangerous hours. Most cers are slain in robbery pursor in attempting other arrs. Last year saw 29 officers d in responding to "disturze calls." It is a shocking ction on our violent society 25 policemen were killed hey made routine traffic s.
he composite image of the dead officer indicates that he was white (10 percent were black, 3 per cent other races); that he was in his late twenties or early thirties (median police service, 5½ years); and that he most probably died on regular patrol duty in his squad car. But of the 127 slain last year, 11 actually were off-duty at the time. They died in the highest tradition of law enforcement, which holds that an officer of the law is never "off duty."

Who were their killers? All but six of last year's killings were cleared by arrest. Of the 192 identified offenders, 77 per cent had prior criminal records. 61 percent previously had been convicted and released on parole or probation. Sixteen per cent actually were on parole or probation when they were involved in the killing of an officer.

Some appropriate method should be found, it seems to me, for the living not only to honor these dead but also to honor the profession in which they served. Perhaps a deserved tribute could be arranged if the President annually were to invite to the White House the families of the slain officers, there to receive medals in memoriam.

ANOTHER APPROACH is suggested in a bill sponsored briefly by Senators John McClellan of Arkansas and Roman Hruska of Nebraska to provide for $50,000 memorial stipends to the families of police and firemen killed by felonious action or by accident in the line of duty.

The McClellan-Hruska bill would cost an estimated $20 million a year. It is a large sum, perhaps unwisely large. But the basic idea has merit. Police officers know little of public honor or respect in life; in some fashion we ought to honor those who pursued law and found death instead.

Reprint from Washington Star

HOLLOW-POINT BULLET VICTIM

Policemen Protest Gun Death of Officer

By JAY WHEARLEY, PAT BRAY
and RYKKEN JOHNSON
Denver Post Staff Writers

About 350 Denver policemen, including many who left their posts, met Thursday to protest the death of a fellow officer who was fatally shot earlier in the day with a hollow-point bullet when he answered a disturbance call at a bar.

The officers, many wearing black arm bands, were angry because they have been prevented from carrying hollow-point ammunition by a public outcry over Police Chief Art Dill's plans to issue it.

Chief Dill met with the 350 protesting policemen during the morning in the City Auditorium, across the street from police headquarters at 13th and Champa Sts. The meeting had been moved from the headquarters when the crowd increased to hundreds. The press was barred from the meeting.

Dill later said the officers asked for shotguns for each Denver patrol car, and their request will be granted immediately.

Other demands, he said, are to be

presented to him by the Denver Police Union, Police Protective Association and The Brotherhood, an organization of policemen. They will be acted upon "one by one," Dill said.

'Want to Protect Selves'

The policemen, he said, want only "the right to protect themselves and the citizens of Denver."

Some officers left the meeting to join an informal march on the State Capitol, where the legislature is to consider banning police use of hollow-point bullets. Others returned to their duties.

On their way to the Capitol, the policemen walked through the City and County Building seeking an audience with Denver Mayor Bill McNichols. When they discovered he wasn't in his office, the policemen continued toward the Capitol.

During the march, a Brotherhood spokesman said police will begin using hollow-point ammunition "until some sort of legislation is passed against it."

He said Dill and the department administration agreed not to take action against officers using hollow-point bullets unless the patrolman uses that type of ammunition wrongly.

Didn't Draw His Gun

The slain police officer, Patrolman William E. Smith, 26, was shot before he had a chance to draw his gun when he walked in on a robbery at Pier 11, 3730 Federal Blvd., Detective Capt. Robert Shaughnessy reported.

Other officers answering the call arrested one suspect in the bar and wounded another as he fled, Shaughnessy said.

He identified the suspects as James A. Lang, 24, a transient, who was jailed for investigation of homicide, and David L. Bridges, 25, no known address, who was listed in fair condition at Denver General Hospital with bullet wounds in the chest and abdomen.

A hold order was placed at the hospital against Bridges for investigation of homicide, Shaughnessy said.

Smith was shot at 2:11 a.m. and died at 3:17 a.m. at DGH. Shaughnessy said the patrolman was hit in the chest by a .357-magnum hollow-point bullet that burst his aorta.

Cops put job, safety on line

July 6, 1997

Because my son was once a Denver city policeman, I can empathize with cops having to deal with violent criminals who may kill when they're in a jam.

One day while my son was driving to work in Denver, he heard on the radio that a cop he had been riding with was shot and killed when he answered a call to a bar room brawl. He was shot in the chest but was not wearing his bullet proof vest. He had left it home that day for his wife to wash it.

Thus I was touched to receive a letter the other day from a young Grand Prairie, Texas, cop's wife, Michelle Hubbard. She was pleading for help to defend her husband from a murder charge, the victim of a "witchhunt" in her view.

The shooting occurred when police responded to the report that a black man was walking down the street, yelling at motorists and waving a knife. The man lunged at an officer, and Blake, just arriving on the scene, drew his gun and fired twice, killing the man — Joe Lee Calloway. Tragically, Blake did not learn until later that Calloway had a history of mental illness and that the other officer had already sprayed him with mace.

Hubbard's wife Michelle says Blake saved his fellow officer's life. But there were sit-ins and protests at the police headquarters, which were covered by the media. The police department fired Hubbard, saying he was not justified in his use of force.

Michelle claims the original assistant prosecutor assigned to the case was a white female, but she was replaced with a black male at the insistence of the NAACP.

Hubbard is being tried this August for murder. If the jury in his trial is as racially stacked as it was in the Simpson trial, Hubbard faces a bleak future behind bars.

MY TURN

ED HAROLDSEN

Moreover, the Calloway family is suing the police department, and has hired the famous Simpson defense attorney Johnnie Cochran as their lawyer in the case.

Meanwhile, Hubbard's wife Michelle, is expecting a baby this summer but still working at her job and trying to raise money to defend him. Aiding her is the Law Enforcement Legal Defense Fund, Washington DC 20069-0563.

It's a sad story. A young cop's life destroyed in a few seconds in what he thought was action in the line of duty. But regardless of whether Hubbard was right or wrong in shooting when he did the fact remains that the police regularly face a near impossible dilemma in meeting deadly force by criminals. Do they hesitate and perhaps get killed themselves, or do they pull their guns to protect themselves?

I'm glad my son is no longer a cop. Now I don't have to wonder each day if he will make it home alive. Considering the wages policemen get and the nasty criticism they have to suffer, it's a wonder any intelligent, qualified young person would ever want to became a cop. But many do, and I'm glad. What would society be without them?

Ed Haroldsen is a Brigham Young University professor emeritus of communications.

18

.357 MAGNUM TRAFFIC STOP

WE WERE DRIVING ON LARIMER Street and saw a 56 Chevy in front of us going back-and forth all over the road. We finally got the car stopped at 19th and Lawrence. As I approached the vehicle on the driver's side, the driver was pulling something out of his pants and put it under the car seat. Mike Luceroo was the driver of the car, and we knew him always to be packing a gun. We had him step out of the vehicle along with Mike Paddilla and Don Cavannagh. When Luceroo got out of the car, I saw the handle of a 357-magnum sticking out from under the seat. The revolver was a Ruger serial number 305189. All three suspects said they didn't know whose gun it was. I arrested Luceroo for carrying a concealed weapon and advised him of his rights and handcuffed him. We asked Paddilla if we could look in the trunk of the car, and he said yes. We found a 7 mm Savage rifle that had been stolen in a burglary. Cavanagh and Lucero, we're both convicted felons, and therefore we charged them as felons in possession of weapons. Detective Burkhart advised us to charge all three of them for the investigation of burglary. We also recovered a large pair of channel locks with brass filings on them, which are usually used to twist off doorknobs. We took all the parties to jail. All the evidence was clearly marked and placed in the custodian.

I was a member of SCAT (Special Crime Attack Team), which was a special unit assigned to burglaries and armed robberies. We were driving in the 2300 block of Holly Street, which had a very high burglary rate. We observed a car with three parties sitting in it parked in front of the residence at 2373 Holly Street. We saw Gerry Jenkens, who was sitting in the backseat and had a history of burglaries and was presently wanted. I flipped a U-turn just as the car sped away from the curb. We finally got the car pulled over and approached very cautiously, knowing that Jenkens had a history of caring weapons. We ordered all the parties to get out of the vehicle and started to search for weapons. An NCIC, radio check came back that Jenkens was wanted on a narcotics warrant, #78312. I arrested Jenkens and handcuffed him and advised him of his rights. All three parties exhibited physical symptoms of heroin use. They all had glazed eyes with constricted pupils, and their attention span was limited, and they were drowsy and yawning and scratching. We placed Steven Brittoon and John Lee Lewiston under arrest for investigation of illegal use of narcotics.

I also advised Jenkens that he, too, was going to be charged with the investigation of the illegal use of narcotics. I called for a backup car to haul the suspect to jail. I called for a tow, and we begin to inventory the items in the car. I found a .22 caliber Ruger automatic under the driver's seat. Two gulf credit cards were found on the front seat as well as a Fina credit card on the dashboard on the driver's side. We also found a soot-blackened spoon on the rear seat. We also advised all three that they were being arrested for carrying concealed weapons.

We were able to determine that one of the credit cards was stolen in an aggravated robbery, and one in a burglary. Additional holds were placed on all three for the investigation of aggravated robbery and burglary. Detective Parisi said the cards had been fraudulently used, and we would charge them with forgery as well. The soot-covered spoon was found next to where Jenkens had been sitting.

We found out that Jenkens and Brittoon were both out on an appeal bond. Their presence on the street with the pistol, narcotics, and stolen property indicates that they are a severe threat to the well-being of the general public. I made up my mind as soon as I found out they're both out on bond that I would go to the judge and get them revoked based on the recent arrests. It would be an excellent service to the community to have the bonds revoked.

On June 17, 1973, while working car 117, we received a call of a burglary in progress at 942 Bryant Street. It was just after 10 PM, and therefore it was very dark. We checked the front door, which was locked and secure, and went around and checked the back door. The glass in the door had been broken out, and the door was barricaded with all kinds of furniture. After a fair amount of effort, we finally got the door opened and entered the house. I quickly checked downstairs and saw the whole area was totally ransacked. Since we didn't find anybody downstairs, we went upstairs to look. We found the suspect Chris Lobato hiding under a bed. We handcuffed him and advised him of his rights and took him into headquarters to the burglary detail. Lobato was advised of his rights again by the detectives. What was a little odd was that he stated several times, "I'm guilty! I'm guilty!"

Lobato had a very long record of burglaries. My partner and I had exhausted several leads on the whereabouts of Tony Leafibre, who was wanted on an outstanding warrant for selling narcotics. We had two good possibilities and spent the next five days after our regular tour of duty using our own car. After two or three hours on one address, we would go and watch the other address for Leafibre. We finally spotted him inside the DQ Delicatessen at E. 28th Ave. and Fairfax Street. We found out that his wife was working next door in the Malcolm X Center for Mental Health. We quickly exited our private vehicle and ran in and grabbed him and placed him under arrest. We handcuffed him and advised him of his rights. We were in full uniform when we placed him under arrest. Car 216 came to transport him to headquarters, where they verified that the warrant was still outstanding, and he was taken to the city jail.

Cops: 8. Bad guys: 0.

NAME: Michael E. Lucero
DOB: 7/16/52
D P D #: 161329
AKA:
ADDRESS: 1036 Hooker
POSS. VEHICLE: 65' Chev, BC-5610
GENERAL INFO.:

CCW gun .357

Bad Bad guy

CRIME SPECIALTY	NAME
Aggravated Robbery	Jerry Jenkins /06

ALIAS: "J=pup"
DESCRIPTION: NM, 6=0, 170, brn, brn
DPD # 96076
F.B.I. NO. 51 834 E

Likes Boulder

ASSOCIATES / RELATIVES: Archie Murrell, McNeal brothers
M.O.: Likes to rob motels & car rentals

Denver Robbery = @DM

LA FEBRE, Anthony Theodore   brn. blk.

DOB : 7-29-52
ADD : 4255 Navajo St.
REC : heroin user. burg.
      D.U.S.

LOVATO, Christopher, DPD 115280,
DOB 8-14-47, S/A, 5'8", 130, Brn.
eyes, Blk. hair. Paroled
1-11-72.

19

FBI'S MOST WANTED

I LOVED MY JOB AS a Denver police officer. I looked forward to going to work every single day. I would polish my brass, polish, and my boots and have my uniforms dry cleaned, so they looked sharp. The starting pay at that time was $600 a month, which at the time seemed to be a terrific paycheck. When we had our fourth child, it was challenging to make ends meet. I decided I wanted to be an FBI agent that paid a lot more. I talked to a friend of mine who was an FBI agent, and he said that they were not hiring, but there would be one way I would for sure get on their agency. He said if I could arrest Cammy Dave Bishup, I would have a free pass for sure. He didn't have to tell me who Bishup was because, like any other police officer, they knew that name and face very well. Bishup had been on the Ten Most Wanted list for seven years. He had blown up power plants and may have killed a police officer. I studied his mug shot for a long time and knew every detail about him.

The Denver Police Department had recently added the new special task force, which had special federal funding. The unit was called SCAT (special crime attack team). I wanted to become a member of this elite group. The problem was I hadn't been a police officer long enough to be considered a real veteran. I applied anyway and was very thrilled when I was picked to be a member of the SCAT team. I found out later that because of my numerous official commendations for outstanding police work, they had waived the veteran police officer requirements.

I loved the camaraderie in the unit. The federal funding made it possible for us to have access to all the latest and greatest guns, ammo, and equipment. We had a van with one-way glass, which made it possible for us to go on stakeouts for hours without being uncomfortable. One of the targets of our SCAT team was to stop armed robberies of convenience stores. Our unit used a computer to determine what store would be a likely target for the next armed robbery.

Our unit became quite well-known for the numerous armed robberies that we were able to stop. Working in the SCAT unit one night, I found out that a 7-Eleven store was on the list of most likely to be hit next, but we didn't have the manpower to sit on that particular store. Since I had the next day off, I went to the store manager and told him I would like to work off duty because it was very likely his store was going to be robbed. He liked the idea and offered to pay me for my time, which I happily accepted.

I took up a position in the back of the store where there was a curtain that allowed me to see what was going on without being seen. After several hours with nothing going on, two suspicious-looking guys came in the store wearing big trench coats, and it was a hot summer day. The store manager had told me earlier that the payphone in the store was out of service, and I should use the phone behind the counter if I needed to call for backup. One of the guys wearing a trench coat went over and started to act like he was talking on the phone.

The other guy approached the cashier at the counter. As he got closer to the counter, he opened his coat and started to reach in to get his sawed-off shotgun, which was hanging from his shoulder. I was in a dilemma as to what actions I should take. If I stopped him at that point, I could only get him for possession of an illegal weapon, and I really wanted to be able to charge him with armed robbery. I couldn't call for backup because the phone was right behind the cashier. With only a few seconds to make this difficult decision, I sprang into action. Jumping out behind the curtain, I was able to disarm the first suspect with the sawed-off shotgun. I slammed him down against the counter and aimed my gun at the second suspect who had the phone up to his ear. I figured he probably was right-handed since he was holding the phone in his right hand and would probably find it difficult to reach for a gun with his left hand. I yelled at him to get his hands in the air, or he was a dead man.

With only one pair of handcuffs, I secured one suspect and held the other one on the floor until backup arrived. I felt great about my decision, thinking that an illegal weapons violation was far better than a dead or wounded cashier.

A few days later, I was working the night shift with our SCAT unit when our Sergeant invited us to have dinner with him at Denny's restaurant. Earlier that day before I went to work, I had been studying mug shots and was concentrating on Cammy David Bishup, the guy on the FBI's Ten Most Wanted list. After sitting down with the Sergeant and several other uniformed officers, I immediately noticed a man sitting four tables away who looked rather suspicious. There was something familiar about him, which I couldn't quite place until he removed his sunglasses. Although he was wearing a hat and had a beard, I knew those eyes. I slowly leaned across the table and whispered to the Sergeant, "Cammy Dave Bishup is sitting four tables behind you!" I didn't have to tell him or the other officers who Bishup was. He calmly said OK, nobody looks that way. We will finish up our dinner, and everyone acts like we're having a good fun time with plenty of laughter and jokes.

We all had a hard time not gulping down our food. We didn't care about eating with the number one most wanted guy in America sitting so close to us. We all got up and went over to the cashier to pay for our meal. Once outside, the Sergeant assigned two officers to each of the four roads leading away from Denny's restaurant. As good luck would have it, the Sergeant advised my partner and me that Mr. Bishup was going down the road where we were sent about a block away hidden behind a garage. The Sergeant gave us a description of the car, and as it passed us, we drove in behind, and I lit up the lights and siren. Bishup immediately pulled over. I approached him on the driver's side, I remembered something crucial to my safety. He always had a gun and would not hesitate to use it. I approached the car very cautiously with my service revolver drawn and with the hammer back ready to fire. Bishups' window was down, and I stuck my gun hard against his temple and said if he made one wrong move, his brains would be all over the car. Much to my surprise, he calmly said, "Okay, you got me, you don't need to kill me!"

We got Bishup in the backseat of our car. I sat on one side of him, my partner on the other, and two other officers in the front. We also had officers in front of us, leading the way and a car behind us as we took him to the Federal Building lock up. I turned and looked at him and asked, "How did you stay underground for seven years?"

He looked at me with cold empty dark eyes and said, "Rookie, I would shoot you in a second while you would be debating whether to pull the trigger or not!"

After we got him in the Federal lockup, we met outside in front of the building. Instead of laughing and doing high-fives and all that stuff and celebrating the big win, we told the other officers about his comment to me and those cold dark black empty eyes. We said to them it was like we just had an encounter with the devil himself.

I could have become an FBI agent, but I loved being a uniformed officer too much.

Cops: 3. Bad guys: 0. One really bad guy: no longer a threat.

DENVER POLICE DEPARTMENT, DENVER, COLORADO

SPECIAL BULLETIN

On Death Row

Descriptions on every death row inmate in the USA. Including every USA execution since 1977

SUBSCRIBE

WOMEN ON DEATH ROW   STATES   EXECUTIONS 2000 TO PRESENT

Cameron David Bishop FBI Most Wanted

- June 23, 2017

CAMERON DAVID BISHOP

Cameron David Bishop FBI Most Wanted

Cameron David Bishop was placed on the FBI Most Wanted List for multiple counts of sabotage. According to the FBI Cameron Bishop and a group of others blew up four high powered voltage lines outside of Denver Colorado. Cameron David Bishop would be added to the FBI Most Wanted List in April 1969 and would not be caught for six years. Bishop was sentenced to seven years in prison

Return To The FBI Most Wanted List

Judge Arraj could become annoyed with attorneys who were unprepared or made fatuous arguments. Sometimes he handled the situation with humor; other times with thunder. Once, when a bumbling barrister ducked into the hallway during a recess, the Judge told his courtroom deputy to lock the door and keep him out. The press reported that Johnny Carson would have envied the laugh.[20] Lawyers knew they were in for it when the Judge Arraj's face began to turn red. If the redness reached the top of his bald dome, a verbal lashing was the order of the day. For the most part, however, the Judge was known as a kind hearted man who loved the law, the people he worked with and his family. Lawyers generally referred to him as Triple A.[21]

Of the thousands of cases over which he presided in his 35 years on the federal bench, Judge Arraj pointed to two as highlights. The first was a highly publicized criminal case during the Vietnam War. In January 1969 Cameron David Bishop and three co-conspirators bombed a tower in Golden that provided power to the Coors Porcelain plant which manufactured nose cones for military missiles. Bishop fled the country and was not apprehended until March 1975. Michael E. Tigar, who later defended Terry Lynn Nichols in the Oklahoma City bombing case, represented Bishop.

[20] Proceedings in Memoriam, Honorable Alfred A. Arraj Judge, United States District Court, 855 F. Supp. At LXXXI-LXXXII (May 11, 1993).

[21] Mike Monroe, *Justice White Praises Arraj, Judicial Tenure*, The Denver Post, June 15, 1987, at 2B.

20

130 MPH PRANK

Because of the many outstanding arrests that my partner and I had made, we were assigned for the first time to what was called "The Wild Car!" This assignment meant that we could cover any area anywhere in the city of Denver regardless of how far away a crime might be occurring. Because we were not restricted in any way to stay in a given area, we were able to cover calls of stick-ups in progress, bank robberies, officers calling for help, and other exciting, action-packed calls. We received information from a confidential informant who had been accurate in the past on numerous arrests. He told us that a particular party had a considerable quantity of heroin and morphine in his apartment. Because of the nature of this information, our lieutenant said for us to go home and put on regular civilian clothes and wanted to find an unmarked police car for the upcoming raid. We told him that from the information gathered from our CI, that we would have to use a vehicle that would not be spotted as easily as one of our typical undercover or unmarked police cars. My partner volunteered to have us use his green Porsche, and the lieutenant said that's a great idea.

With our clothes changed, we were driving the Porsche heading to the courthouse to get the judge to sign the Warrant. Since we didn't have a police unit, we had a portable radio with us, and we're monitoring all the channels in case of a hot call. We then heard a traffic radar unit come over the radio stating the different speeds cars were going under an overpass. We had seen the setup before and knew exactly what the traffic guys were doing to write people for speeding. The speed limit on that particular road was 45 miles an hour. As we came over the rise and started to dip down to drive under the overpass, we saw the radar car up above with his radar gun and heard him calling out "brown Ford right lane 49 miles an hour let him go!" Then he said, "red Chevy station wagon left lane 47 miles an hour let him go!" He then said, "green Porsche 51 miles an hour right lane let him go!" We both smiled at each other and had the same little prank in mind. It took us a few minutes to get off of the highway come back around on the same road as we approached the radar set up. We heard the same traffic car calling out different colors of cars and their speeds. The last call on the radio came out just before we got within range of the radar gun coming over the hill, "Black Cadillac, right lane, 56 miles an hour—get him!"

Only a couple of seconds after that, we heard a loud hysterical voice scream, "Green Porsche 130 miles an hour get that maniac!"

As we came to the bottom of the overpass going like a bullet, we saw two motorcycle cops as they were slamming their feet down, starting their motorcycles. The two motorcycles came screaming after us, probably thinking we were some bank robbers or something terrible like that. We sped up a little more just to make things a little more exciting and heard them calling out our speed as they were having a hard time catching us. Fearing one of them might get injured or we could have an unfortunate accident, I finally came over the radio and said, "Back off, guys, we're part of the same team!"

The dispatcher screamed into the mic, "Who in the blank is this?"

I calmly said, "Hey, we're cops just like you tell your motorcycle cops they can go back under the overpass and catch some real speeders!"

I won't repeat some of the nasty comments the motorcycle cops said over the radio, but we sure did have a nice laugh about the whole thing! Needless to say, we were the talk at the roll calls for a few days after that, with a lot of laughs and jokes being made about the traffic guys. Once in a while, our Sergeant or lieutenant would interrupt the laughter and jokes and speak kind of sternly but always had a half-smirk on their faces!

When we got downtown, I had my partner get the Warrant signed, and I wanted to go up to the DEA floor in the federal building to check on the possibility of a better-paying job. I rode the lockup elevators that were used to transport prisoners and as it opened onto the DEA floor when things got kind of crazy. I quickly drew my gun and yelled, "Freeze, or you're a dead man!" when I saw a long-haired creepy-looking scumbag with a 45 in the back of his waist. The next few seconds were very tense as he's very slowly turned around to face me. I was always good at recognizing faces and knew I had seen this creep somewhere before.

He slowly started to drop his hands, and I was ready to fire when a detective yelled at me, "He's one of us put your gun away!"

It turned out he was a deep undercover narcotics detective who had put numerous bad guys away because he looked like the worst person in the world you would run into. I quickly apologized to him, and he took it rather well. We talked for a few minutes, and things got a lot friendlier. I still could not get over what a bad-looking dude he really was, but was also one of the best undercover cops you would ever know. He looked like such a bad guy that he would testify in court and put some terrible guys in prison. Oftentimes, years later, he would bust the same dumb bad guys because they did not remember that he was actually an undercover cop.

Cops: a bit of fun. Traffic cops: not so much. (DEA guys: a bit of excitement.)

21

WORLD'S BEST LIAR

POLICE OFFICERS QUICKLY LEARN THAT intuition and gut feelings are crucial in making good stops and good arrests. The suspect's body language often helps in assessing a situation. Working in car 109, which had the highest crime rate of any precinct, was always a great experience because I loved the action. One of the many ways I was able to make so many good arrests was a technique I learned from my training officer Mad Dog Burton. Driving around in our assigned area when we would see a suspiciouslooking person walking down the sidewalk, we put our plan into action. We would drive our police car slowly close to the curb at the same speed as the person walking. Every single time we did that, if the person didn't turn and look at the car, we knew we were on to a good stop and possible arrest. Without exception, if we slammed on the brakes, the suspect would boogie.

It was a beautiful summer day in late May when we spotted a suspicious-looking guy walking down the sidewalk. Like clockwork, after putting our plan in motion, the guy took off on a dead run. I bailed out of the car and caught him a block and a half down the street. My partner pulled the police car up, and we started to question him. When we asked him why he took off running, he turned red in the face and reached his hand in his pocket. I grabbed his arm as he pulled out several small balloons, probably containing heroin. Before I could stop him, he stuffed his mouth full and started to swallow them. I tried to stop him, but it didn't work. We arrested him and took him downtown. We told the sheriff about the balloons, and he said he would make sure that he used the toilet with the screen. The next day they retrieved the balloons from the toilet, and we picked them up and took them to the lab to be tested. A few days later, we got the report back that the balloons contained heroin just as we suspected. We went to the jail and talked to the suspect about the heroin. With his past arrest, this latest narcotics violation would send him to prison for at least ten years. We told him that we would put a good word to the district attorney if he would give us the name and address of his suppliers. We told him that we couldn't promise anything, but if his information leads to a big drug bust, he could possibly only serve a year. He quickly agreed to the deal and gave us the information we needed. Since this was our first dealing with him as a confidential informant, we had to get another source to verify the drug dealer he gave us was for real. With a bit of good luck and being at the right place at the right time, we ran into an old Cl. When he saw the police car, he took off running but gave up when I yelled at him who I was and that I knew him. We patted him down for weapons and found methamphetamines in his pocket, which would've been enough to put him back in prison. With the promise that we would not file charges on him, if you could verify some information, he quickly agreed. We went to the judge and got a no-knock search warrant. The warrant included every type of illegal street drug, and possible weapons and cash.

Because of the likelihood of weapons being in the house, we had an additional four other officers go with us. I went to the front door with two officers, and my partner went to the back door with two other officers. We communicated by radio and said, "Go now!" As we charged through the door, we found numerous suspects sleeping on the floor. We searched them all and had them sit on the couch. We confiscated drugs on the table and syringes and other drug paraphernalia. Two narcotics detectives came into the house and started giving me a hard time. They asked me where the big stash was that we heard you were supposed to find here. So far, at that time, we had seen only a small amount of drugs in different rooms. Detectives did not let up with their sarcastic comments saying, "So, Supercop Haroldsen, you call this a major drug bust, give us a break?" I was starting to feel really bad about the drug raid because I was so sure we were going to hit pay dirt.

Right at the moment, the two detectives started to give me some more crap my partner said, "I think I found it get in here!"

Under the stairs was a large metal storage locker. It had a heavy-duty padlock on it. Since we had the steel door ram for the no-knock search warrant, it quickly broke off the lock. I literally held my breath as the lid was opened on the storage chest. Just before it was open enough to see in it, one of the detectives said, "You really think you're going to find anything in that?"

It was crammed full to the very top with packaged drugs. I turned to the two detectives standing there looking rather sheepish. I said, "So, I guess, you guys aren't stupid enough to try to take credit for this bust?"

With that comment, the two of them walked out without saying a single word. We determined from some mail on the table whose house this was. We separated all the guys in the place to question them. It soon became somewhat clear who lived there and some of the people who were just visiting. One of the suspects I was questioning, Dale Hineman, was a very clean-cut guy who seemed to be quite intelligent and didn't fit in with the others. He told me that he just stopped to see a friend, but since he wasn't there, he was actually on his way out when we came in the door. He said he was in law school and hoped this incident wouldn't cause him any problems with his scholarship. After talking to him for a while, I could tell he was very well educated and smart and told him I would speak to the district attorney about dropping charges on him. We took the suspects in to have them booked and put in jail.

The next morning, I got a phone call from the district attorney who asked me to meet him in the courtroom. He told me it was crucial and I should get there as soon as possible. As I was walking down the hall in the building, two uniformed officers that I did not know stopped me and said, "You're Officer Haroldsen, right?" I asked them how they knew my name. They replied, "Your picture is on the front page of the Rocky Mountain News!" I said to them that they had to be kidding me because that would not be possible. Then One of the officers took a newspaper folded under his arm and opened it up to the front page of the paper was a picture of me holding a rifle. On the table was a shoulder holster with a handgun, several pounds of drugs, and a cash deposit bag from the recently robbed drive-in theater. There was also evidence that these suspects were involved in a pharmacy robbery.

The officers wanted to have all the details, and I started to tell them when I remembered I had to meet the district attorney in the courtroom. As I was walking into the courtroom, I was feeling pretty good about myself. A front page story on the Rocky Mountains newspaper with my picture and story was pretty impressive. I was starting to feel like the nickname the narcotics detectives had given me. Supercop Haroldsen is in the news again with another big drug bust. I thought to myself smiling. My smile quickly faded when I saw the face of the district attorney frowning. He told me to sit down so we could talk. He said," officer Haroldsen, are you familiar with the Organized Crime book that was issued to you?" Feeling a little bit surer of myself, I answered absolutely!" He then asked me to tell him about Dale Hineman, who I had arrested on a narcotics raid. I told him about our conversation and then wanted to know if he agreed with me that we should not file charges against him. He then pulled the Organized Crime book out of his briefcase. He flipped through a few pages and stopped and turned the book around so I could see it and pointed to a picture of Dale Hineman. I quickly read about him being arrested for selling $288,000 worth of cocaine to some undercover narcotics detective. Supercop Haroldsen suddenly became Super Sad Cop Haroldsen. Hineman was the best liar I've ever met in my life. Finding out later that he was involved in an armed robbery of a pharmacy in Pocatello, Idaho, in which an officer was killed did not make me any happier. I spent the next several days studying the Organize Crime book, so I would not make another stupid mistake.

Cop: 5. Bad guys: 0. (It was almost "cops: 4; bad guys: 1.")

Suspected narcotics seized

Patrolman Scott Haroldsen surveys about 20 pounds of suspected marijuana and various quantities of other suspected narcotics which Denver police confiscated Sunday in a raid at 233 W. Third Ave. Five persons were arrested. Also taken was .22 caliber rifle and a deposit bag belonging to a Lakewood drive-in theater. Those arrested are suspected of involvement in a recent hospital pharmacy robbery. **STORY ON PAGE 33.**

Three Arrested On Suspicion of Selling Cocaine

Three persons were arrested and suspected cocaine police said had a street value of $288,000 was confiscated early Saturday, Detective Robert Cantwell of the Organized Crime Strike Force reported.

Cantwell said the arrests were made after the three suspects allegedly sold 5½ ounces of cocaine to undercover officers at Ramada Inn, 3737 Quebec St.

Arrested for investigation of narcotics for sale were Dale Hinman, 21, and Margaret Newton, 18, both of 3300 W. Iowa Ave., and Tom Miles, 21, of 2073 S. Walcott St., Cantwell said.

In addition, Cantwell reported, his group, the North Metro Enforcement Group and the Special Crime Attack Team executed arrest warrants on five of 19 persons charged in connec-

DALE M. HINMAN
DOB - 8/7/52

MARGARET D. NEWTON
DOB - 4/26/55

THOMAS F. MILLS
DOB - 1/27/52

DENVER POLICE DEPARTMENT

OFFICIAL COMMENDATION

TO: Office of the Chief of Police

Date May 14, 1974

FROM: Patrol Division-Dist. One
Division — District — Bureau

I wish to commend Officer Scott Haroldsen , Serial No. 72-33 .
who is presently assigned to Car 125 Dist. One
for the following:

- ☒ Class Two Award
- ☐ Class Three Award
- ☐ Class Four Award

WHEREAS it is realized that the great bulk of police work is done routinely by good policemen, let it be known that the above-named officer displayed initiative and alertness decidedly in excess of the norm in this particular instance.

Fact Situation: On May 12, 1974 Officers Haroldsen and Meyer received information from an informant that the parties living at 233 W. 3rd Ave were selling narcotics. Officers obtained a search warrant and on this date a raid was conducted resulting in the recovery of over ten pounds of marijuana and other drugs, as well as evidence possibly connected to several stick-ups. These officers are commended for thier initiative which led to the recovery and the arrest of five parties involved in the sale of narcotics and several robberies.

Commending Officer Tech. M. Walker 68-104 A/Sgt.

Command Officer's Approval Capt. J. Lahey

Read and Approved Paul a Montye
Division Chief

Arthur G. Dill
Chief of Police

DISTRIBUTION
Original and one copy to Commendations Board

(Separate set for each officer mentioned)

— DO NOT FOLD —

DPD 139 (Rev. 6/70)

22

LET'S MAKE A DEAL

THERE WAS A BIG DIAMOND heist of one of the high-end jewelry stores in downtown Denver. I contacted some of my reliable, confidential informants to see if any of them had any information about the big diamond heist. Up to this point, we had struck out, but we are driving slowly around the residential area that was known to have criminals active in the area, and we spotted a guy walking down the sidewalk. I mediately knew that he had not been out of prison very long because of the way he shuffled his feet as he walked. Inmates who spend time in the Buena Vista prison in southern Colorado kind of pick up a certain way they walk, which we nicknamed the Buena shuffle. This guy definitely had recently been released from the Buena Vista prison. The second we slammed on the brakes on the car, the chase was on. My partner ran him down on the sidewalk at the same time that I used the police car to pin him up against the fence. As luck would have it, our search revealed a switchblade knife in one pocket and a bag of cocaine in the other pocket. As soon as we brought up Mike "Black" Montoya's name, it was apparent from his reaction that he knew him and also knew about the diamond heist.

After the arrest, we finally negotiated a deal that we would not send him to prison if he could give us some information about the heist. After a couple of hours of intense questioning, he finally told us that he did not know where Montoya lived, but he had his phone number. I had an individual contact in the phone company who had helped me numerous times in the past, so I gave her a call. I gave her the phone number, and after only a minute or two, she had the address. She asked me if I was ready to write it down and I said you bet and she gave it to me. I went to the judge and got a no knock search warrant, because of the danger Black Montoya would be. My confidential informant who gave us the phone number had proved to be reliable on confidential informant search warrants in the past, so we had no trouble getting this one. I called my sergeant and told him the situation, and that I would need at least six other officers because this guy was known to be armed and very dangerous. We met at a store a couple of blocks from the suspect and put our plan together. We figured the house would have the front door and back door, so I assigned four officers to the back, and three officers and I took the front. Because of the danger that we could easily face, I told everyone that we would hit both doors precisely at the same time, which would cause a little bit of confusion and give us time to get the drop on "Black."

Everyone was in place, and so I barked out the order on the radio, "Go hard now!" We hit the front door so hard with our RAM that the door fell flat on the floor off its hinges. I was the first one through the front with the shotgun and got the drop on a woman and two children sitting on the living room couch. My very first thought was this cannot be the right house. We had eight officers with their guns all aimed at two small children and a woman who looked like a very ordinary housewife, definitely not a girlfriend of a scumbag like Montoya. I shouted at the officers to all put their guns down. I was amazed when I saw her reaction as well as the two kids as they glanced at us and then back to the television where they were watching the show "Let's Make a Deal!" They kept watching the TV show with the greatest of interest and then would glance at us for a second, and they would look back at the TV.

We had knocked down the door in the wrong house! I could hardly believe such little reaction she and the two kids had to eight police officers with their guns aimed at them after just smashing into their home. They seemed to be mesmerized by what they were watching on television and had no concern at all about their door getting busted down and their living room full of armed police officers. When I approached the woman on the couch, she seemed only irritated that I was interrupting what must've been her favorite TV show. I told her that I apologized for the interruption and said the Denver Police Department would gladly pay to have her doors repaired and or replaced. She glanced at me for a second and said thank you and quickly turned back to her show. Even her two small children seemed to be way more entertained with what was on the television than the sight of heavily armed police officers in their living room. We all left the house and drove back to the store where we had initially met so that I could use the phone. As soon as the particular operator answered the phone and I told her it was Officer Haroldsen, she immediately replied, "Oh, I am so sorry I was off one line when I gave you the address. She then gave me the correct address and said that she hoped that she hadn't caused us any problems. I told her that she wouldn't believe what happened, but I said I had to get going to the right address. After assuring all the officers that we now had the correct address, we headed to Black Montoya's house. So once again, I gave the order "go hard now!" Just as we went crashing through the doors, we heard the car engine revving up in the garage. Black had a car in the garage that we did not know about. Because we had a police car parked in front of it, he could not make a run for it. Well, at least we knew we had the right house this time. We were able to recover most of the diamonds. One more nice official commendation for the robbery division was the icing on the cake.

Cop: 1. Bad guys: 0. (I sure hope the nice lady got the department to pay for new doors.)

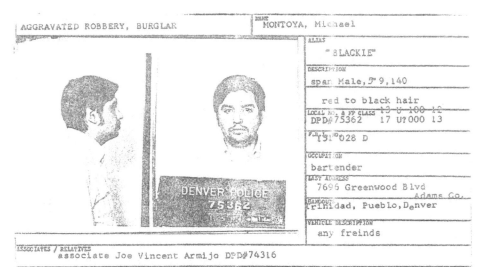

AGGRAVATED ROBBERY, BURGLAR	NAME MONTOYA, Michael
	ALIAS "BLACKIE"
	DESCRIPTION span Male, 5'9, 140 red to black hair
	LOCAL NO. & FP CLASS DPD#75362 17 U?000 13
	F.B.I. 151 028 D
	OCCUPATION bartender
	LAST ADDRESS 7696 Greenwood Blvd Adams Co.
	HANGOUT Trinidad, Pueblo, Denver
	VEHICLE DESCRIPTION any freinds

ASSOCIATES / RELATIVES associate Joe Vincent Armijo DPD#74316

M.O. driver on big jobs, wears disquises, likes jewelry robberies

LET'S MAKE A DEAL

Editorial Comment by Scott Haroldsen

Innocent, Innocent, NoLo Deferred, Deferred, Case Dismissed, Suspended Sentence, Not Guilty, Aquitted—Guilty—oops, how did that slip in? Exaggeration? *I don't think so.*

How many times have you testified in court other than on minor traffic cases? I used to think I was the only cop on the department who hardly ever testified—twice in three years. I've since found many cops with similar track records.

Now comes the old argument of plea bargaining. I am going to call it LMAD—Let's Make A Deal. True, there are not enough court rooms, judges, and lawyers to try all cases. That's the whole idea behind LMAD—I catch an armed robbery in progress, the case is filed (maybe), the DA says "Let's go over this case real thoroughly so we'll be ready for trial."—Wrong—He says, "How about letting him plead out to unlawful carrying of a weapon?" Exaggeration? I don't think so.

What about our limited court rooms, judges, and lawyers? Too often you see empty court rooms, and see judges and lawyers leaving at 10 or 11 in the morning for the rest of the day. LMAD has gone too far. Under our present system *all* cases cannot be tried—but how about *some* of them? Our judges and lawyers are being well paid, but for what? They shouldn't be paid to see how fast they can shuffle their cases into quick dispositions. They are paid to try cases! It's like someone playing solitaire with 52 cards in their hand. They cheat so they can get rid of all the cards and have a place to put them.

At the In-service Training, we learned that it takes the average cop 3 years patrolling to catch one burglar and 14 years patrolling to catch one stick-up. If I spend those 14 years getting my once-in-a-lifetime stick-up in progress, would it be too much to ask that he be *tried* for stick-up?

I heard a DA reporting on "what a poor job of testifying a veteran officer had just done on the witness stand." Practice makes perfect—there's no substitute for experience. We all would like to be good at testifying but how can we if we spend all of our time in court watching LMAD, Let's Make a Deal".

How many sharp trial lawyers have you seen in the DA's and CA's office? Their super good at playing "LMAD" but what about trying cases?

A few days ago my partner had a court case. Knowing how fast the cases are dealt out I went in to wait for him. Much to my surprise he said the case was going to trial. "Today?" I asked. "Yes." "When?" "Now," he stated. I couldn't believe it—a real trial. I jokingly said, "Oh the DA will probably blow the case it's been so long since they've actually tried one." Guess what? The DA forgot to have the officer identify the suspect and the case was dismissed.

DENVER POLICE DEPARTMENT
COMMENDATORY LETTER

From: PATROL - DISTRICT ONE
Division - District - Bureau

Date: January 9, 1974

Recognition is hereby given to J.S. Haroldsen, serial number 72-33,

who is presently assigned to District One - Detail Two,

for the following described activity: While citing a G.J. Martinez for a traffic

violation at West 44th Avenue and Stuart Street on January 5, 1973

at 1:30 PM, did discover stolen items in Martinez' car, with a pas-

senger Michael Montoya. Both parties arrested for Investigation

Burglary.

A further check by Officer Haroldsen revealed Martinez was

wanted on warrant-bond jumping.

Submitted By: Sergeant F.L. Chapman, #51-27

Approval of Command Officer:

DISTRIBUTION:

Original - Recipient Officer
Copy - Officer's Personnel File
Copy - Commendations Board

Form 139A (4/70) DPD

23

ONE TOUGH FEMALE COP

WORKING THE DAY SHIFT, MY regular partner got the day off, and so the sergeant assigned me to work with a female officer who had been in the department for over ten years. After about an hour with very little going on, we got a call about a man threatening to kill a woman with a knife. We knocked on the door and got no answer but heard some screaming and so we crashed down the door. Across the room next to the kitchen was a huge man holding a large butcher knife against a woman's throat. I drew my gun, and since I was an expert marksman, I was ready to shoot the suspect. My partner surprised the suspect and me when she went walking across the room without her gun drawn and told the guy, "Hey, you big ugly creep put the knife down, or you'll have me to settle with, you don't treat women that way, you idiot!" The guy was so shocked that he remained stunned and didn't move a muscle, which allowed my partner to a couple of seconds to hit him right in the face and grab the knife from him. Her calmness and obvious self-confidence made our suspect totally freeze, dumbfounded by the very presence of this female officer who so quickly took charge of an awful situation. I slapped the handcuffs on the suspect and took him out to the car and my companion got a signed statement from the victim. We took him into the station to be booked for aggravated assault and attempted murder and went back to work. A vehicle ran a red light right in front of us and headed for the railroad tracks. He turned onto the tracks and started to go down them. There were times when he almost got high-centered by the height of the rails. My partner turned onto the rails, and then after about ten yards, the tires were spinning, and the car was high centered.

After a few minutes of desperately trying to get moving, she turned me and said, "I suppose you think you could do better?" I said I would sure give it a try, and we changed places. Once I got the car rocking back and forth, I got free of the rails and caught up to our suspect, who had got permanently high-centered. We arrested him for running the light and added felony, eluding police officers, and driving illegally down the railroad tracks. Finally, back in our unit, patrolling in our area, we started up a conversation regarding the man with a butcher knife. I asked her what she would've done if the guy hadn't frozen in his tracks where he had the blade very close to the woman's throat and not far from my partner. She admitted it could've gone wrong, but she had a feeling he would not take any action. We continued on the subject of female versus male officers in a police department. At first, she was adamant that a woman could do the same job as a man until I posed a kind-of-hard-to-answer question. I asked her if a guy was beating her up in her home alone would she rather have a female officer her size comes through the door or a great big tough male officer come to her rescue. She thought about it for a couple of minutes and finally admitted in some cases, bigger and stronger was better. Sometimes even real bad guys are indeed in a state of shock when they see a female officer making an arrest.

A stick-up in progress at a bank came out over the air, and the dispatcher said they had confirmation that the stick-up was still in the bank at this very minute. It's usually police officers who stop bank robbers, but in this case, a teller did a fantastic thing. The stick-up approached one of the many Bank tellers placing a note down on the counter that said this is a stick-up put all the money in the bag, at which time he lifted his shirt so that she could see a gun in his waistband. This happened to be that particular teller's very first day on the job, and she was a hyper young lady. She picked up the note and threw her hands in the air and screamed in a booming voice and said, "This is my first day on the job you idiot why don't you pick on another teller, there's plenty of them in this huge bank!"

She continued screaming at him to pick on someone else, not her. "You want me to get fired my very first day on the job give me a break!"

The bank robber was so shocked by what he had just encountered that he could barely move. She, as well as other tellers, pushed their silent stick-up alarm while this bozo was walking almost in slow motion backward. As good luck would have it, and the timing couldn't have been better since two police cars were only a block away. He backed out of the bank so slowly that he was met outside by none other than four armed officers. He came through the doors backward and didn't even see the men in blue. Bank employees, including tellers, are always told to cooperate fully with any attempted robbery. This new teller didn't follow that rule, but everyone ended up safe, and of course, the bank's money was never even picked up by the stupid, incompetent bank robber. She could've quickly been shot or injured, but on this day, good luck was on the good guy's side.

A few months later, we got a similar call of a bank robbery in progress, and since it was in the downtown Denver area, it was a very slow process getting there. We would get jammed up at a red light and would use our PA system, directing the people in front of us to get out of our way. Many of them wouldn't do that since it meant they would have to run the red light to get out of our way. When we got close to the bank, we would turn off our siren so as not to alert the stick-ups of our presence, which could cause a hostage situation. This bank was enormous and had probably twenty-five or more teller windows. We entered the bank with our guns drawn, and there were dozens and dozens of people behind all the teller windows. We had no idea which teller was being robbed. The bank manager ran over to us and said he had bad news and some excellent news. Thank goodness for really stupid criminals who make our job so much easier. He took us to the teller who had been robbed so we could question her. We asked him what the good news was, and he said, "I'll let her tell you!"

She handed us a note that said, "This is a stick-up; don't push any alarms put all the money in this bag, and you might live!"

The good news was right there in my hands! The stick-up note was written on the opposite side of a deposit slip, which listed the name address and phone number. My first thought was it couldn't possibly belong to the stick-up. We had the dispatcher run the name through the NCIC, and it came back the guy just got out of prison for armed robbery three weeks ago. I kept thinking to myself; this is way too good to be true, but we would follow up anyway.

We arrived at the address with plenty of backup officers and knocked on the door. We stayed to either side of the door because officers have been killed standing in the doorway when a bad guy would shoot them right through the door. This particular door did not have a peephole, so the perp wouldn't know who was there without asking. The door opened up, but there was a chain that kept it from going all the way open. It only took three of us ramming into it, sending the door slamming the suspect against the wall. The guy was naked except for a gun in his hand, but he gave no resistance since he was almost out cold from the impact of the door. His first dumb words out of his mouth were music to our ears and would be to the DA's office when he said, "How did you find me so fast?"

We asked him his name, and magically it was the same one recovered at the bank on a deposit slip.

Cops: 3. Really dumb bad guys: 0.

24

HOW TO HANDLE A WOMAN

THE NIGHT SHIFT, WHICH WAS from seven o'clock in the evening to three o'clock in the morning, was always my favorite shift because that's when most of the action happens. One summer night, my partner and I had a rather dull shift with very little action. We were heading into District one station when we got a call to check on a person down in the middle of the road. Because we were both drained, we sure didn't want any overtime. We hurried to the call, hoping we could make it very short and get back to the station and get off duty and head home. After getting close to the area, we went slowly down the street when we saw a woman sprawled out in the middle of the road, apparently unconscious.

We got out of the car and checked to make sure she was breathing. She really reeked of a lot of bad booze. We did not want to arrest her and take her into the station. It would take a couple of hours to go through the booking process, and we'd end up taking her downtown to the jail. It took us several minutes to finally get her to wake up enough to move. We were looking around at different houses to see if anyone was out on the porch or had any lights on since it was about 3 AM. We were hoping that we could find out which house she had come from. Even though we got her awake, she could not stand up or walk. About that time right in front of where she was, a porch light came on, and a guy came on the porch and yelled something. I asked her if that was her husband yelling, and she said yes. My partner and I lifted her partway with her arms and partially lifted and partially drug her towards the house. We heard the door slam and saw the porch light go off. Since we had stopped pulling her across the road to look at the home, we turned to get a better hold on her arms. To our dismay, her pants, including her panties, had come down almost to her ankles. We quickly glanced around at all the porches hoping no one was watching this lousy scene. I told my partner to pull up her clothes, and he said no way. He said you are the senior officer, so you get to do it. I told him I am not going to touch her. As the two of us were arguing back and forth, a cool breeze came blowing down the road and brought the woman around enough that she reached down and pulled up her panties and pants. Thinking things could definitely not get any worse as we got to the sidewalk, we were quickly proven so wrong.

A little dog came running around the house and sunk his teeth deep in my partner's leg. Being distracted by the dog, he forgot about the woman's arm and let go of it at the same time as I reached for my mace to get the dog, and I let go of her other arm, and her head went clunk on the sidewalk. When I started spraying the mace at the dog, but my partner's head got in the way, and he really got it bad. After a few minutes, his eyes started to clear, and he stopped coughing. Finally, getting her up the steps at the front door, we took a breather and finally rang the doorbell. Her husband came to the door and said he didn't want her in the house, but we finally talked him into it and carefully helped her into the living room. Once inside the house, she suddenly stood up, screaming his name, and attacked him with her fingernails on his face like a wild animal. He yelled at us to get the crazy drunk woman out of his house, or he would kill her. In a flash, she went from a wild woman to an unconscious heap on the floor. Her husband kept yelling at us to get her out of the house before she came around again. He didn't even turn on the porch light for us when we took her down the stairs.

The second we got to the sidewalk the stupid little mean dog came running around and nailed my partner on the leg again. This time I was more accurate with the mace, but we both ended up dropping her arms, and her head went clunk on the concrete again. She was still out cold as we carefully dragged her towards the police car. With her close to the back door of the police cruiser, we turned to lift her in and realized her panties and pants were again down to her ankles.

We both quickly looked around at the neighbors' porches, and we are relieved to see not a light was on, and more importantly, we didn't see a single person watching this awful scene. Once again, we both argued over who was going to pull her clothes up.

Neither one of us wanted to touch her anywhere except on her wrist to load her into the car. Once again, a cool breeze blew down the road hitting her bare skin, and she reached down and pulled up her clothes. Very relieved because of mother nature's help, we loaded her in the car and headed for the station. We both thought we would have to take her downtown to the jail, but the Paddy wagon was getting ready to leave the district station, and we got her loaded in it. Although we didn't get to go home when we wanted to, we are both relieved that we didn't have to go downtown to do a bunch more paperwork.

It just so happened that the next day because District one was short on manpower, we both had to work the day shift. We were standing at attention for roll call when the sergeant called out in a very gruff voice, "Officer Haroldsen, my office immediately!" At that point, it never occurred to me what the problem could possibly be. I walked into his office, and he told me to shut the door. He then asked me about a medical report from Denver General Hospital regarding some gravel that was embedded in a woman's butt. He said you and your partner arrested her for drunk and disorderly last night, and you sent her to jail. He said he wanted to know how in the world some gravel ended up in her backside. I was at a loss for words and didn't know what I could possibly say to get out of this jamb. He told me to get my partner and get right back in the office. We didn't have time to get our story straight, so we told the sergeant the truth and precisely what had happened. The good thing was he said we could never make up such a far-fetched story, so he believed us.

He told us to get back to the roll call, which we immediately did. My partner and I were not standing next to each other, and halfway through roll call some of the other officers obviously had heard a little about what happened. Some whispering started to go on but quickly turned into snickering. I made the mistake of leaning forward and looking down the line of officers and saw my partner with a big smile on his face. The next thing before I knew it, we both broke out laughing very hysterically. The sergeant yelled at us to get into our cars, and get to work.

Cops: 0. Drunk woman: 1 (well, she kind of won).

25

DON'T ROCK THE BOAT

AFTER A LITTLE TIME AS a police officer, I realized I was only interested in stopping the bad guys. I spent countless hours studying mug shots of wanted guys and criminals who were actively breaking the law. I developed a terrific memory of faces, which made my day fighting crime exciting. If I saw someone run a red light or stop sign, I would pull them over, and the first question I asked them was, "Where do you work?" I quickly realized that the best way to make felony arrests was to let good, hard working people off the hook. Very seldom would I write a ticket to a person who had a regular job and admitted to speeding, running a red light, or whatever the violation was? If they would lie to me or argue with me, then I would give them a ticket. Any active or wanted criminals were the ones that I spent my time going after. My sergeant called me into his office one day and told me that I should not be pulling over ex-cons or other criminals just because of their past. He told me that although I had made a lot of great felony arrests, some of the guns and drugs were not admitted in court because I lacked probable cause for the initial stop. I immediately but sarcastically asked him if the judges in those cases ever returned the drugs and guns to those felons!

He did not answer my question but said that I was violating their rights. I argued with him vehemently that as far as I was concerned, a known active criminal had no rights. Once in a great while, I would come across a felon who was trying to turn their life around, so in cases like that, which were few, I would cut them some slack. Over the years after being given the nickname Supercop Haroldsen, the bigger narcotics arrest, I made the more I was harassed by narcotics detectives and some other officers. One day after I made a huge narcotic bust; I was called into the Captain's office. I assumed that I was going to be getting another of my many Official Denver Police Commendations for another outstanding arrest. I was absolutely dumbfounded and speechless when the Captain told me to just write some tickets and let the narcotics detectives handle the big felony arrests. At first, I thought he was kidding! Then he said to me words that I'll never forget and did not understand at the time, "don't rock the boat!" I finally said to him, "I thought we are on the same side, and our objective was to take drugs and guns and bad guys off the street!" He said, "you are a uniformed patrol officer, so that's what your job is write tickets and patrol your area and leave the rest to the detectives, put your 20 years in without getting yourself hurt, and you can retire!" I left his office feeling pretty down, but that all changed when I went back to work on the street.

We received a call of a burglary in progress and raced to the address. When we approached the front door, we could hear a dog barking and saw the glass on the door shattered and blood everywhere. The homeowner yelled to give him a minute to get his dog restrained. He let us in and told us what happened. He said he had been sleeping when the vicious dogs barking woke him up. He said he then heard the front door glass shattered, and his dogs barking turned into vicious growling. He turned on the lights and saw his dog biting viciously on a hand that had reached through the broken glass to unlock the front door. The man was screaming in agonizing pain and finally pulled his arm loose. There were bloody chunks of flesh on the glass and the doorknob inside. He didn't want to open the door because he was afraid the dog would disappear and maybe even be shot. Because of the large amount of blood everywhere, we were sure the suspect would head straight to the hospital. Denver General Hospital was fairly close, so we headed there. We were almost positive we would have our suspect in the ER being treated for his wounds. We found our guy and handcuffed his good arm to the bed and read him his rights. I remember very well telling him," when you get out of prison many years from now, I don't think you'll ever again break some window glass and reach through to unlock a door, and with a little luck maybe the dog taught you a good lesson!" As we were heading out the door in the breezeway, there was a man on a gurney being brought into the hospital. A doctor and a nurse ran into the breezeway and ripped open his shirt and tried to stop the bleeding from a bullet wound to the chest. There was glass between the entrance and exit breezeway. I watched the Doctor take a scalpel and make a long incision down the man's chest and then put some ribs spreaders to give him room to work on the guy's heart. The bullet had gone right through his aorta. My partner started to get sick and went outside, but I was too fascinated watching with my face pushed up against the glass. Blood started spurting all the way up to the ceiling and on the glass when the Doctor got his ribs spread. He was finally able to stop the spurting blood and yelled for the paramedics to wheel him into the emergency room. I never did find out if the man pulled through or not.

Working solo on the night shift rarely happened unless we were short of officers. I was thrilled to work alone so I could respond to any call I wanted to cover. A call came out of a burglary in progress in an industrial park area. I proceeded to the business and was the only car on the scene. The back door was open a little, and there were signs of forced entry with some type of a pry bar. The dispatcher called me again and said the burglar was actually the one who called for the police! I opened the door and used my flashlight to find my way around. I could hear a dog barking and headed in that direction. Why would a guy pulling a burglary call for the police? The loud, barking dog gave me a pretty good idea of why. I found the burglar climbing on top of some boxes kicking at the Doberman pinscher biting at his feet. We were taught in the police academy to always wear our hats with the badge showing because police dogs and guard dogs are often taught not to attack someone wearing that type of hat. I was sure grateful that I was wearing my police hat when the dog turned and came towards me. He sniffed my hands and sat down, breathing heavily. The burglary yelled, "please keep that crazy dog away from me, he already got me on the leg!" I called the emergency number listed on the phone on the wall to have them come and take care of the dog, so I could arrest the burglar. Never in my career as a police officer had I run into a burglar so happy to be handcuffed and taken to jail. After booking him for burglary, the sergeant suggested I call an ambulance to have him taking to the hospital to treat the injury to his leg.

Police: 2. Bad guys: 0. (Sergeant & Captain's advice disregarded.) (Attention: all felons—Supercop Haroldsen is coming after you.)

26

LOOTING DOWNTOWN

A POWER OUTAGE HAPPENED IN downtown Denver one evening when there were a lot of people. We immediately heard glass breaking all over the downtown area. There was an electronics store not more than fifty feet from where my partner and I were walking the downtown beat. As we approached the front door, several guys came running out with big televisions. I erroneously thought that as soon as they saw two uniformed officers that they would set the TVs down or take them back inside and run. When they went past me and kept going, I quickly drew my gun and yelled, "Police Officer, freeze!"

Some of them kept going, and a couple of them turned around and awkwardly held the television so they could flip me the bird. One of them yelled, "You think you're going to shoot one of us?"

They taught us in the police academy never to draw our gun unless we were going to shoot someone. This situation was the most frustrating position you could ever find yourself in. Very reluctantly, I holstered my weapon and started grabbing people carrying stolen merchandise out the door. We were so outnumbered that we were only able to stop some of the thieves physically. The whole downtown area became a large target for looters. We started using our mace, which was very effective in this situation although a lot of the TVs and stereos were dropped on the floor and the looters ran out blindly into the crowd.

We called for backup, and within minutes we had a swarm of officers making hundreds of arrests. We had to use zip ties to secure prisoners. Or Paddy wagons were not sufficient to hold the prisoners, so we used prison buses. Just try to imagine how difficult it was to have the paperwork correct for which thief was stealing what TV, stereo, camera, or other merchandise from which store. It was a paperwork nightmare, but at least we got a lot of looters hauled off to jail. It was an unfortunate thing to witness possible law-abiding people turning into looters because of a dumb mob mentality. Some of the people we arrested made comments like, "Well, everyone else was doing it!"

Cops: 273. Bad guys: 0.

27

TRICKS OF THE TRADE

WHEN IT COMES TO MAKING felony arrests, sometimes you have to get real creative. We received information from an informant of the location of a guy who was wanted on several outstanding felony warrants. Because the informant that we were using did not have a past record of accurate information, we could only get a search warrant from a judge if we found another informant to collaborate the same information. We decided on the hundred-dollar bill trick. With the sergeant's approval, we went home and got changed into civilian clothes and got a very ordinary-looking car and went to the address to get the felon. We knocked on the door and asked the girl who answered for Joe Martinez. She said she was sorry, but he was not at home at the time. I took a hundred-dollar bill out of my pocket and reached it out to her and said, tell him that Freddy wanted to pay him for the deal we made the other night. When she reached out to take the money, I pulled it back and said, you know I wanted to give it to him in person, so never mind, I'll stop by later. With that said, she said just a minute and yelled his name, and within a few seconds, he came to the door. We grabbed him and put the cuffs on him and advised him of his rights and said there were several outstanding warrants for his arrest and thanked the young lady for her help.

Another little trick we used to pull with narcotics dealers worked just as well. When we had good information on a narcotics dealer that we had failed to get a search warrant for, we did our knock-knock flush the toilet trick. We used this little trick only when we were very confident that a drug dealer had a large stash of illegal narcotics in his pad. We would pull up to the house with our red light and siren going. After slamming on the brakes, we would run up to the house and pound on the door, and yell police officers open the door! The sounds we would hear were music to our ears. The garbage disposal was going, and the toilet flushing, and people running around in total chaos. We would wait two or three minutes and then pound on the door again. It usually didn't take more than two or three minutes before the door would be open, and we would be smiling and would say, "Oh, did you guys think we had a search warrant?" We would continue to smile and laugh a little while they were turning red in the face mad as can be. We would then thank them for getting rid of all the drugs in the house and to have a very nice day, bye-bye! I couldn't even guess how many times we did that and how well it worked.

We received information from two very reliable informants about a huge stash of narcotics at a residence. After getting our search warrant signed by the Judge, we talked to one of the informants again as to the location of the drugs. He told us that they kept them right by the sink next to the garbage disposal and the other big stash in the bathroom by the toilet. He also said that they had heavy steel doors and door jams that would not open easily even with our large steel ramming device. With that valuable information, we decided on a plan to make sure we were able to get the drugs before they went down the drains. We got permission from the Judge to do a little plumbing alteration at the house. We got a plumber to turn off the water to that house and some others on the block. The plumber called our suspects and told them that there were problems that he had to go under the house and repair. He located the sink drain and the toilet drain and installed mesh screens so that anything flushed or garbage disposal used would be caught in the mesh screen. The next day with search warrants in hand, we knocked on the door and said police officers we have a search warrant. We didn't even bother

COP LIVING ON THE EDGE

breaking down or attempting to break down the steel door. After a few minutes, a guy opened the door with a big smile on his face. We told him it sounds like your garbage disposal and toilet work really well, and he just laughed at us. I then said, "I guess you think you pulled a fast one on us, huh?"

I let him laugh for another minute or so, and then I said, "I think we are going to have the last laugh!"

He had a very puzzled look on his face until I explained to him about the plumbing work that we so carefully put in place. We had one of our officers wearing coveralls and knew a little about plumbing climb under the house and brought out a considerable stash of wet drugs. lucky for us, the heroin and cocaine were all sealed in plastic so, or evidence remained well in tack. We then had the privilege of arresting three bad guys for possession with intent to sell narcotics. The quantities involved were so significant that not only were they felonies, but they would be spending many years in prison.

What does a good police officer do if they are on the way to an important call and have a drunk driver in their way? My seasoned partner had just the right plan. We stopped a very drunk driver in front of us on the way to a burglary. There were no DUI traffic cars available at the time, so I said we would have to arrest him, or he could end up in an unfortunate accident hurting someone. He told me he had a better plan. He took the driver's keys, and when the driver was not looking, he threw them into a bunch of sick weeds. I asked him if we at least should not write him a ticket for reckless or careless driving. He said you never want to put your name and date and time on a traffic ticket for somebody like that. I didn't realize how right he was.

How do good police officers conserve their ammo? What I am about to tell you really happened just like all of the other stories in this book. I was chasing two armed robbery suspects fleeing from the store that I happen to be nearby. The chase was high-speed and dangerous through heavy downtown Denver traffic. Every time my police car became airborne, dirt would fly right into my eyes, nose, and mouth. I did an excellent job calling in the chase, with correct directions, streets, and descriptions of the suspect and car. lucky for me, the suspects got blocked in at a red light with nowhere to go.

Two detectives in an unmarked car had been listening to the chase and had a description of the vehicle and the stick-ups. When I said where the suspect's car had gotten stalled in traffic, they realized they were sitting at the same intersection. They looked at the car to their right and realized the stick-ups were right next to them. The driver of the armed robbers saw the unmarked police car and saw the passenger talking on the police radio. The driver rolled down his window and pointed his gun at the detective. The detective had already drawn his gun and fired one shot before the stick-up could get off a single round. I was only two cars back and saw the whole thing. The single-round went through the driver and hit the passenger and killed both stick-ups. An old lady sitting in the car behind the detective's car tried to tell someone or anyone who would listen to her that the two detectives had killed two innocent people for no reason. She, of course, had no idea what had just transpired. Like many civilians who only see half the real picture, she did not know anything about the incident.

A call came over the radio that there was a stick-up in progress at a 7-Eleven store. Two younger guys were working in the store at the time of the robbery. The stick-ups came on both sides of the cashier's area, where there was one cash register on each side. Both suspects had 45 caliber automatics aimed at the two clerks working in the middle area. Without saying a single word to each other, the two clerks fearing they would be shot at any second, both dived down onto the floor. The instant the cashiers started to move, both stick-ups fired multiple shots hitting each other instead of the store clerks. One died right where he had been standing bleeding out on the floor. The other suspect who was severely wounded made his way out of the store and started moving very awkwardly down the sidewalk. Although no description of the second wounded suspect was aired on the radio, he was very easily spotted trying to make his way with great effort down the sidewalk, still holding a gun in his hand and leaving a trail of blood from the scene. He put up no resistance at all but died before an ambulance could get to him.

Cops: 4. Bad guys: 0. (Four bad guys: gone forever with only one round fired by police.)

28

I GOT STABBED

WHILE ON ROUTINE PATROL IN November 1973, I was in the 3200 block of W. 38th Ave. I saw a guy running wildly down the middle of the street. When I pulled the police car up alongside him, he turned and started running toward the opposite direction still in the middle of the street. I was following him down the road in my police car when suddenly he turned around and ran right into the front of the vehicle and ended sprawled on the hood. His face was pushed up against the windshield where I could easily see his eyes were very bloodshot. I called for backup and followed him halfway down the block when he darted to the left and ran right into a house and slammed the door. Officer Torres arrived at the house, and I told him to take the back door, and I would take the front. With guns drawn, we careful he entered the house, which was pitch black because of coverings over the windows. Although we could not see the suspect, we could hear him breathing very heavily in the corner of the living room.

There was a sliver of light coming through the edge of one of the curtains, which reflected off of what appeared to be a large knife in his hands. Without even saying a word to each other, we both had the same idea and holstered our guns and charged the suspect. During the ensuing struggle, one of the curtains opened a little, and we could see a large butcher knife he was slashing at us. In the process of getting him subdued and handcuffed, we both ended up getting stabbed with what turned out to be a 12-inch butcher knife. The suspect had aluminum-colored paint residue around his nose and mouth, and a sock saturated with that paint in his pocket. Huffing paint causes a person to be delirious, super high, and often act out in violent ways. It also somehow makes the person stronger than you could imagine. We placed him under arrest and advised him of his rights, but he no doubt had no idea what we're saying.

The next day right after roll call, we were told to report to the captain's office. In the past, every time I was called into his office, I was receiving another commendation for an outstanding arrest. Assuming I was going to get another award, I was smiling all the way. When we walked through the door, the captain had a frown on his face, and I wondered what could be wrong. In a very gruff voice with a frown on his face, he told us to take a seat. The first words out of his mouth were shocking! "I should suspend you two for two weeks without pay for your actions yesterday! What in the world were you thinking of fighting with a man who is holding a twelve-inch butcher knife! And to make things even worse, you both got stabbed during the scuffle!"

He then asked us what we should've done. We were both speechless and didn't know what to say. He said, "If a guy is holding a butcher knife and slashing at you, shoot him!" He asked us how many times do you shoot, and where do you aim? When we didn't respond, he answered his own question saying, "You aim at his center mass and fire five rounds into him!" He told us that's what they teach in the police academy, and that the two of us were obviously not paying attention.

The captain looked through my file and, after a couple of minutes, looked up at me. "Officer Haroldsen, because of your record with numerous commendations for outstanding police work, I'm going to let this pass. If it ever happens again and you don't kill the suspect, I'm going to suspend you for a month!" Officer Torres and I went out into the hallway after shutting the captain's door and talked over what just happened. We both agreed that since the boy was 16 years old and we would've killed him if we would've done as we were told. If we had to do it over again, we wouldn't have changed a thing. We happily celebrated an outstanding arrest and not the fact that we had just killed someone. Very few police officers feel good after killing someone, no matter what the circumstances. However, there are indeed times where deadly force is the only way to save yourself or someone else.

Cops: 1. Bad guys: 0. (In this case, we were glad that it wasn't one dead bad guy.)

29

BULLET BARELY MISSED

WHILE WORKING THE DAY SHIFT with a new partner who was giving me a hard time about my nickname Supercop Haroldsen, I made a quick U-turn and chased after a wanted felon. My partner officer Wheeler said, "What the heck are you doing?"

After I told him that the guy we were chasing was a wanted felon, he agreed to let me pull him over. It turned out there were two guys in the car, and we put them in the backseat of the police car. He told me to run an id check on them while he searched their vehicle. I always searched for weapons on anyone before I placed them in the backseat of my car. Since this was our first time working together, I wasn't sure if my new partner had searched the other suspects who were wanted. The dispatcher said, "Your party is wanted on several outstanding felony warrants!"

The very second those words came out on my radio, I heard the back door open and our guy was trying to make a speedy escape When you call the dispatcher to see if there are any outstanding arrest warrants, the dispatcher is supposed to use a code to give you a chance to get them in custody. I told the other suspect he would be a dead man if he moved as I was bailing out of the car! I screamed at my partner, "I need your help!"

As I started chasing our escapee. I started gaining some ground as he ran around the fourth house on the street. He slowed down a little as he reached awkwardly into his pocket. The first thing I saw was a large shiny object that looked like a gun. Since I didn't know if my new partner had searched him, I quickly drew my gun as he brought the object up and turned looking at me. I saw him bring a gun toward me, and just as I was pulling the trigger, he threw it into the air. The same instant I pulled the trigger, I jerked my gun up when he threw the object away. He came to a 6-foot-high fence and quickly climbed over it running across the backyard. A large Saint Bernard bit at his legs as he started climbing over the other fence. When I started to climb over the fence the dog jumped up biting at me. The dog forced me to run around the fence in the backyard and continue the chase. My partner watched me chasing the suspect as we both disappeared around the house. He heard one shot fired and then saw the suspect running towards the next house. Since I hadn't gone over the fence and had run in a different direction, he didn't see me, so he thought I had been shot! He called over the radio "my partner was shot send help!" I continued chasing the suspect in the last direction I'd seen him fleeing. I caught a glimpse of him running around another house, and when I came around the corner onto the street, he had disappeared. Several police cars arrived, and the helicopter was overhead. My partner came around the corner in the police car and was very relieved when he saw I was all right. He asked me who fired the shot, and I told him exactly what happened. We knew our guy could not have gotten very far and commenced the search. With so many police officers so quickly in the area and with the helicopter overhead, we knew it would be only a matter of minutes before we could find him. After a couple of hours checking everywhere, we finally gave up. Two days later, working the night shift, I got a call from the district 1 station to meet someone there. My partner and I went to the station, and I couldn't believe who was sitting there waiting for me. Our wanted fleeing felon stood up and held his hands out for me to handcuff him. I placed the handcuffs on him and advised him of his rites and asked him, "why did you run and now turning yourself in?" He told me that he had a date with a really hot chick and wouldn't have missed it for the world." Why am I here now? You tried to kill me! I felt the bullet zinging right through my hair!"

What was really hilarious in my mind was what the repercussions were because of this. During the next few weeks, almost every time I would stop someone to question them or arrest them, they would immediately throw their hands up in the air when they read my name tag. They would say very excitedly," Officer Haroldsen, we've heard about you, please don't shoot me!" Sometimes even when I would be arresting some big-time hardened criminals, once they saw my name tag, they would quickly become very submissive and do exactly what I told them.

One busy Saturday night around midnight, three quick buzzing alarm sounds came over the radio, followed by officers calling for help. There is a horrible crime area called five points in Denver. The area is very dangerous, and only the worst criminals live in that part of town. Two of Denver's most hardened police officers work in that scary neighborhood. They had black belts in several different styles of martial arts, and one of them did hand-to-hand combat training in the police academy. When we realized that they were the ones calling for help, we knew things must be horrible. We were the first car arriving on the scene, coming to a screeching halt right in front of them. They were chasing a suspect down the middle of the street. One of them stopped and started throwing ninja-type stars at the suspect. When those all missed, he took a handheld police radio and hit the guy dropping him in the street.

We handcuffed the subject and arrested him for aggravated robbery and assault on a police officer. One of the officers had a pair of numb chucks he started twirling around like a real pro. Our police car was really filthy, and he reached out in the middle of the hood and made a small X. He then started the numb chucks going as fast as lightning and with "hi-ya!" hit the X on the police car with incredible precision.

We then got a call to a bar fight that sounded like it could be a nasty one. We arrived there behind one other police car.

The place was utter chaos when we walked in the door, with bottles, cue sticks, and people flying all over. One woman was attacking a man, and I started pulling her back when she turned on me, going at my face with her fingernails. Another officer punched her right in the face and knocked her out. Most of the fighting was happening in the back room around the pool tables. Several guys were using pool sticks and started beating on other guys in the bar. When my partner and I got to the door to enter the poolroom, an enormous guy about 6-10 weighing well over 300 pounds stood in our way. I looked up at him and said, "I sure hope you're not part of this problem!" He answered by saying, "oh, you need me to help you with these guys?" With that said, he turned and started going through the guys fighting, grabbing them one at a time and throwing them against the wall or onto the pool tables. We didn't have to lift a finger, and within a few minutes, all the fighting guys were out cold. We thanked him for his help and started loading all of them into the paddy wagon. Most of them were really beat up and bleeding, but we didn't have a single scratch.

Cops: 21. Bad guys: 0.

30

GUN ON PLANE

I LOVED BEING A POLICE officer, but the pay made it kind of tough, and I still thought of getting in the FBI or the DEA. Periodically officers are brought in to take a lie detector test to ensure only the best of the best are performing their duties. When I went in to take my test, I was not worried at all because I did not have any skeletons in my closet. I went through answering all the questions without a problem until, towards the end, I was asked, "Are you now or have you ever been wanted by the FBI?" I answered no, and the officer administering the test said, "I'm getting a big response that you're not telling us the truth!" I didn't have to think hard at all to know that my answer was correct until it dawned on me what the problem could be. I told him that I wanted to be very honest, so I admitted that I had turned in an application hoping to get a job with the FBI. He then rephrases the question saying, have you ever been or are you now wanted by the FBI for a crime that you have committed. This time my answer indicated that I was telling the truth. He followed it up with a question concerning me applying for a job with the FBI, which of course, my answer showed I was telling the truth.

Because of the many times, I was almost killed on duty, and my wife asked me if I couldn't get a job in a safer city such as Salt Lake City, Utah. Giving it a try seemed like a reasonable request, so I packed a few things and headed to the Denver airport. When I went through the metal detector, it went off because I was wearing a gun. There were two Denver police officers there that knew me and said go ahead and get on the plane. After arriving in Salt Lake City, I rode with an officer on an eight-hour shift and decided it was way too boring for me. I thrived on the action, which is one of the reasons I loved my job, so I thanked him and went back to the airport to head for Denver. I had my 357-magnum service revolver in a high riding holster in the center of my lower back under a jacket. The metal detector I was approaching was being manned by three or four rent-a-cops, not regular police officers. Just before I entered the metal detector, I told one of the gentlemen I had a gun and was a police officer. The only thing he heard was, "I have a gun!"

When the metal detector went off, and the alarm was going, he screamed, "He's got a gun!" Several other rent-a-cops came running over and started patting me down. Because of the position, my gun was in riding high up in the lower part of my back; they never even found it. I told them that the gun was loaded and before I could say to them again, I was a police officer; they all came unglued, screaming, "He's got a loaded gun!"

I was the only one who remained calm and finally got them to listen for a second when I told him my badge was in my inside coat pocket, and I could show them where my gun was. I again reminded them that I was a Denver Police Officer. When I reached back to get my 357, they all became hysterical. As I was slowly pulling it out of my holster, a couple of them grabbed my arm, and I reminded them that the gun was loaded. They held my weapon like it was a stick of dynamite ready to explode, and it was pretty hilarious. I then reached into my inside coat pocket and gave them my wallet, which had my shield and identification with it. One of the guys finally said, "I think he is a cop!" They took my gun and unloaded it like they were handling an explosive. They put my gun into a box and wrapped it up using a lot of paper and tape. They then put the ammo in a separate box and wrapped it up in the same way. I reached in my pocket and handed them a handful of more ammo, which really surprised them, and they wrapped it up. And then they said, "You can't take the gun on the plane. It will have to go in a checked bag!"

I told them that I did not have any checked bags, and I wanted to talk to the pilot of the aircraft. They very reluctantly went on the plane, and the pilot came to talk to me. He studied my badge and ID for several minutes and said, "I just want to know where you're seated, so if we have a problem, I know where the firepower will be!"

The rent-a-cops were very disappointed that I was going to get to board the plane with my gun. As soon as I got seated, I open the boxes loaded my gun, and put it in my holster. A little boy about eight years old, sitting right across the aisle from me saw what I was doing and had a very fearful look on his face. I pulled out my badge and held it over close enough for him to see. I had a big smile on my face, and he quickly grinned at me and shook his head like it's okay. After I got my year in on the Denver Police Department unknown to me, there were some initiation steps I would have to confront. The first one wasn't bad, just kind of funny. My partner stopped at a little hotdog stand and asked me if I would like a hotdog, and I said yeah, that would be great. He told me he wanted to pay for it. I have never been one who liked spicy foods. I was starving, and so when my partner handed me my hotdog, I took a big bite as he pulled away from the Hot dog stand. In about three seconds, my mouth was burning so hot I thought I was going to die, and his laughter couldn't have been more irritating. I can't remember what the hotdog was called, but that was the first and last one I ever ate. The next initiation was repulsive and disgusting, to say the least.

I'm glad to this day I can't remember what officer I was working with when we went down an alley and stopped and he beeped the horn a couple of times, and we just sat there for a few minutes. I saw a porch light come on the back of a house, and a woman dressed in a long robe came walking out to the police car. He told me to roll my window down, which I did. The woman then untied her robe and opened it up wide, and she was standing there bare-naked. My partner said he would be back in a while to pick me up, and she reached down and opened my door. I very firmly said, "No thanks, I am a happily married man, and I'm going to stay that way!"

As soon as I said that, my partner insisted I get out of the car right now, and I said no, and the woman reached down and started to unbutton my pants. I told him to get me out of here right now, or I would report this to the sergeant. He only laughed and said, "So you think the Sergeant doesn't know all about this?"

With some difficulty, I finally got him to see I was in no way going to go along with their stupid sick game. He then got out of the car and said pick me up in about 45 minutes I'll be right here in the alley. I never once doubted that I did the right thing and hoped many other officers did likewise. We received a call to cover a bar fight that was reported as almost a riot situation and headed for the call. There were way more guys fighting than cops trying to break up things. When there's a bar fight going on, you never really can tell who the bad guys and who are the good guys if there are any good guys. One woman was taking beer bottles and hitting people over the head with them. I went over and grabbed her arm, and she started to fight with me. Since she was a woman, I was trying to be careful where and how I grabbed onto her body. My sergeant pushed me aside and with one punch, hit her in the face breaking her nose and knocking her out. When he saw the incredulous look on my face, he explained to me the proper way to handle that kind of woman. First of all, he said, "Remember, this is a woman, not a lady!"

He told me it was easy to know the difference. Remember this during such an encounter if you punch a woman in the face or knock her out, you'll never be charged or accused of molesting or touching her in the wrong place.

31

MILITANT MOB

My partner and I, with the help of an informant, found out that Lee Valdez, who was wanted on Federal Drug Violation Warrants, was in Columbus Park, also known as la Raza Park. Our lieutenant had us go home and put on regular clothes and gave us an unmarked police car so that we would have a little time as we drove into the park before we were recognized as police officers. We had other police officers stay a couple of blocks away so they would not be spotted but would be available if we called for help. We drove into the park, passed a large group of very belligerent people, and snatched up Valdez and shoved him into the backseat before driving out of the park. The crowd of people in the park we're so taken by surprise that they did not react because everything happened so fast.

With Valdez in custody, we took him into the narcotics bureau for questioning. After advising him of his rights, we told him that we would put in a word to the district attorney if he would give us information about where Joe Marquez was hanging out.

He finally told us he was going to be in Columbus Park the day after tomorrow. We gave the information to our lieutenant. We said that we would need an unmarked car that did not look at all like a police unit. He said he would get whatever it would take and told us, of course, to come to work that day in civilian clothes. We needed to wear bulky clothes, so that our bulletproof vests would not be noticed.

Two days later, we went down an alley a block away from the park. Even with a pair of binoculars, it took us over an hour before we spotted Marquez sitting on a park bench in the middle of a wicked-looking crowd. We met with our lieutenant and Sergeant and went over our plan on how we could snatch him out of there without getting any of us injured. We had four police cars a couple of blocks away, ready to assist us if we ran into any problems.

As soon as all the backup units were in position, the lieutenant gave us the green light. We drove around one part of the park and drove over the curb and straight into the middle of the crowd. We bailed out of the car, and I had my gun out while my partner grabbed Marquez, and we shoved him into our police car and started to peel out. The crowd of people was much bigger than before, and rocks and bottles were crashing through the glass on our unit. We couldn't go very fast because so many guys surrounded the car. Some of them stood right in front of the police car until the bumper of the car was touching their legs. I kept watching for any guns aimed at us. My partner kept Marquez sitting up straight to act as a shield. I saw two or three guys with guns, but it was apparent that they were afraid they might shoot our prisoner. We didn't have time to handcuff Marquez, so I kept my gun aimed at him until we got a couple of blocks away where all of our backup officers were waiting. I thought the lieutenant would bring in our SWAT unit and arrest the whole gang of bad guys. When I mentioned it to him, he said he did not want to start a riot, with tensions being so high in that area.

We took Joe D. Marquez to the narcotics bureau. One of the detectives advised me to do a strip search of him because he was always known to be packing a gun and narcotics. He told me that was something they would normally do, but they were shorthanded. We took him into a holding cell where we did the strip search. When we had him remove his shoes, his socks were glued to his feet. Some of his skin stuck to his socks as he pulled them off his feet. He told us that he hadn't taken off his socks for at least a couple of months.

COP LIVING ON THE EDGE

Once he pulled his socks off, the smell was so overwhelming that the whole narcotics bureau moved up to the next floor.

All of the detectives were so angry with me. I didn't know what to do. When we first brought him in, they were all congratulating us on such a significant arrest. But the nauseating toxic gut-wrenching smell quickly made us the bad guys. When we first brought him in, they did, however, make it very clear that he was their prisoner even though we had made the arrest they would take over from there. The next several narcotics arrest I made were very challenging because of the way I was treated when I brought them into the Narcotics Bureau. They referred to me as Smelly Supercop Haroldsen. Despite their bad attitude towards me, I still received an official Denver Police Department Official Commendation for devotion to duty and bravery in the face of a hostile crowd.

Cops: 2. Bad guys: 0. (Narcotics bureau fumigated and the smell gone, but their bad attitude—not so much).

DENVER POLICE DEPARTMENT

OFFICIAL COMMENDATION

TO: Office of the Chief of Police

Date __July 18, 1974__

FROM: __Vice/Drug Control Bureau__
                    Division — District — Bureau

I wish to commend Officer __Jon Haroldsen__ , Serial No. __72-33__ ,

who is presently assigned to __District One__

for the following:

- [X] Class Two Award
- [ ] Class Three Award
- [ ] Class Four Award

WHEREAS it is realized that the great bulk of police work is done routinely by good policemen, let it be known that the above-named officer displayed initiative and alertness decidedly in excess of the norm in this particular instance.

Fact Situation: __On June 22, 1974 OfficersG. Meyer and J. Haroldsen received__ __information that Leroy J. Valdez, wanted on a Federal Drug Violation Warrant,__ __was in Columbus Park, West 38th Avenue and Pecos Street. The two officers__ __made the arrest of Valdez without incident even though the park was full of__ __belligerent people.__
       __On June 24, 1974 the officers received word that George D.__ __Marquez, wanted on a Federal Drug Violation Warrant, was in the same Columbus__ __Park. Due to the mood of the people the help of Cruiser 11, Command Car 1A,__ __and another car was asked. Officers Meyer and Haroldsen drove into the park__ __and made the arrest of Marquez, despite the rain of bottles and rocks from__ __the protesting crowd.__
       __The officers are to be commended for their devotion to duty__ __and bravery in the face of a hostile crowd.__

Commending Officer ___J. McCormick, Sergeant___
                                            J. McCormick, Sergeant

Command Officer's Approval _____
                                            C. J. Kennedy, Captain

Read and Approved _____
                                            T. E. Rowe
                                                                                        Division Chief
                                            ___Arthur G. Dill___
                                                                                        Chief of Police
                                            Arthur G. Dill

DISTRIBUTION
       Original and one copy to Commendations Board

(Separate set for each officer mentioned)
– DO NOT FOLD –

DPD 139 (Rev. 6/70)

32

FELON WITH A GUN

On July 8, 1974, we saw a known felon, Lee Velardei, acting very suspiciously in a residential neighborhood. He took off running as soon as he spotted our police car. We caught up to him by Sloan's lake and handcuffed him and placed him in the back of the police car. We took him back to the house he was seen walking from at 2601 Quitman. We found the home had been burglarized by a person matching his description exactly. He was packing a gun, had fresh needle marks on his arm, and found drugs in his pocket along with a hypo. We also found items taken in the burglary on him. We informed him that we were arresting him for burglary, carrying a concealed weapon, and illegal use of narcotics.

On February 18, 1974, a call came out over the radio of a stick-up in progress, and my partner and I were working in car 116, went to cover the call. When we got to the address of 3480 W. Colfax, we placed Bob Gallego under arrest for armed robbery and advised him of his rights. We found out that Tom L. Mendeze was also in on the robbery and arrested him at 1366 Meade. We recovered a blue coat that we found out was used during the robbery. He stated that the jacket belonged to Luceroo, who also was in on the robbery. Mendeze made several spontaneous statements while en route to headquarters. He said he committed the robbery with Luceroo and Gallego and noted that the gun and mask belonged to Luceroo. He further stated that he and Gallego ran into his sister's house at 1329 King where they left a red coat that he had worn during the robbery. Suspects were all charged with the investigation of armed robbery and also possible attempted auto theft since the keys to a car were taken from the victim's purse.

We found the keys in the left coat pocket of Gallego. On November 25, 1972, we responded to 3801 W. Colfax's best car sales on reported auto theft. A 67 Dodge charger was stolen. A little later in the day, I spotted a car matching that exact description leaving the alley not far from the stolen car scene. We chased down the car and stopped at 33rd and Shoshone. We ordered the six occupants out of the vehicle to search them for weapons. All parties were handcuffed and placed in the police cars. We had called for another car to come and help transport them to headquarters. An NCIC check came back that the vehicle had been stolen. All the adult parties were taken to the city jail and the minors to the juvenile hall. One of the parties turned out to be an escapee.

In May 1973, we spotted a Chevrolet pickup truck that matches the description of the vehicle used in a stick-up at Alameda and Zuni. We finally got the car stopped in the 2800 block of FederalBoulevard and ordered all four occupants out of the vehicle. All four parties had fresh needle marks in their arms and were arrested for investigation of illegal use of narcotics. We also placed a hold on all the parties and turned them over to the stickup detail and the vice bureau. They were all advised of the rights at the scene as well as when they were taking to headquarters.

We later received a call from Eighth and Broadway on two suspects seen prowling around vehicles in a used and new car sales lot. The two suspects we saw fit the description given out by the radio. They said they were looking at cars with the idea of buying one. We took a look at the one vehicle they were walking away from and quickly saw that the tape deck had been torn out, and the wires were still hanging. The witness that had called said he saw them break into two different cars, which had the tape decks torn out of them. We placed both suspects under arrest and advised them of their rights. The two suspects, Ellie Janet Jarkowe and Mike Steve Jarkowe, both unknown to the department, cleared up more than 30 other such break-ins. A consent to search waiver was signed, and we found very sophisticated burglary tools and a whole bunch of stolen tape decks. Mike Jarkowe told us after being advised of his rights that they always went out on Sundays and hit large car dealers. We had their car towed to the pound and all evidence taking into the custodian's office.

We were working car 117 when we heard a burglary had just been committed at 3838 W. 25th Ave. A description of the vehicle was aired with a license plate also given. After finishing the report, we went back out, patrolling the area when another call came out of a burglary. The car description and license plate number were an exact match of the earlier burglary. Only a couple of hours later, we spotted the car just pulling out onto Federal Boulevard. After a brief chase, we got the car stopped. The car was being driven by a female by the name of Angel Marrie Rice a.k.a. Pizzalato. Najera and Ivy Rice were also in the vehicle. The driver, Marie, had her haircut short and looked like a guy and would have been mistaken by the burglary witness. The three were arrested for investigation of burglary and their car towed to the pound.

Cops: 13. Bad guys: 0.

CRIME SPECIALTY	NAME
AGGRAVATED ROBBERY	LEE VELARD

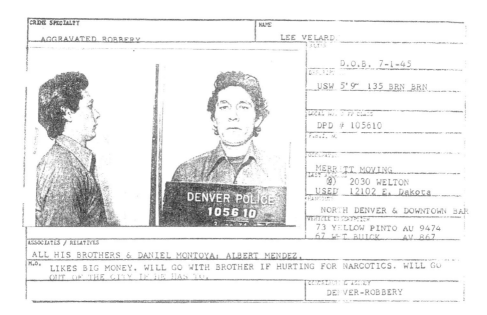

D.O.B. 7-1-45
USW 5'9" 135 BRN BRN

DPD # 105610

MERRITT MOVING
2030 WELTON
USED 12102 E. Dakota
NORTH DENVER & DOWNTOWN BAR
73 YELLOW PINTO AU 9474
67 WHT BUICK AV 867

ASSOCIATES / RELATIVES: ALL HIS BROTHERS & DANIEL MONTOYA, ALBERT MENDEZ.

M.O.: LIKES BIG MONEY. WILL GO WITH BROTHER IF HURTING FOR NARCOTICS. WILL GO OUT OF THE CITY IF HE HAS TO.

DENVER-ROBBERY

DENVER POLICE DEPARTMENT
COMMENDATORY LETTER

From: Patrol - District One
Division - District - Bureau
Date July 8, 1974

Recognition is hereby given to Officer J.S. Haroldsen ,serial number 72-33 ,

who is presently assigned to District One - Detail Two ,

for the following described activity: Officers Walker and Haroldsen observed a known felon (Lee Velarde) in a residential area acting suspicious. Velarde upon seeing the police unit, broke and ran, later being arrested near Sloans Lake. A residence near where Velarde was seen (2601 Quitman) was found burglarized with the description of the suspect matching Velarde. Items from the crime were discovered on Velarde who was jailed for Burglary, C.C.W. and Illegal Use of Narcotics.

This fine police work, knowledge of the area and people, and the alertness of the officers resulted in the apprehension of the suspect and the stolen property recovered.

Submitted By: Sgt W.L. Morris 55-3
Sgt. W.L. Morris, #55-03

Approval of Command Officer: Capt. 2. Lake

DISTRIBUTION:

Original - Recipient Officer
Copy - Officer's Personnel File
Copy - Commendations Board

Form 139A (4/70) DPD

33

GIRLS HITCHHIKING MURDERED

You don't often see a pretty young girl hitchhiking on the highway. There had been a rash of hitchhikers picked up along the road on the way to Boulder that had been kidnapped, raped, and murdered. The police at that time had no suspects and no evidence as to who was committing these heinous crimes. One beautiful summer day, I was off duty driving on that highway, when I came upon two very cute young girls hitchhiking. I was cruising that stretch of highway back-and-forth, hoping to see a suspect picking up some young girl. Slowing my car down as I passed these two girls, a thought came to me of what I can do to help them not become victims of such a horrid crime. I stopped the car a little past them, and they came running up to get a ride. I had my service revolver tucked between the console and my seat out of plain view. I greeted the two girls as they got in the car and asked what their names were. When I got up to the speed limit, I changed from being a smiling happy guy to a mean slow-talking creepy person. I asked them where they were headed and said we are going to have to take a detour. As soon as I made that comment in as creepy voice as I could muster, they both became noticeably very scared. I reached down and lifted my gun for just a couple of seconds letting the terror get to them. Then, I quickly held up my badge and told them that I was a Denver police officer.

I told them about the numerous recent girls murdered and wanted to make sure it didn't happen to them. I asked them where they lived and headed towards their homes. During the drive to their homes, I related a couple of incidents of women that had been raped and what a terrible thing for a girl to go through. They both promised me that they would never hitchhike again, and I believed them. I had scared them to the point they were both listening intently to what I was telling them. When I got to one of their homes, I escorted the girls to the front door and talked to one of the girls' parents. The parents were very thankful that I picked them up, and I felt great that I was able to get them safely back home. The other girl assured me that she would tell her parents all about what had happened when she got to her house. I left the house feeling I may have possibly saved their lives.

Cop: won. Two girls: safe. (Bad guy: hopefully in prison or executed.)

34

AMBUSH SETUP

A CALL WENT OUT THAT there was an injured person down in the middle of the street. Officer Dick Barber and his partner went to the location given where the injured party was seen. They saw the person lying in the middle of the road and stopped to assist. It turned out that the person lying in the street was part of the ambush that was planned to kill as many police officers as possible. The so-called injured party jumped up and ran down the alley, and Officer Barber ran after him. The guy pulled out a gun, and during the struggle, Officer Barber was shot in the cheek, his chest, and his leg, yet still managed to return fire and killed the guy. His partner called for backup, stating an officer was down, and shots fired. There was a large apartment complex that appeared to be abandoned, where the shooting started. All of the windows looked like they had been boarded closed. When the officer started arriving, the boarded-up windows were hinged and were dropped open. It was like a fortress structure. Every car available went to the scene as hundreds and hundreds of rounds were fired at the arriving officers. Most of the bullets fired from the building were from machine guns. None of the officers arriving even had shotguns in their cars. My partner, CD Burton, a.k.a. Mad Dog.

Burton had a violin case that held a machine gun with at least 1000 rounds of ammunition. He was the only officer that had firepower equal to or better than the bad guys were using. The Denver swat team was out of town on a special training mission, so they were not available that night. As each of the police cars arrived at the scene, they were riddled with automatic gunfire from the building. Only the sergeants coming to the shooting had shotguns in their vehicles. Officer Gene Gold that was in the police academy with me was directed to go up a stairway and check for shooters on the second floor. When he got up to the second floor and opened the door, he was hit by automatic gunfire and fell down the stairs. The gun battle lasted several hours until daybreak. Thousands of rounds were fired between the police and the ambushing criminals. Several police officers were wounded and taken to the hospital.

Miraculously not one police officer died that night. Finally, when the gunfire coming from the building stopped, the officers very cautiously entered the complex and were very shocked at what they found. They were more upset that they did not find any dead bodies. There were thousands of rounds on the floor and blood everywhere, but not a single suspect was found in the building. After doing a lot of searching, they finally found a secret passageway underground that went from this building underground to another building far enough away not to draw any attention. Again, to everyone's surprise, the secret tunnel that ended in another building was empty of anyone dead, wounded, or alive. So much blood in the tunnel and the buildings made it clear some of the criminals who set up the ambush had died. No one could figure out how so many people wounded, dead, or alive could have gotten away without anyone seeing them. My partner and I were assigned to stay in our car in front of the buildings. We stopped a lot of people in the area who looked suspicious at all and questioned them and searched them for weapons and any gunshot injuries.

This seven-hour gun battle drove the point home of the need for every officer to have a shotgun in the car and to carry more rounds on them and have speed loaders. We also finally convinced the chief of police of the need for hollow point ammunition so they would drop suspects instead of only slowing them down.

Cops: 1. Bad guys: several?

Ready on the Firing Line
by Dick Barber

In January 1975, the president and secretary-treasurer of the PPA Council initiated a lawsuit against the city, manager of safety and the chief of police. The suit called for city-provided and issued safety equipment. The present status on these items is as follows:

1. Hollow-points: HP's are allowed except for magnum HP's. The city council study done by the University of Colorado has been completed. The preferred round is no longer manufactured nor will it be in the future. Apparently instead of stepping down to the next round on the list and ordering it now, the chief will wait until after the mayoral run-off election.

2. Shotguns: Shotguns have been purchased on a rush order. They have been received, assembled, marked, test fired and cleaned by range personnel. Car mounts have been received and installed, while the shotguns have been gathering dust in the range for two months while we wait for gun lockers for district stations. We are told the weapons will be distributed when the gun lockers arrive.

3. Holsters: Everything in the world except clamshells and cowboy tie-downs are okay, provided it looks like one of the eight holsters pictured in the range.

4. Front-back car screens: These are still being tested.

5. Vests: After shooting holes in most of them at the range, the department is still leaning toward a $25 reimbursement if an officer now has one or will purchase one. Prices vary from $50 to $120 plus. Is $25 sufficient?

35

SHAKING GUN

THEY TOLD US IN THE Denver police academy that we most likely would never catch a burglary in progress. Thanks to some good luck and also a fair amount of good police work, we did exactly what they said would never happen. I was assigned to work with a female officer Conroy. We quickly gained a good rapport, and I have great faith in her ability. We got a call of a possible burglary in progress and headed to the house to check it out. So often calls end up being not for real or you get there, and the suspects are long gone.

On a beautiful day in April, we arrived at the possible burglary. I dropped off officer Conroy at the back door and went to the front of the house. Not seeing any sign of forced entry at the door, I checked out the windows, glanced down in the basement, and saw a suspect. Suddenly, there was a scream coming from the back of the house. As I ran around to the back porch, two suspects were standing there while officer Conroy had her gun pointed at them. Although her revolver was shaking quite a bit, she had the two suspects frozen in their tracks. They pleaded with me to please hurry and handcuff them before she shot them. I had to try very hard not to laugh out loud because these two dumb burglars had been scared to death by my partner, who was a great female officer. I figured these two bozos would've taken off running if I would've got to drop on them with a gun, thinking I would not shoot.

It was no problem finding the third burglar who was hiding down in the basement. These arrests cleared up five other burglaries that these lowlifes committed. I complemented officer Conroy who was only six weeks out of the police academy for doing a great job. I told her that the fact that her gun wasn't real steady scared those guys so bad they wouldn't blink.

Cops: 3. Scared bad guys: 3.

36

GUNSHOT GUY PUNCHES MD

ONE OF THE MANY LOW-INCOME projects in Denver is kind of like a breeding ground for criminals. Over the years, I often would go into one of the units to make an arrest and find out more things about the burglar, stick-up, or drug dealers. The dad was also an active criminal as was the grandfather. That being said, you can easily understand why it was a dangerous place to go and always required additional backup units. A call came to us to respond to multiple shootings in the projects. The action was a big part of the reason I joined the Denver Police Department, so I was excited as we headed to the call. I was a little concerned when the dispatcher advised us to be careful because there were no additional units available for cover. When we pulled up to the projects. The rapid sound of gunfire told us exactly where things were happening. There was a large grassy area between the four projects where we quickly spotted several suspects firing at each other. Because we were so badly outnumbered with firepower, I hit the siren for one quick blast, which sent the shooters fleeing the area. One suspect was down on the grass wounded. We approached him consciously and started to check him for any injuries. He was bleeding quite badly from a gunshot in the back. When we rolled him over, there was a .38 underneath him, and he suddenly became very violent. We could not believe the power that he had, considering he had been seriously wounded. After a tough long and drawn-out struggle, we got him handcuffed. Advising the dispatcher that we were headed to Denver General Hospital with a severely injured party, we went red light and siren. We were met in the breezeway by the emergency team of medical people. We placed him on a gurney and quickly rolled him into one of the emergency surgery rooms. During the drive and going into the surgery room, he had remained quite calm and was not moving at all. The Surgeon on duty walked into the room and kind of came unglued when he saw the handcuffs. He yelled at us in a very disgusted loud voice, "Get those blankety blank handcuffs off of him right now him!"

We tried our very best to convince him that it was a very, very bad idea because of the struggle we encounter getting them on him. Ignoring what we just told him, he said, "Take them off right now!"

With the handcuffs removed, he seemed to be wide-awake and rubbed his wrist for a few seconds, and in a flash, he punches the doctor right in the face. The doctor fell backward into the carefully laid-out tray of sterilized surgical instruments. The doctor quickly stood up and screamed, "Get those handcuffs on him now!"

The struggle we had earlier putting on the handcuffs was nothing compared to what we now were going through in a room full of breakable glass, medical equipment, and sharp instruments. A police officer working in the hallway rushed in to give us some very much-needed assistance. It is challenging to imagine trying to subdue a severely wounded person who is fighting like a tiger without causing further injury. After several minutes with three police officers and one maniac flying all over the room, we finally got the cuffs on him. At that point, the sterile well-organized surgical room looked like a tornado had ripped through it. The blood from the wounded guy and our blood was all over everything. Even the Surgeon was bleeding from his possible broken nose. Speaking to us now in a very subdued somewhat strained voice, he said, "Would you good officers please stay nearby while I remove this bullet?"

We convinced him that the officer working there in the hospital should be able to handle things now, especially since they would be sedating the guy for the surgery. Since he was handcuffed lying on the gurney, we took the opportunity to ask him if he knew who shot him. Past experiences with guys like this helped us not to be too surprised when he said, "Don't worry about it. When I get better, I'm gonna go kill the guy!"

We wished him good luck with that and went back into service. At the end of our shift, when we headed back into the station, our sergeant told us that we had done a great job considering how many shooters there were.

Cops: 2. Bad guy: 0. (We got one extra point by saving the surgeon!)

37

BIG DRUG BUST

I OBSERVED A VERY SUSPICIOUS party walking down the sidewalk doing the Buena Vista shuffle. I could tell he had just got out of prison by the way he was walking. A good police office easily recognizes people who end up in prison in Buena Vista, Colorado, because they develop a certain way they walk. I did one of my maneuvers slamming the brakes on the car, knowing the suspect would take off running. He only got about a half a block when I yelled, "police officer freeze!" He turned and glanced at me and continued running, and I tackled him. He was an informant I had used in the past who was out on parole. I searched him for weapons and found his pockets full of several bags of suspected heroin. He also had a .32 automatic handgun in his waistband. It didn't take very long for us to convince him he could either go back to prison or turn us on to a significant drug arrest. He gave us two addresses on Quitman Street, where he had bought his drugs. I got a search warrant signed by Judge Ursa. I got three other officers to execute the search warrants with me.

The first house we hit with our no-knock search warrant revealed a large stash of drugs. We arrested Carlo Makintoshes for illegal possession with intent to sell drugs. We confiscated five large bricks of marijuana, some hashish, a weight scale, a gun, and $5949 in cash. We seized 100 packages of speed as well as a brick of marijuana in the second house, but the owner was not home at the time. While we were searching at the other house, I saw a blue van I had seen the night before parking in front of the same residence. The driver sped off when he saw us coming out of the house. The van stopped at 3900 Stewart St. and both occupants jumped out and ran into the residence with us right behind. Carrie Lynche, who was the driver, was trying to hide the drugs inside the house as we entered. The smell of marijuana was overwhelming. We immediately arrested Lynche for possession of narcotics for sale. We saw several joints, roaches, and some more hand roll joints, hypos and syringes, and hashish in plastic bags on the table as well as bags of marijuana. He agreed to sign a consent to search form #372, stating he didn't have hardly any drugs in the house. We did not arrest his wife Priscilla because she was a minor, and she had two small children with her, one only two weeks old. Our arrests took some big-time drug dealers off the street. I made the front page of the Rocky Mountain News for our successful raid.

Cops: 3. Bad guys: 0.

To make our day even better, we got a call from one of the informants we had used in the past who told us he had some hot information on a big-time drug dealer. We met with our informant, who gave us the name and two different addresses next to each other where he had been buying his drugs. Based on our informants past, we got Judge P. Widick to sign our search warrants. We went to the two addresses 2701 Federal Boulevard #201 and #101 and watched the traffic for a couple of days.

Many vehicles were coming in and leaving in a hurry a few minutes later. We knew that this was going to be a righteous drug raid. We got our sergeant and several other officers to go with us as we went to execute the search warrant. Since the doors were metal frames and metal doors, we got the manager to get the suspects to unlock the doors for us. Arguello came to the door, and we showed him the search warrants. We found a large amount of every type of drug imaginable, as well as weapons and cash in both units. We then placed Arguello and Blas Luceroo under arrest. After we advised them of their rights, we took them into the narcotics bureau and took all the evidence to the property bureau.

Since both addresses ended up with the confiscation of a large number of drugs, I received two different commendations.

Cops: 5. Bad guys: 0.

Rocky Mountain News   Fri., Nov. 22, 1974, Denver, Colo.

NEWS PHOTO BY HOWARD BROCK

Confiscated drugs and cash inspected

Patrolman J. Scot Haroldsen inventories some of nearly $6,000 in cash and six pounds of suspected marijuana he and Patrolman Greg Meyer confiscated Thursday night at 3876 Quitman St. Arrested there for investigation of possession for sale was Carlos McIntosh, 22. During the raid, a car seen near the house was pursued to 3900 Stuart St., where Terry L. Lynch, 20, was arrested after police found four pounds of suspected marijuana and seeds and 91 grams of suspected hashish.

166

DENVER POLICE DEPARTMENT
OFFICIAL COMMENDATION

TO: Office of the Chief of Police

Date: December 2, 1974

FROM: Vice/Drug Control
Division — District — Bureau

I wish to commend Officer Jon S. Haroldsen , Serial No. 72-33

who is presently assigned to District One

for the following:

Official Commendation

☐ Class Two Award

☐ Class Three Award

☐ Class Four Award

WHEREAS it is realized that the great bulk of police work is done routinely by good policemen, let it be known that the above-named officer displayed initiative and alertness decidedly in excess of the norm in this particular instance.

Fact Situation: The above Officer executed search warrants at 3784 and 3876 Quitman Street, recovering five kilos of marijuana and three ounces of hashish. As a result of the recoveries, three major marijuana peddlers were arrested and have been filed on for Sale of Narcotics. The alertness and initiative of this Officer was beyond his realm as a uniform patrol officer.

Commending Officer D. DeNovellis, Sergeant

Command Officer's Approval C. J. Kennedy, Captain

Read and Approved T. E. Rowe, Division Chief

Arthur G. Dill, Chief of Police

DISTRIBUTION:
Original and one copy to Commendations Board

Separate set for each officer mentioned)

— DO NOT FOLD —

DPD 139 (Rev. 6/70)

DENVER POLICE DEPARTMENT

OFFICIAL COMMENDATION

TO: Office of the Chief of Police

Date October 29, 1974

FROM: PATROL - District One
_____
Division — District — Bureau

I wish to commend Officer _____ J.S. Haroldsen _____ , Serial No. ___ 72-33 _____

who is presently assigned to _____ District One - Detail Two _____

for the following:

COMMENDATORY LETTER
☐ Class Two Award
☐ Class Three Award
☐ Class Four Award

WHEREAS it is realized that the great bulk of police work is done routinely by good policemen, let it be known that the above-named officer displayed initiative and alertness decidedly in excess of the norm in this particular instance.

Fact Situation: On October 28, 1974 above officers received information from an informant regarding the location of a large amount of
Marijuana. After obtaining the information the officers watched
the traffic in and out of the apartment house at 2701 Federal Blvd.
for some time. They then obtained a Search Warrant for Apt. 201
at this location. Two parties were arrested, Floyd Arguello and
Blas Lucero, after 40 plastic bags and one 2.2 lb. brick of Mari-
(Continued on Back of Page)

Commending Officer _____ Sgt. D.J. Lawless 60-24
Sergeant D. Lawless, #60-24

Command Officer's Approval _____ JJ Britton 56-35

Read and Approved _____ D/c Paul A. Montoya 50-10
Division Chief

_____
Chief of Police

DISTRIBUTION:
Original and one copy to Commendations Board

(Separate set for each officer mentioned)
– DO NOT FOLD –

DPD 139 (Rev. 6/70)

DENVER POLICE DEPARTMENT

OFFICIAL COMMENDATION

TO: Office of the Chief of Police

Date   November 7, 1974

FROM: Vice/Drug Control
Division — District — Bureau

I wish to commend Officer   Jon Haroldson   , Serial No.   72-33   .

who is presently assigned to   District One

for the following:

OFFICIAL COMMENDATION

☐ Class Two Award

☐ Class Three Award

☐ Class Four Award

WHEREAS it is realized that the great bulk of police work is done routinely by good policemen, let it be known that the above-named officer displayed initiative and alertness decidedly in excess of the norm in this particular instance.

Fact Situation: On information received from a confidential informant Officers Burton and Haroldson executed a search warrant at 2701 Federal Blvd. #1, which led to the recovery of 136 grams of marijuana, 12 marijuana cigarettes, 50 tabs of amphetamine and eight capsules of codeine. These officers are to be commended for their initiative in the recovery of these drugs and the arrest of two parties for Possession and Sale of Dangerous Drugs.

Commending Officer _____
D. L. Simmons, Sergeant   53-15

Command Officer's Approval _____
C. J. Kennedy, Captain

Read and Approved _____
T. E. Rowe   Division Chief

_____
Arthur G. Dill   Chief of Police

DISTRIBUTION:
Original and one copy to Commendations Board

(Separate set for each officer mentioned)

– DO NOT FOLD –

DPD 139 (Rev. 6/70)

38

GIVEN SHOTGUN ORDERS TO KILL

THERE ARE TWO TYPES OF calls over the police radio that are considered most urgent. One is an officer calling for help, and the other is a stick-up in progress. Because these two calls require your immediate attention, they are preceded by three very loud and distinct alarm-type buzzing sounds. When an officer hears these three distinct sounds, they immediately turn up the radio, so they are prepared to respond. Working solo one summer day, I heard what had to be either an officer calling for help or a stick-up in progress, come out over the radio. The dispatcher came on the air and said we have an officer calling for help and request cars to cover. Since I was the closest officer to the call, the dispatcher told me to respond to Code Ten (red light and siren)! I turned the radio up even louder so that I could hear it over the sound of my siren as I raced to the call. Officer Martinez came on the radio and shouted, "They're all dead; their bodies splattered all over the walls!"

The problem when you let your emotions affect the way you're talking on the radio is it instantly becomes contagious to the other officers responding to the call. Although I was already going very fast, I automatically pressed the gas pedal to the floor as I was busting through red lights and stop signs, sometimes going over 100 mph. Some of the intersections that were jammed with cars were very frustrating as I could barely go through at 20 miles an hour. I went through the police academy with Officer Martinez and knew he was not the type of person to exaggerate a bad crime scene. Martinez came on the radio again and screamed, "The shooter may still be somewhere in the house; get me help right now!"

The brakes in my car were starting to fade because of the extreme breaking I had been doing at all the red lights and stop sign intersections. My brakes had completely faded when I was a little more than a block away. I tried using the emergency brake as I came flying up to the front yard of the house. It helped slow me down, but I finally had to slam the car into parking mode to avoid running into the house. I jumped out of the car with my gun in hand as I ran up to the front porch. Officer Martinez came running out the front door yelling, "Don't go in there. The kids and their moms' guts are splattered all over!"

He blocked me from going through the front door and assured me that the shooter was nowhere to be found. We called for the medical examiner, our sergeant, lieutenant, and homicide detectives. The sergeant came and told me to be sure and protect the crime scene by not letting any other officers enter the house unless they were there to investigate the crime scene. Our captain and some other ranking officers insisted on going inside even though they were not there to help with the investigation. Most of the officers who went inside came back out looking very sick with pale-colored faces. They threw up as soon as they got off the front porch. No number of years as a police officer would prepare anyone for what they witnessed. After a couple of hours, I told Officer Martinez that I wanted to go upstairs and see the crime scene. I am very thankful, to this very day, that he would not let me get past him at the front door. He later told me that he had nightmares almost every night of the horrid crime scene he had witnessed. My sergeant took me aside and told me he had a critical special assignment that he knew I could handle. He gave me a shotgun and said that there was an unmarked police car that he wanted me to park in the alley across the street from the house. He told me that the homicide detectives had determined from talking to the neighbors and the crime scene that the husband had murdered his wife and children and fled the scene in his car. He showed me a picture of the husband and gave me a description of the car. The instructions he gave were very clear. "You stay in that unmarked unit with that shotgun ready, and when he returns, you get as close as you safely can, and you blast that murdering piece of trash to bits!"

Hours passed very slowly as I contemplated my assignment. One part of me wanted to kill that guy the second he showed up. The other part of me wanted to get the drop on him, get him handcuffed, and get him sent to prison for the rest of his rotten life. I remembered what they taught us in the police academy about shooting a suspect. When confronted with an armed suspect who had a gun aimed at us, we were told to fire five rounds into their center mass, leaving one round in the cylinder. We were told that real life in the world of criminals is different than the movies. You never shoot to wound or disable the suspect because of the numerous police officers and innocent victims who have been shot that way. They told us it is better to be tried by twelve than carried by six. "We want all of you officers to return home safely to your families at the end of your shift, and don't ever forget that!"

All of these things kept running through my mind over and over again as I sat there, armed and ready to take out one of the bad guys. Every time a car came by the house, my heart pounded, and my adrenaline was rushing through my system like a fire with gasoline being poured on it. I knew deep down inside me that I could kill this guy if he didn't give up instantly. I remember very well praying that when he showed up, I could arrest him instead of killing him. Just a few minutes before my shift ended, the sergeant called me and said we want you to stay there, and you'll get overtime pay. Normally I loved getting paid for overtime, but this night was completely different.

A couple of hours into the overtime, I was called on the radio, and given the best news, I could possibly have heard. The suspect has been arrested by Colorado State police officers without incident.

Because of Officer Martinez, I don't have any vivid images of that horrific crime scene. I cannot imagine the bloody gory scene that he had to deal with that night and for the rest of his life.

Cops: 1. Bad guys: 0. (Innocent mother and precious children are safely in heaven with God.)

39

NO KNOCK WARRANT

My partner and I had observed a lot of traffic in front of 999 Pearl St., Apt. 304. We were sure that there was a big drug dealer there, so we tried to find an informant that could confirm the information so we can get a search warrant. We saw a car in front of us run a stop sign, and when we pulled the car over, luck was on our side. The suspect turned out to be a confidential informant that we had used on numerous occasions. To sweeten up the deal when we searched him, he had a .38 caliber handgun in his coat as well as some drugs. Since he was on parole, he quickly gave us the information we needed to get a search warrant at the Pearl Street address. He said that the really good stuff was hidden in the toilet tank in a waterproof package. We told him since he was packing a gun we would have to arrest him, but we put in a good word with the DA's office. He got mad about that situation thinking we're going just to turn them loose. Also, by doing it this way, if the information turned out to be erroneous, we would still have him in custody. Because of his reliability in the past, we were able to get a judge to sign the no-knock search warrant. To protect our confidential informant, we did not put anything in the search warrant about the toilet tank.

We went to the Pearl Street address and apartment 304 and discovered that there was a steel door. Since there was no peephole, we lightly knocked on the door and heard a voice ask, "who is there?" Since we had observed a lot of traffic going to and from that address, there were several known drug users that we knew on site. I said with a Hispanic accent, "It's Joe Martinez, and I am really in bad need of a fix right now!"

With that said, she immediately opened the door, and we pushed our way into the apartment and showed her the search warrant. We saw several joints on the coffee table and promptly arrested her, Debie Bubier, and Mary Fente. We found a large quantity of marijuana as well as heroin in the bedroom. We searched the apartment very thoroughly and at the very last, finally looked in the toilet tank like we didn't know if we'd find anything there. We advised both suspects of their rights and took them to jail without any further incident.

For about five weeks, we were getting information from two or three informants about a big-time drug dealer at 2740 Park Pl. Two of our informants gave us the same information, and so we went and observed the address for a few hours. Because of the fast traffic coming and going, we were sure we had an excellent drug raid coming up. We got our search warrant signed by a judge and went to the house.

We knocked on the door, and a lady opened it without even asking who was there. We figured because everybody going to the door was there to buy drugs, she dropped her guard down. We showed her the search warrant and told her to sit down on the couch. We found 20 one- hundred lot bags of amphetamines in the kitchen. We placed Pearle Montoya under arrest for possession of drugs with intent to sell. We also discovered marijuana on the table in the kitchen. Mrs. Montoya was very upset and emotional and told us that she had nothing to do with the drugs. We finally got her to agree to call her husband, Erneste Montoya, in order to get him to return home immediately. She told him that her daughter was hurt, and she needed him. We had two other officers pick her up and take her to jail while we waited inside the house. About 20 minutes later, he pulled into the driveway, walked into the house, and was immediately arrested. Both suspects were advised of their rights at the house.

Neither party was known to the narcotics bureau or any other officers as drug dealers. There were two small children at home, and Mr. Montoya called his brother Joe who came to watch them.

Cops: 6. Bad Guys: 0.

DENVER POLICE DEPARTMENT

OFFICIAL COMMENDATION

TO: Office of the Chief of Police

Date _____ May 14, 1974 _____

FROM: _____ Vice/Drug Control _____
                Division – District – Bureau

I wish to commend Officer _J. Haroldson_ , Serial No. _72-33_ ,
who is presently assigned to _District One_
for the following:

- [X] Class Two Award
- [ ] Class Three Award
- [ ] Class Four Award

WHEREAS it is realized that the great bulk of police work is done routinely by good policemen,
let it be known that the above-named officer displayed initiative and alertness decidedly in excess
of the norm in this particular instance.

Fact Situation: On May 11, 1974 Officers Meyer and Haroldson executed
a search warrant for narcotics at 2740 Park Place. This warrant
resulted in the recovery of 2,029 tablets of amphetamine and 28
grams of marijuana. Because of the fine work of these officers
two parties were filed on in District Court.

Commending Officer _____
                D. L. Simmons, Sergeant   53-15

Command Officer's Approval _____
                C. J. Kennedy, Captain

Read and Approved _____
                T. E. Rowe   Division Chief

Arthur G. Dill   Chief of Police

DISTRIBUTION:
        Original and one copy to Commendations Board

(Separate set for each officer mentioned)

– DO NOT FOLD –

DPD 139 (Rev. 6/70)

DENVER POLICE DEPARTMENT

OFFICIAL COMMENDATION

TO: Office of the Chief of Police

Date May 6, 1974

FROM: Vice/Drug Control
          Division – District – Bureau

I wish to commend Officer   Scott Haroldson   , Serial No.   72-33   ,
who is presently assigned to   District One
for the following:

- [X] Class Two Award
- [ ] Class Three Award
- [ ] Class Four Award

WHEREAS it is realized that the great bulk of police work is done routinely by good policemen, let it be known that the above-named officer displayed initiative and alertness decidedly in excess of the norm in this particular instance.

Fact Situation: On April 30, 1974 Officers Meyer and Haroldson obtained a search warrant for a residence at 999 Pearl apartment #2. Recovered in this search was marijuana, a cigarette rolling machine, roach clips and three vials of morphine were found floating in the toilet tank, wrapped in baggies. Through the fine work of these officers, two parties were filed on in District Court.

Commending Officer _D. L. Simmons, Sergeant_   53-15

Command Officer's Approval _C. J. Kennedy, Captain_

Read and Approved _T. E. Rowe_   Division Chief

Arthur G. Dill   Chief of Police

DISTRIBUTION
      Original and one copy to Commendations Board

(Separate set for each officer mentioned)
– DO NOT FOLD –

DPD 139 (Rev. 6/70)

DENVER POLICE DEPARTMENT
COMMENDATORY LETTER

From: __Patrol - District One__   Date __May 3, 1974__
Division - District - Bureau

Recognition is hereby given to __Officer J.S. Haroldsen__, serial number __72-33__,

who is presently assigned to __District One - Detail Two__,

for the following described activity: __The above officers received information from__

__a reliable informant as to the location of dangerous drugs and the__

__persons in charge of the drugs. Acting upon this information the__

__officers obtained a search warrant and executed the same at 999__

__Pearl St., #304. In conducting the search a quantity of marijuana,__

__and heroin was discovered. In addition two persons were arrested__

__and jailed without incident.__

__On May 2, 1974 the District Attorney filed two felony counts__

__against the two mentioned suspects for the unlawful possession of__

__marijuana and heroin.__

__The two suspects that were arrested in this matter are:__

__Debie Bubier, DOB 1-8-53 and Mary Fent, DOB 12-29-52.__

Submitted By: _Sgt W.L.Morris 55-3_
Sergeant W.L. Morris, #55-03

Approval of Command Officer: _Lt J.J. Britton 56-35_

DISTRIBUTION:

Original - Recipient Officer
   Copy - Officer's Personnel File
   Copy - Commendations Board

Form 139A (4/70) DPD

179

40

BURGLAR PUTS KNIFE TO THROAT

WE GOT A CALL REGARDING a burglary and immediately responded. We were talking to a man and his wife about what had happened. The woman was so shaken up she could hardly speak to us. She finally said that she was sound asleep in bed with her husband when she woke up with a knife being held against her throat. She didn't even have to tell us any more details because we knew exactly who the burglar was. Very reluctantly, she said to us that the burglar told her he would come back and slit her throat if she told the police anything. This burglary fit the MO of a young guy we knew very well. He would break into a house and collect all the things he was taking in a bag by the door. He would then go into the bedroom and put a knife against the throat of the woman of the house. He often did this even when the woman's husband was asleep right next to her. He would wake her up and tell her who he was, and if she called the police, he would come back and slit her throat. The woman would be so terrorized that she would not dare testify in court. Even though we knew of the numerous burglaries, he had committed every time he got arrested, the DA's office could not prove a single one. We just keep waiting for one of the many victims to come forward and testify against him. A call came over the radio of a burglary, and since we were so close to the house, we got there in less than a minute. Just as we approached the house, we saw Geronimo Sanchex running around the back of one of the neighbor's houses. We immediately called for backup and started chasing our little notorious burglar. Because of some amazing good luck, we were able to catch him. We handcuffed him and advised him of his rights, but since he didn't have any stolen items on him, we knew this could end up like all the other cases. We found out when we took him in to have him booked for burglary, he had dozens of arrests in the past but no convictions because of the threats he made to all his victims.

We got a call to cover the fire department going to school where there was a reported fire. We were right behind the fire truck, going very fast with red lights and sirens going. Back in those days, the fireman would ride on the back end of the fire truck, which was equipped with a platform and grab bars for them to hold onto. The fire truck was just entering an intersection when a car hit the back end of the fire truck, killing one of the firemen. To make the story even sadder, some kid in the school pulled the fire alarm as a prank. The driver of the car was seriously injured but did not die. Fire trucks now are equipped with a large cab where all the firemen ride inside.

In our district 1 station, we had a terrific lieutenant who had been a street cop for many years before moving up in the ranks. Most of the criminal element knew him very well and stayed out of his way. He requested my partner and me to meet him at a very well-known bar that was always full of criminals. We walked into the very poorly lit bar, and he told the bartender to turn on all the lights. With the lights on, he said it in a rather loud voice "I'm Lieutenant Britton, and I want every one of you up against the wall spread eagle!"

It was not too surprising that we recovered guns knives and drugs from almost everyone. We were prepared with zip ties as we arrested numerous criminals. We called for the patty wagon to have them transported to the jail downtown. It was always very exciting to work with our lieutenant, who always knew where the action was. My partner and I returned to the same bar the next day, thinking that we might make some more felony arrests. As soon as we pulled into the parking lot, I spotted a guy that I knew was wanted. We were just in the process of handcuffing him when some guys a few cars away had us ducking below our police car as we were getting showered with rounds from some .32 automatics. One round creased my head, causing a large red welt. We were so outnumbered they had us pinned down. We didn't dare fire in their direction because there were homes right behind where they were at and also a daycare center. By the time backup, cars arrived they were all gone. We never got a good enough look at any of them in order to get arrest warrants issued.

The next day was a Sunday, and I was working the dayshift. This particular day was very boring, with very little criminal activity going on. That was all about to change as a group of hell's angels came riding through Denver on their motorcycles. There were eight of them, and two of us driving right behind them. We called for cars to back us up before we pulled them over. Because it had been a very slow day as far as any action, we quickly had a whole gang of officers with us. We pulled the gang over and had them outnumbered—two to one. Because of the number of police officers killed by hells angels, we approached the gang with the greatest of caution. We searched them and had them empty their bags on the street. Not surprising at all, we ended up with a number of guns and drugs.

One thing I discovered turned my blood cold. One motorcycle had a twelve-gauge shotgun rigged as part of the handlebars with the trigger connected to a wire with a loop in the end. By watching the mirror mounted on the motorcycle; the rider could turn the handlebars and aim the 12-gauge shotgun at an approaching officer. This particular stop made our Sunday a lot more exciting and ruined it for some really bad dudes. This was definitely that kind of stop you would only make with plenty of good police officers. This also was a very good day for several tow trucks to help us out. Two of the gang were clean and we had to let them go but not before really hassling them. They sure did not have smiles on their faces as they rode off on their motorcycles.

COP LIVING ON THE EDGE

While working the night shift we got a call that Baner Molinare, who had several outstanding arrest warrants had just been spotted. He was a very dangerous criminal who always carried a gun. Several cars responded to the area and my partner let me off in an alley where he had been seen. I had my gun out and stepped back behind a dumpster watching for him. One of the officers came on the air and said he just saw Molinare get into a car which he then described. I heard the car approaching and saw it coming down the alley with its lights off. Even though it was fairly dark as he got close to the dumpster, I could clearly see it was him. It was summertime and his window was rolled down and he didn't see me quickly move over next to his car. I stuck my gun against his temple and cocked it. When I shined my flashlight in his face, I saw he was holding a 45 in his right hand. I told him that if he even twitched a muscle, whatever little bit of brains he had would be splattered all over the car. It felt really good to have taken down such a bad guy so easily.

I was working solo when I got a call about a burglary in progress. I got about a block away and I was watching the area for the guy they described over the radio. I pulled the car next to the curb close to where he was walking on the sidewalk. The second I stopped the car he took off running in the other direction. Since he got such a good head start on me, I decided to chase him backward in my police car. He stayed on the sidewalk as he ran. Just as I caught up with him and was getting ready to bail out of my car to grab him, I slammed into a flatbed truck parked on the road. I had been watching him in my rearview mirror and the truck was totally in my blind spot as I came to a smashing halt. Just a few seconds before I crashed into the truck the guy who called about the burglary was standing on the sidewalk watching me with a lot of apprehension on his face. About one second before I hit the truck he yelled, "Look out, behind you!"

And I thought he meant I had just caught up to the burglar, but he was trying to tell me I was about to hit the parked truck. The truck I hit was a very heavy-duty steel flatbed truck and it completely totaled the backend of my police cruiser. There was no damage to the truck, but it ended the opportunity I had of catching the burglar. I asked the guy on the sidewalk why didn't he warn me sooner about the truck. He replied, "You are a policeman, and I was sure you weren't going to run right into it!"

I took the burglary report and I had a tow take my unit to the motor pool. I was relieved that the car I was driving was an old piece of junk and was ready for the scrap yard. Hundreds of new police cars were just being delivered the next week so I got lucky on my timing. The new police cars had air-conditioning which was really great in the summertime. The one big drawback was they were gutless Ramblers. When you put the pedal to the metal, they sounded like a vacuum cleaner winding up. We were told not to go over 60 miles an hour for the first 3000 miles in order to break them in. We were specifically told to not get in any high-speed chases. A few weeks later car 107 spotted a stolen car and started chasing after it. The chase ended up on the interstate as the officers were calling in directions and speed. They said over the radio we're now going 75 mph, and now up to 90 trying to close the gap. The sergeant came on the radio and told them to call off the chase or they would blow up the engine. They obviously did not hear the sergeant because then they said, "We are now going to 105 mph, oh crap the engine just blew up!"

They called for a tow and the sergeant came on and said in a very angry voice, "I'll be picking you guys up in a few minutes!"

Several cars came on the air, all of them laughing hysterically. When I went back on the night shift my partner and I always had a plan on how to get a hot set of wheels. We would disable our Rambler by pulling the spark plug wire off just enough to make a couple of cylinders not work. Then we would grab the keys to an unmarked .426 Hemi-head with a modified police interceptor engine. We always hid the keys so nobody else would be able to get our really fast unit.

The three quick buzzing alarm sounds came on the radio with an officer calling for help! Since we had the fastest car, we made it to the junior high school where the call originated. A gang of junior high kids jumped a uniformed officer and tried desperately to get his gun and shoot him. Luckily, he was wearing a clamshell holster that only police officers know how to open. We arrived at the scene along with several others police cars. The gang of teenagers took off the second the other officers and ourselves arrived. We were able to arrest some of them as they were fleeing the scene. It didn't take too much persuasion to get them to rat out the other guys involved. The officer was beaten up pretty badly but was alive because of the holster he was using. After the incident occurred, we never entered any junior high or high school without backup and being totally on guard.

Working the dayshift, the dispatcher had been using a lot of abbreviations (acronyms) which we were not familiar with. We had come upon an abandoned car and asked the dispatcher to run the plate to see if it was a stolen vehicle. He responded saying, "Is the vehicle APC?"

He then said, "Last night, a suspect was charged with AGGDWI and also AEO while driving that vehicle. I responded to the dispatchers that I did not know what any of those letters meant.

He told me, "APC stands for Actual Physical Control, AGGDWI stands for Aggravated Driving While Intoxicated, and that AEO stands for Attempt to Elude and Officer!"

I then said to him, "So you wanted to know if we actually had the vehicle and that it had been driven by a man driving intoxicated trying to allude to the police?"

He told me, "Yes, that's what he was trying to convey using a much shorter method!"

My partner and I could not believe all the crazy acronyms the dispatchers used all the time. About an hour later, we saw a cat that had been run over in the road. I thought I'd have a little fun with the dispatcher and called to report a FLCOTRJ. The dispatcher asked me to repeat what I had just said over the air. I then said we have a FLCOTRJ in the 200 blocks of federal.

He then asked me, "What on earth do those letters stand for?"

I told him they stand for a Flat Cat On The Road, John. The dispatcher's name was John! And as soon as I told him what the letters stood for, there were numerous cat calls and laughing coming from numerous police cars all over the city. Life is definitely too short to take everything so seriously!

NAME: MOLINAR, Banner L.

DOB: 7-22-53

ADDRESS: 4225 Umatilla St.

VEHICLE: 66 Chev, Blue, AZ-9990(73)
Wrecked in Chase--Now in Jail

O: Vice Grip Burglars

ASSOCIATES: Richard Luna-Lute Casias

SANCHEZ, Geronimo
4-4 90lbs. Brn. Bl.
DOB 9-8-58 DPD #198825
1247 Tennyson St.

@ Leonard Garcia, Dale Cordova, Michael Deffert, Steve Houghton and David Lucero.

Numerous arrests for Burg. and Assault. These parties have pulled many burglaries where the victims have been held at gun-point and have threatened the victims to keep them from prosecuting them.

IS THIS OUR OWN OFFICER SCOTT ALIAS "JOHN" HAROLDSECHVER

policemen patrol on foot during car crisis

Some Denver policemen spent nearly as much time Monday waiting for their cars to come out of the police repair shop as they did on patrol. Patrolman J. S. Pieratt, left, stands next to the patrol car he discovered had no safety inspection sticker. Right, four officers kill some time waiting for cars. From left, Sgt. J. L. Pinda and Patrolmen Gregg Meyer, John Smith and John Haroldsen.

By TED CAREY
News Staff

Six Denver policemen Monday patrolled the downtown area on foot because the department didn't have enough patrol cars to go around.

Meanwhile their assigned areas of responsibility either went uncovered or were partially patrolled by cars from neighboring precincts.

That was just one of several embarrassing — consequences of the problems police are having with their aging fleet of squad cars, which the News observed Monday while spending a few hours at the Denver police garage, Speer Boulevard and Larimer Street.

Policemen who were hanging around in the garage's back lot, waiting for a pool car to become available, said these kinds of several hours in waiting at the beginnings of shifts have become the norm over the past few months.

Two of the affected policemen, Patrolmen Gregg Meyer and John Haroldsen, finally left the garage around 1:30 p.m. after waiting since 10 a.m. for a car that never came.

'WILD CARD' ROUTE

Meyer and Haroldsen normally patrol a "wild card" route without a particular precinct assignment in District 1, which includes Northwest Denver and downtown.

Monday afternoon they headed out from the garage in Meyer's rented Audi, which they said they planned to park and then walk around the downtown area.

District 1 Sgt. W. L. Morris said he had four more men on foot Monday for the same reason. The problem was similar in Denver's other three police districts, he said.

A District 4 patrolman, John Smith, who was at the garage for more than an hour trying to get his car fixed, said at least four patrolmen in his district were without cars Monday.

Smith's precinct, which stretches from Alameda Avenue to Florida Avenue and from Downing Street to the South Platte River, was unpatrolled while he was at the garage.

SUPERVISION AFFECTED

Morris said the problem has begun to affect police supervision, too. In his district over the past few days there have been only two cars available for three sergeants and a lieutenant, he said.

Normally these officers each cruise the district in separate cars, ready to dispense advice and supervision. But since Friday they've been forced to "double up" in the cars, effectively cutting supervision in half, Morris said.

Patrolman J. S. Pieratt had the most embarrassing experience. He said he had stopped a woman driver and was writing her a citation for driving with an expired safety inspection sticker when the woman noticed that Pieratt's patrol car didn't have a sticker at all.

Pieratt, who had picked up the vehicle from the garage pool that morning and had been driving it for more than three hours without noticing the blank spot on its windshield,

---

IS THAT MEANY CHIEF ART DILL GOING TO MAKE A "FLATFOOT" OF OUR BOY?

OR WILL THE TAX PAYERS COME TO HIS RESCUE?

OR... WILL OUR YOUNG OFFICER SCOTT ALIAS "JOHN" HAVE TO DRIVE HIS OWN AUTO? AND MAKE HIS POOR FAMILY SUFFER?

FOLLOW THESE EXCITING DETAILS IN YOUR LOCAL PAPERS

"I swear I'll NEVER volunteer for an assignment again..."

41

SAWED-OFF SHOTGUN

MY PARTNER AND I RECEIVED information from an excellent confidential informant of a party that was selling heroin. From the past history with this informant, we were able to obtain a no-knock search warrant for 4507 West Nevada Place. Officer Martinez and Laska of the narcotics bureau assisted us in executing the search warrant. We knocked on the door, but no one answered, so we kicked in the door. We found balloons of heroin, aluminum packages of heroin, packages of marijuana, and the barrel of a sawed-off shotgun. We also found numerous narcotic implements, including a hypo containing suspected heroin. While we were searching the house, we saw the suspects Rae Santiago and Willy Santiago pull up in their car.

We rushed outside and grabbed them before they could get away. They both had fresh needle marks on their arms and were arrested for illegal possession and use of narcotics. They were handcuffed and advised of their rights. I tagged all the evidence and took it into the custodian's office and the drugs to the lab for analysis. They were again advised of their rights in the narcotics bureau. I told the detectives when I was in the house, I picked up the phone and could hear people talking on the line. I had found out earlier their phone at that address had been disconnected for nonpayment of their bills. When I questioned Rae Santiago about the phone, he said he just hooked it up into a line going into the next apartment. And the additional phone was found in the closet with several telephone wires going from it. The detectives advised us to add the charge of felony wiretapping to both parties. We were commended for making such a good arrest while in the narcotics bureau.

While on routine patrol, we spotted several people standing around a station wagon near 33rd and Holly Street in front of Juniors Food Store. The minute they spotted our marked police car they all took off running, and three of them went into the store. We walked past the station wagon and observed stereo equipment on the seat. An older man Hoskins said the stereo equipment belonged to another party. Marve Jenkens said the equipment was his, and he had brought it with him when he just got out of the Army. We asked him to Identify the equipment giving us the name and other information. He couldn't tell us anything about it without looking at it closely, so we knew he was lying. We found the address of 1200 Stout St. on the back of the Bell & Howell tape player.

We placed Jenkens under arrest for theft. When we took him into headquarters detective, Flos told us that the equipment had been taken in a burglary from 2108 Lafayette Street. After the detective called the victim of the burglary, she described all of the equipment which was an exact match of what we had recovered. When we arrested Jenkens, he had a Wallet containing a Social Security card and a Red Shield Community card with the name of Vernis Crews of 2700 Josephine St. The detective said they would probably add carrying false identification as well as the other charges.

On February 4, 1974, we got a call of a burglary in progress at 2861 Mead Street. We drove around for a few minutes in the area where the burglary occurred, waiting for a description of the suspects. We immediately observed two suspects matching the description aired northbound in the 2800 Block Alley between law and King Street. We stopped them both and asked for identification. A revised description with more details matched the two perfectly. We separated the two and questioned them about where they had been and where they were going, and there were numerous discrepancies. We returned them to the scene in front of the premises where the complainant had seen them earlier. She said that they were the same ones who had broken into her house. We placed the two, Rae Rose Fuentes and Dave M. Casado, under arrest for investigation of burglary and advised them of their rights. While we are searching the area, we saw a 1972 Plymouth duster yellow in color plate number AT 9127 was right close to where the suspects were walking from. We found a pair of vice grips on the front seat of the vehicle the suspects used to twist off the doorknob. We had the car towed to the pound and continued looking in the area the suspects were walking. We found a portable stereo radio in the trash dumpster a few feet from where we stopped the suspects. The items were placed in the custodians' office as evidence. The victim identified the stereo radio as the one taken from her house.

We were patrolling the area of the Quigg Newton Projects, and we spotted two suspects that we knew to be very active heroin users and drug dealers. They were driving a blue Pinto which we finally got stopped in the 4500 blocks of Mariposa way. They jumped out of the car and started running, but we quickly caught up to Martinez aka Fat Fairy. During the rundown, Martinez threw down a tinfoil package that had heroin in it as well as a hypo. Pat Trujillo was able to escape from us and never was found. We found fresh needle marks in Martinez's arm and placed him under arrest for possession of narcotics and illegal use of narcotics. We found out when we took him into headquarters that he was already out on bond for possession of heroin from a narcotics raid made earlier in the year.

Cops: 6. Bad guys: 0.

DENVER POLICE DEPARTMENT
OFFICIAL COMMENDATION

TO: Office of the Chief of Police

Date ____August 29, 1974____

FROM: ____Vice/Drug Control____
Division – District – Bureau

I wish to commend Officer __J. S. Haroldson__ , Serial No. __72-33__ ,
who is presently assigned to __District Four__
for the following:

COMMENDATORY AWARD
- [ ] Class Two Award
- [ ] Class Three Award
- [ ] Class Four Award

WHEREAS it is realized that the great bulk of police work is done routinely by good policemen, let it be known that the above-named officer displayed initiative and alertness decidedly in excess of the norm in this particular instance.

Fact Situation: On July 31, 1974 Officer Wheeler and Haroldson assisted by Officer Meyer, initiated and executed a search warrant at 4507 W. Nevada Pl. 4.8 grams of marijuana and .430 grams of heroin were recovered. These officers are to be commended for their iniative and dilligence which resulted in the recovery of narcotics and the arrest of two parties who were filed on in Denver District Court for Felony Possession of Narcotics.

Commending Officer _____
D. L. Simmons, Sergeant   53-15

Command Officer's Approval _____
J. Kennedy, Captain

Read and Approved _____
T. E. Rowe   Division Chief

_____
Arthur G. Dill   Chief of Police

DISTRIBUTION:
Original and one copy to Commendations Board

(Separate set for each officer mentioned)

– DO NOT FOLD –

DPD 139 (Rev. 6/70)

42

OUTNUMBERED SIX TO ONE

WHILE WORKING A NIGHT SHIFT, I came upon a man lying partly in the road, I stopped to check on him, and he had no signs of life. I started doing CPR on him, and I felt so bad that his breath made me throw up several times. I continued doing it and got no response, so I did the compressions harder and harder. After several compressions, I heard his sternum crack and felt awful. The paramedics arrived and used the electrified paddles on him and everything possible and said he was gone. I told them I was sure I had broken his ribs or his sternum, and they said it happens very often even when you're doing it right. Even though my CPR training was up to date, everyone should keep their skills very sharp when it comes to life-saving techniques. I have personally had my life saved many times over the past two years by first responders who knew precisely how to do life-saving techniques. I never go to bed without thanking first responders in my prayers. I have saved lives in the past by doing the Heimlich maneuver and CPR.

Working the dayshift, I got a call about a man with a gun running from the scene of an armed robbery. I was just pulling up to the building when I saw the guy with a 45-automatic running around the building across the parking lot. He didn't see me un till the very last minute, because I was driving an unmarked police cruiser. He aimed the gun at me as I reached down to unbuckle my seatbelt. The seatbelt was stuck, and no matter how hard I pulled on it, it wouldn't release. The shooter also realized I was stuck in my car and started to back away, but still had his gun aimed at me. I opened the door, still fighting to unbuckle my seat belt. Since I was using both hands to release the seatbelt, he moved further away but kept his gun pointed at me. I finally got the seatbelt released, and as I was drawing my gun, he took off running. I think all of my buildup adrenaline finally kicked in, and I caught up to him and screamed, "Drop your gun, or I will shoot!" I always felt that the jammed seat belt might've saved my life when he was right next to my Police car. I think if I would've tried pulling my gun out at that point, he would've been able to shoot me before I had a chance. It seemed like he felt safe as long as I was stuck in the police car. When I took him downtown to have him booked, I couldn't believe all the shootings he had been involved in and was amazed that he didn't shoot me when he was right there so close.

I was working in car 112 in a more upscale neighborhood when I got a call on a burglary. The homeowners had been on a three-week vacation when they returned to their home and found it totally empty. I talked to the next-door neighbor and found out how everything in the house had been taken without anyone calling the police. Apparently, a fake moving van was backed up in their driveway. The curious neighbor walked over and talked to the burglars and asked them where the Hendersons had moved. The burglars were wearing uniforms with the name of the moving company printed on their backs. She told them that she was really good friends and was surprised that they hadn't told her they were moving. One of the guys said to her that it was a last-minute thing because of a new job offer Mr. Henderson had just taken. The neighbor felt bad that she had been so easily conned by these criminals. Since they had been working so hard, she had taken them over a picture of punch and a plate of homemade cookies. We got an excellent description of the three but had no other leads to go on. This was definitely a very well-planned out and gutsy move on the part of these burglars.

We were experiencing a near-riot downtown when the lights went out. There was a guy with a large bulge at his waistline. I approached him from behind and reached out and grabbed a .45 caliber automatic that was fully loaded and had the hammer cocked. I asked him what he was doing with that gun, and he replied, "I'm here to shoot any looters that I see coming out of the stores!" I arrested him for carrying a concealed weapon with intent to do bodily harm. I explained that if he would've drawn his gun, one of the police officers would've probably shot him thinking he was one of the bad guys. I put some heavy-duty zip ties on his wrists and put him in the paddy wagon.

Three zip alarm sounds came over the radio, followed by, "We had an officer who has been shot!" A state police officer had stopped a car on the highway and placed the subject in the backseat of his car while he was running a ID check. Back in those days, there was not any protection between the backseat and the front seat of police cars. The suspect fought with the officer and somehow ended up with his gun and shot him in the head. The officer's six-inch Colt Python was taken by the suspect.

Every officer on duty tried to track him down for the next several days with no success. Sad cases like this finally led the police departments into installing bulletproof glass or heavy-duty wire mesh between the front and backseat. After my partner Bill Smith was murdered by a recently paroled criminal, we finally got shotguns installed and all of our police cars. We also were issued bulletproof vests and much better ammunition. It was really too bad that it took another officer being murdered to get the proper gear we should've always had!

During my first year on the job, I was working with a very professional training officer. He taught me a lot of very valuable lessons that helped save my life and also the lives of innocent bystanders. One thing he taught me was if you draw your gun and start shooting, make sure that there is no one in that direction you're shooting at other than the bag guys. A call went out of a man with a gun creeping around the back of some houses. My training officer went around the right side of one of those houses just as a guy came around the corner walking backward with his gun out. He yelled, "Police officer! Drop the gun!"

Instead of dropping it, he quickly turned his body, facing the officer aiming the gun right at him. Fearing for his life, my training officer fired quickly taking down the suspect. The facts that came out over the next hour were tragic and life-changing and sadly unalterable. It turned out the boy was only 15 years old and was playing cops and robbers with his friends with plastic toy guns. My training officer told me that the same situation could happen to any police officer. In one case if they hesitate their dead, and in another case, they may shoot an innocent person. The really tough part about it is you only have a split second to make a life-changing decision. I remembered in the police academy that they told us it's better to be tried by twelve than carried by six! What they could never teach you is how to be certain, when you shoot someone that it was the right thing to do. I was awarded the highest rating possible, Distinguished Expert Marksman. One day I was working solo when I stopped a car with six guys in it. They were driving very slowly checking out some warehouses down by the railroad tracks. When I pulled them over to see what they were doing all six guys got out of the car. I told them to all get back into the car. They kept walking towards me and started to spread out. Some of them had big knives and the others had their hands in their pockets. I knew I could shoot two or three of them, but I wasn't sure about the others. As they got closer, I was ready to start shooting. A couple of them put their hands in the air but still kept moving towards me. I aimed my gun at each of them going back and forth as they moved closer and closer to me. One of them yelled, "Hey pig, you can't get all of us and will take you down!"

Just as I was ready to start pulling the trigger the thought came to me to jump in my car and get the heck out of there. I quickly walked back towards my police car while keeping my gun pointed at them. I really wished that one of them would've pulled out a gun or attacked me with a knife so that I could have shot them. And I always wondered after that what another police officer would have done in the same situation! I never told this story before to anyone, especially friends who were police officers.

43

ATTEMPTED RAPE

A HUSBAND AND HIS WIFE had a terrible argument that made her so mad she went running out the door to leave in her car. It was about one o'clock AM, and she was so tired she decided just to try to sleep it off in her car. A guy came along and shined his flashlight in the backseat and saw this woman sleeping. She had forgotten to lock the car doors. He opened the door and started trying to rip her clothes off. She quickly realized that she could not fight off this attacker, but by keeping a real cool head, she came up with a fantastic plan. She said in a very calm voice, "Hey, why don't we just go in the house and use my upstairs bedroom, which will be way better than the backseat!" The guy agreed and grabbed her by the arm and walked up to the house and went up the stairs to her bedroom door. Just as they stepped through the door, she screamed her husband's name at the top of her lungs and said, "this man is trying to rape me!" Her husband was not actually asleep, and he sprang from the bed, grabbed the guy, and slammed him to the floor. He yelled at his wife to call the police as he started pounding on the low life. Since it had been a slow evening as far as crime goes, several cars showed up at the house. The attacker was pretty beat up when we took him into custody. The other officers on the front porch all wanted to pound on this creep. The woman's husband had done an outstanding job detaining him until we all arrived. We handcuffed him and put him in the back seat of the car and then talked to the couple about precisely what transpired.

We told the woman what an amazing cool head she had and that her plan was ingenious. We informed the couple that because of the circumstances, this scumbag would not see the light of day for many years. When we returned to our police car, some of the other officers had taken him out of our police cruiser, and we're questioning him! We realized that his injuries were too severe, and he was bleeding everywhere, so we called an ambulance. The District Attorney's Office could hardly wait to prosecute this criminal. The husband-and-wife team was excellent witnesses on the stand. The defense attorney was almost speechless at every turn, and the judge sentenced him to a maximum of twenty years in prison.

Several weeks later, we got another call of attempted rape. The woman who was the victim said she had some evidence that she knew would put this guy away. She was beaten up and covered with blood. Her injuries did not look like they could be the source of so much bleeding. She went over to the nightstand and picked up the totally mind-boggling evidence. In her bloody hands, she was holding a big chunk of her attacker's ear, which she had bit off. I immediately called Denver General Hospital and asked if they had someone being treated for a serious injury to their ear. After a couple of minutes, a nurse came back on the phone and said that there was a man in the ER who had lost so much blood he had fainted. I asked her if the victim had a big part of his right ear missing. She said the doctors were stitching up the jagged piece of what was left of his ear. She told us when he came in, he said he had injured it trying to shave with a knife. The doctors did not believe him because the injury looked more like a dog had bit off his ear. We explained to her what had really happened and told her we would bring in the remaining part of his ear to see if it matched. We later learned that it was a perfect match, and the doctors had attempted to sew it back on. Once again, the district attorney was anxious to try this scumbag.

I was working the night shift with a training partner when I spotted a car being driven by a guy that I knew was a big-time drug user and always carried a gun. We pulled the car over and took the driver Albert Spahne out of the car to search him. I was surprised when I didn't find a gun during the search. He was wearing a hat, and my training officer quickly reached up, grabbed it off of his head, and showed me the .32 automatic he had hidden in his hat. I knew he was a heroin user, and I found fresh needle marks on his arms. We arrested him for carrying a concealed weapon and illegal use of heroin.

My partner and I were very aware of the rioting and fighting going on in la Raza Park. Our Sergeant had told us to stay clear of that area which we did most of the shift. Things had gotten very quiet with very little crime going on. We were getting rather bored with no action other than at the off-limits park. We decided to have a little fun driving through the park. We had some CS gas grenades in the trunk and put them on the front seat of our police car and drove slowly through the park. When we came to a large group of militant criminals fighting, we started throwing the gas grenades out of the car right in the middle of the group and sped out of the area. Our little fun had a very positive result in that all those bad guys took off running to get away from the CS gas and the fighting ended. We ignored several calls over the radio asking if anyone knew what officers had driven through the park, throwing out gas grenades.

The quiet day ended when we got a call of a young boy bleeding very severely from a large cut on his wrist. We got the call that occurred in our area and drove red light and siren to the house which was only 50 yards away. I knew at that moment that the Lord had guided my driving. The six-year-old boy had fallen through a glass window and was bleeding profusely. Because this was a life-threatening injury, we informed the dispatchers we would be transporting the boy to the hospital since no ambulance was even near. I held the boy on my lap, applying direct pressure to the wound with a clean towel to try and stop the massive bleeding. My partner did an excellent job busting through red lights and stop signs at a breakneck speed avoiding numerous accidents. We felt very blessed to have saved this young boy's life when the doctors told us he would've died in a matter of only a few minutes had we not got him there so quickly. I could not believe how much blood he lost even though I did direct pressure so firmly against his deep wound. There is no doubt that or Heavenly Father looked down kindly on this young child and because of him he lived.

Only a few weeks later we got another emergency call of a young two-year-old girl who was choking and could hardly breathe. Once again, we were blessed to be very close to this house and were able to arrive in a matter of only three or four seconds. The two-year-old was barely breathing, and when I got close to her mouth, I could smell a powerful chemical odor. I looked around on the floor and under the couch was a bottle of a liquid plumber. We got poison control on the phone, and they said to give her a little bit of milk with some burnt toast and get her to the hospital as soon as possible. I did remember from first aid training that burnt toast and milk act as an absorbent for poison. I also remembered something that burns going down would also burn coming up, so you don't ever make them throw up. Because there was no ambulance close, we took her to the hospital as fast as we could safely drive. I remembered the first aid training in the police academy on how to do CPR on a tiny child or baby. The doctor and nurses were right at the ER entrance when we pulled up. Once again, our Heavenly Father saved this precious little one.

Cops: 3. Bad guys: 0. (Militant bad guys in La Raza Park: 75 to 100—sick coughing and throwing up. The Lord saved one sweet innocent little boy and a precious little girl.)

NAME: SPAHN, Albert J.

DOB: 11-8-54

ADDRESS:

VEHICLE: 65 Ford Van, Wht/Blue, AC-4511(73trk)

MO: Heroin-Burglary-CCW

ASSOCIATES:

44

AMUSEMENT PARK RIDE SENDS SEVERAL RIDERS FLYING TO THEIR DEATH

THERE WAS A HORRIBLE ACCIDENT at Elitch Gardens Amusement Park. Serval people were killed on the flying spider when it came apart. We had numerous fire department personnel ambulances and police officers on the scene. We were finishing our report when a car crashed into a parked vehicle and left the scene. The most upsetting part about it was that the car narrowly missed hitting several kids who had just witnessed the flying terrible spider accident.

We didn't see the crash, but we were able to follow the car because the tires had blown, and the rims were making grooves in the asphalt. After a few blocks, we saw the car with the rims spinning and not getting any traction. He had the pedal to the metal, and the big engine was wound up spinning the tires so fast they were shooting sparks everywhere. The driver was so drunk he didn't know where he was. We arrested him for driving under the influence and leaving the scene of an accident. We were able to get a DUI traffic car to finish the report so we could return to the accident at the amusement park.

We got another one of those exciting three buzzing alarms of a stick-up in progress and an officer calling for help. The call came from a liquor store on Larimer Street that had been robbed numerous times in the past. The first officer on the scene pulled up just as the stick-up was coming out the door. He yelled at him to drop the gun, and when he didn't, he opened fire. The whole front of the store was floor-to-ceiling storefront glass. None of the glass was broken, and the suspect was not hit. He was pretty much scared to death because of all of the gunfire aimed at him. He quickly gave up and almost seemed relieved when he got handcuffed and hauled downtown to be booked. The owner of the store wanted to know what we thought about him mounting a 12-gauge shotgun above the sales window with a remote trigger.

We told him we knew it was illegal but said he could go ahead and do it. For several weeks, there was not a single attempted robbery because the word was on the street about the wall-mounted shotgun. A few weeks later, a stick-up went in to rob the place, not knowing about the shotgun. The owner even had a sign mounted above the cashier window, stating that the shotgun was loaded and would be used if someone tried to rob him. He pulled out a handgun and proceeded to rob the liquor store and ignored the comment about the shotgun. Just as he turned to leave, the owner said you're going to be dead if you take another step. He told the stick-up to look up above at the shotgun. The guy made a comment that he knew it was just for show. The owner then pulled the wire attached to the trigger and killed the suspect right where he stood. The DA did not file any charges over the shooting. To my knowledge, the liquor store was never robbed again.

Cops: 2. Bad guys: 0. (Several Good people hopefully in heaven.)

45

$97,000 SAFE JOB

I WAS WORKING OFF DUTY with five other officers at the Regency at a dance where there were about eight hundred people. The hotel management informed us that the people giving the party owed them nine hundred dollars and asked if we would keep an eye on the man at the door taking in the money. During the dance nine o'clock PM until two o'clock AM, I observed the man taking the money was only placing one-dollar bills in the cashbox and was putting the larger bills in a wad in his pocket. His right-side pocket was bulging with the large bills. The manager told me that the man taking the money was supposed to take the money to the main office. The manager asked me if I would please keep an eye on the man with the cash box. I knew that he had a large wad of cash in his pocket and only one-dollar bills in the cashbox, I got another officer to come and help me. While the other officer watched the cash box, I have followed the man with the wad of money, go over and talk to some girls at a table. He reached in his pocket and started to pull out the wad of cash when he saw me watching him and then took his empty hand out of his pocket, leaving the wad of cash. He then walked over to the table and picked up the cashbox and said he was going up to his room number 1209. I followed him to the door and then went back downstairs and had Officer Wheeler call Lieutenant O'Hare. He asked him if we could arrest the party for defrauding an innkeeper. He said no but told us to call the district attorney. The DA told us to

COP LIVING ON THE EDGE

contact a man named Proctor who signed the contract and keep him there until he would arrive. Proctor got off the elevator near the desk, holding a large wad of cash in his hand, and walked back towards the ballroom. I asked him to step into the manager's office and get the bill settled. Proctor replied, "Hey, man, I am in a hurry!"

Proctor then stepped to the other side of the desk. I asked him to please step back into the manager's office, and he rushed towards another door and slammed it into my legs, hitting my feet with the steel door. I grabbed him by the arm and said we're going into the manager's office. He then made a fist and swung at my face, and I deflected it into the wall and escorted him into the manager's office. The DA then came into the room with the manager. I wanted very badly to arrest him, but the DA said not at this time. The security manager called for more uniform cars and stated that the people giving the party would not pay their bill, and we're trying to use some bad credit cards. We arrived at their door, and they finally came out and said that they could not pay their bill because the manager wouldn't accept their credit cards.

Per the advice of sergeant Morris, I informed them that if they did not pay their bill immediately with cash, they would be arrested for defrauding an innkeeper. They finally agreed and paid their bill and left the hotel. Wes Hathaway said he would testify that Proctor swung at Officer Haroldsen and also slammed the door into him, causing cuts and bruises He further stated that Proctor received no injuries even though he assaulted Officer Haroldsen. I was commended for doing a great job of restraint under very bad circumstances. I made up my mind right then that I would never again work off duty at any large dances.

Cops: 1. Bad guys: 0 since they had to pay!

$97,000 safe burglary

While on routine patrol, I observed a very well-known felon Al Rivera drive by my police car going in the opposite direction. I immediately flipped a U-turn and started after him. He was driving an older car, and when he accelerated, I quickly passed him up and forced him off the road to the curb. I ordered him out of the car and got him spread eagle and searched him for weapons. Although he had no guns, I did find a bag containing $2600 in gold coins. I placed him under arrest and took him into the burglary detectives. Some of the things I got him to tell me along with information the detectives had cleared up a $97,000 safe burglary. This action took place on November 27, 1973. A short time later, on October 13, 1974, he escaped from jail.

On June 27, 1974, my partner and I were at 4308 Navajo St. on a man with a gun call covering car 109. While we were walking back to our police car, a 1963 black Thunderbird drove by at a high rate of speed swerving all over the road. We pursued the vehicle to the 1200 block of 46th Ave., where the suspect drove on the wrong side of 46th Ave. and parked his car. We approached the car, and I asked Vigil for his license and registration. He responded, saying, "What did I do?" I informed him that he was going to receive a citation for reckless and careless driving! We told him to stay in his vehicle while we were writing him the ticket. As we were writing the ticket, Vigil came back to the police car and stated, "Oh man, my steering is all messed up!"

He then said, "Oh, man, how chicken can you guys get! I don't care if you're going to give me a ticket. I'm going to tear it up!"

I then asked him, "Are you going to go to court on the date we set?"

ESCAPE
COLORADO STATE REFORMATORY
Box R Ph. 395-2418
Buena Vista, Colorado

NCIC WILL-889-755
CCIC 217-777
Denver PD: 118754
FBI NO.: 838-739-G

NAME: RIVERA, Albert
ALIAS: GUERRERO, Albert
C.S.R. NO.: 74-053
SEX: Male   **DOB:** 3-21-48
PLACE OF BIRTH: Denver, Colorado
AGE: 26   **DEGREE OF THREAT:** Caution Advised
HEIGHT: 5'8"
WEIGHT: 142
P.C.: Unknown
SSN: 523-68-7405
SERVICE NO.: None
NATIONALITY: Spanish
RACE: White
HAIR: Black
EYES: Brown

NATURE OF OFFENSE: 2nd Degree Burglary-Escapes-Misd Theft
SCARS, TATTOOS: 2" scar on left pectoral; Scar from gunshot wound, right elbow.

WARRANT: Sentencing Mitt No. 70284 & 70763   **USUAL OCCUPATION:** Waiter
POSSIBLE CONTACTS:
Wife - Lorraine Rivera, 1670 So. Shoshone, Denver, Colorado
Mother - Mary Guerrero, 3038 California, Denver, Colorado
Sister - Phyllis Chavez, 1360 Ebony St., Westminster, Colorado

Escaped 10-13-74 from Montrose Co. Jail, Montrose, Colorado

WILL EXTRADITE
ARREST, HOLD AND TELEPHONE
C. WINSTON TANKSLEY, WARDEN
COLORADO STATE REFORMATORY, BUENA VISTA, COLORADO

When he didn't answer, I asked the question again, "Are you going to go to court?"

Vigil stated, "No, I won't!" He then added some profanity. I then informed him that due to his attitude about not going to appear on the citation that he was under arrest. We called for a backup unit, at which time he started to walk away. Officer Winkler then again advised him that he was under arrest.

Vigil, by this time, was standing at the back of his car and removed his glasses, throwing them on the trunk of his car, and told both officers, "Don't you dare touch me, keep your hands off me!"

He then had both fists clenched, acting like he was going to strike both of us. He kept repeating, "Don't touch me and keep your hands off of me!"

We then grabbed him and turned him around and placed the handcuffs on him.

He then said, "Hey, man. Don't hurt my arm; it's broken!"

His wife or girlfriend came out of the house and started screaming at us not to hurt his broken arm and used a lot of obscenities. The whole time while we were taking him to the district station, he was yelling obscenities at us. We then called for an ambulance to take him to Denver General Hospital. At no time did either one of us strike or hurt the suspect in any way. We found out later that he got his broken arm in a bar fight. Vigil is a very well-known militant felon and has served two terms for aggravated robbery in the state prison. He is a heroin user and also deals heroin.

Cops: 1. Bad guy: big 0. Known militant felon and has served two terms for aggravated robbery in the state prison. He is a heroin user and dealer.

known militant felon and has served two terms for aggravated robbery in the state prison. He is a heroin user and also deals heroin.

Cops One Bad guy big Zero

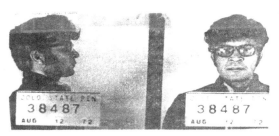

VIGIL, Raymond Joseph
5-11 165lbs. Brn. Brn.
DOB 5-27-40 DPD #60028
665 Perry St.

@Lee Vigil

Served two terms in CSP for Agg. Robbery. Currently using and dealing heroin.

@ Jolly Roger Lounge.

Raymond J. Vigil
5-27-40
resids
665 Perry

U. Rec
Jolly Roger
P. ado Program

Militant and
could be
Dangerous

DENVER POLICE DEPARTMENT

OFFICIAL COMMENDATION

TO: Office of the Chief of Police

Date   November 27, 1973

FROM: PATROL - DISTRICT ONE
  Division — District — Bureau

I wish to commend Officer   J.S. Haroldsen , Serial No. 72-33 ,
who is presently assigned to   District One - Detail Two
for the following:

[X] Class Two Award
[ ] Class Three Award
[ ] Class Four Award

WHEREAS it is realized that the great bulk of police work is done routinely by good policemen, let it be known that the above-named officer displayed initiative and alertness decidedly in excess of the norm in this particular instance.

Fact Situation: Outstanding police action in the arrest of Albert Rivera, DPD #118754. During this arrest twenty-six hundred dollars ($2600.00) in gold coins were recovered. This arrest cleared up a $97,000.00 safe burglary in Jefferson County.

Commending Officer   L.J. Britton
Lieutenant L.J. Britton, #56-25

Command Officer's Approval

Read and Approved
  Division Chief

  Chief of Police

DISTRIBUTION:
  Original and one copy to Commendations Board

Separate set for each officer mentioned)
- DO NOT FOLD -

DPD 139 (Rev. 6/70)

46

FIGHT THE RAPIST

WORKING SOLO ONE DAY, I received a radio call of a man who had just rape a girl and was running from the apartment. I was very close to the area when the dispatcher gave out the description of the suspect. I spotted him heading for the park. By staying in my police car I was able to get right up to him in a matter of only a few seconds. I bailed out of the car and tackled him just in front of the police cruiser. He was bigger and stronger than me and quickly slammed me to the ground and pulled out a knife but missed when he tried to stab me in the throat. My adrenaline kicked in and I was able to push him off me, and he took off running again. I climbed back in my car and called for backup as I continued to chase him through the park. Just as I got right up behind him, he dodged around a tree, and the branches ripped off my overhead lights.

One of the officers I knew very well was coming to my aid red light and siren when he got in a bad accident at an intersection. At that point, I knew no other cars were coming to cover. The fact that he had just raped a young girl and a good friend of mine just got injured in a car accident made me just furious. Since my overhead lights and siren were ripped off, I couldn't even call attention to what was going on for any neighbors nearby. I finally caught up to him with my police car, and I was really tempted to run him over, but I just tapped him hard enough to knock him down. I had been driving my car with the door open, so it only took me a second to jump out.

He was getting up when I tackled him. Since I'm sure, his adrenaline was pumping the same as mine turned into a real battle. About the time I was running out of energy, he was pulling away from me, some guy came from nowhere slammed him to the ground and helped me and get the handcuffs on the scumbag. I took him back to the girl who had been raped, and she screamed, "that's him!"

I sure was tempted to land a few punches on the puke, but I took him downtown to be booked and turning him over to the officer at the jail elevator. When the officer operating the elevator saw how beat up and bloody, I was, and read he was being charged with aggravated rape and assault on a police officer he gave me a big smile and said, "We will take really good care of this creep!"

As soon as the doors on the elevator closed, I could hear a lot of punching, banging, and slamming going on in the elevator. Jailers never like to see their fellow officers injured and especially hate rapists.

Before I knew it, I received a call of an accident with injuries and went with red light and siren racing to the call. The fire department guys were already on the scene. I went over and talked to the driver of one of the wrecked vehicles. He had no physical injuries but was very upset, so I took him over and sat him down in the shade of a tree and told him to calm down, and he would be all right. At first, he was very red in the face, so I kept him sitting up, but then he turned white as a sheet, so I elevated his legs to get some blood to his head. He was suffering from shock, so I asked the paramedics if they could take him into the hospital to keep an eye on him. A traffic car came and wrote up the report of the accident, so I went back into service. The next day at roll call I found out that the guy I had treated for shock died in hospital, even though he had no physical injuries.

My shift was just about to end when I received a call of a possible DOA in a very old hotel downtown. I got a key from the desk and went up and knocked on the door several times. I unlocked the door, and the second I opened it up, I knew for sure the guy was dead. I went out in the hallway and took a deep breath and went in to look for signs of forced entry on the door or the window and found none. Since I didn't have a gas mask, I did as they told us in the police academy to open the gasoline cap on your car and inhale two or three times and then go back to investigate the cause of death. The stench was so penetrating that I waited out in the hallway for the ME. The guy was lying on the bed and bloated two times his normal size. The ME told me that he had been dead for several days, and since the heat was turned on full blast, that sped up the decomposing. Using the car as a temporary office, I got the paperwork finished up and headed to the District 1 station. I never in my life took so long taking a shower using soap and scrub and as hard as I could to try to get the smell off of me. I felt like sticking the showerhead in my mouth and having it shoot through me to clean out all the smelly crap. I thought I would have to burn all my clothes, but the dry cleaner did a great job.

Part of the training in the police academy was to observe two complete autopsies up very close to the corpses. The DOA was much harder to take than watching the two autopsies. As a police officer, you witness a lot of blood and guts, but the autopsies I found to be very fascinating. Quite a few of the other police cadets fainted as soon as the ME started to cut open the bodies. I thought I was going to have a problem with it, but I was just so amazed at the procedure and what they were doing that I didn't have a problem at all. There was so much information that we were learning during the autopsies I knew it would be very valuable in the future determining the cause of death suicides and murder.

Once again, when I was working solo, I received a call of possible suicide and went to an apartment to investigate. There was a young kid about 16 years old that appeared to have no signs of life, but I called an ambulance anyway just to make sure. I knew it would help his mother through the ordeal. Paramedics started doing CPR on him and carried him out to the ambulance. One of them whispered to me that he was gone, but he thought it would make it easier for his mother to deal with the situation. I was always impressed with these paramedics being so kind and thoughtful of how devastating a situation like this had to be to a parent.

Cops: 1. Bad guys: 0. (Good guys gone to heaven: 3.)

47

DOUBLE HOMICIDE

My partner and I were working a downtown car when we stopped at a red light behind a semi-truck trailer. We then noticed a canine unit pull up to the light next to the truck. We could hear the dog barking and saw him jumping up against the window, obviously on to something like drugs. The canine officer pulled out in front to block the truck, and we pulled up close so he couldn't backup. He took the police dog out of the car on a leash, and the dog started going along the truck barking furiously indicating there were drugs inside. We got the driver out of the semi, and immediately, the dog started barking right by the suspect's pockets. A search revealed a loaded .38 gun and a baggie full of what appeared to be cocaine or heroin. It was very easy to obtain a search warrant because this narcotics dog was never wrong when it came to finding drugs. After getting the search warrant, we open the doors to the truck, and it was full of heroin and cocaine millions and millions of dollars' worth.

What happened next is a little bit unbelievable but actually happened. A very high-ranking but idiotic judge ruled that the dog was too perfect in finding drugs and violated the suspect's right of privacy and threw the case out. I didn't really believe it when I heard about it, but then I read it in the paper, and it made me sick! Some judges think if they make police officers do their job with one arm tied behind them, things might work out better for the general public. I'll never forget a judge in New York City who was so lenient on criminals that almost anything other than first-degree murder would not let them end up in prison.

After years of being super lenient and handing out extremely light prison sentences, the judge's daughter was kidnapped, raped, and almost beaten to death. He quickly became known as "The Hanging Judge" for nearly always giving the maximum number of years in prison for convicted felons.

I personally knew of one case where the district attorney did not want to file felony charges against a mother who had molested her child over and over again when he was just a youngster. The stupid attorney said he did not want to brand her for the rest of her life as a child molester. Since that is exactly what she was and will continue to be that guy should be thrown into jail himself. I'm sure if one of his own children were molested as this little one was, he would've had a different view of the whole thing. Lawyers go to school for many years to learn a lot about the law, but one of the things they often are lacking is just plain old good common sense. It's no wonder that our courts are so jammed with cases.

My partner and I were working one night when we spotted a very suspicious car driving into the parking lot of a bar. When we stopped the car and approached the driver, he seemed to be so nervous we knew we were onto something big. We got him out of the car and searched him and found a .38 revolver loaded in his pocket along with some baggies suspected narcotics. We arrested him and advised him of his rights and handcuffed him and asked him if we could look in the car. He seemed to be just fine with us looking in the front and the backseat, but when I asked him if we could look in the trunk, he went absolutely nuts on us and ran and blocked our access to it. He kept telling us there wasn't anything in it. I told him if there wasn't anything in it, then he shouldn't mind if we opened it. He gave us an expression like whatever. As I reached down to open the trunk, he went as white as a ghost, and I quickly found out why as soon as I opened it. A dead man was lying in a pool of his blood. You may have already guessed what happened when the case went to trial. The loaded gun and drugs were admitted as evidence, but the judge threw out the murdered man because we did not have a search warrant that included the trunk. In the state of Colorado, verbal consent to search is as valid as a written signed permission to search. We later found out that the guy we arrested was a hitman for the Smaldon mafia family.

Only a few days later, we got a call of a drive-by shooting and went to the victim's home to investigate. An amiable young Hispanic guy said, "Hurry my dad has been shot!"

We found his dad laying on the floor just inside the front door with very faint signs of life, so we immediately called for an ambulance. The young man was so upset that I got him to sit down and started to ask him a few questions. I gently patted him on the back, and I felt something very sticky. There was blood on his back, coming out of a bullet wound, and he didn't even know he had been shot. I immediately called for another ambulance and got the bleeding stopped from his injury. He told me his dad heard a noise at the front door and when he opened it a guy shot him through the screen barely missing his heart. I figured that when the young man turned to help his dad with his back to the door, the shooter got him also.

We didn't know until the next day at roll call that the father and the son both died at the hospital, and the homicide detectives were taking over.

Cops: 2. Bad guys: 0.

48

SNIPER PINS US DOWN

A STICK-UP IN PROGRESS CAME over the radio, and even though we were not close, we were working what was called a Wild Car and could go anywhere in the city. Our police car was a unmarked 426 Hemi-head special police interceptor engine. When we were going 60 miles an hour, we could burn rubber by putting the pedal to the metal. Because our car was so fast, we were able to get to the donut shop just as a marked unit pulled behind us.

Things didn't seem quite right because as we pulled up, two uniformed officers were coming out into the parking lot walking towards a kind of beat-up older car. We hurried towards the donut shop while the other marked unit stopped to talk to the two officers who just come out of the store. Before we even entered the donut shop, we heard some yelling and commotion coming from the officers behind us. The officers in the arriving police car had the two other officers down on the pavement and were handcuffing them. After talking to the donut store manager, we found out that the two so-called police officers out on the ground were the ones who just robbed the store. The manager said he was kind of suspicious of them when he saw them get out of the car way out in the parking lot. They had cloth sewn on badges on their shirts instead of the standard silver and gold badges. He pushed the silent alarm button before they entered the store. There were some other customers at the counter ahead of them, and they just stayed back by the door, acting very

220

nervous. He said there was just something about their whole uniform and of course, their actions that made him think they were phony cops. The two officers in the parking lot also sensed the same things, plus they did not recognize either one of them. Standard long sleeve issue police shirts are always worn with a tie, which neither officer was wearing. The scariest part of this stick-up was the fake officers had on bulletproof vests and had armor-piercing rounds in their guns. The real clincher was they asked for some donuts, and the bulging donut bag was stuffed with money. I was working solo when I responded to a call of a burglary in progress. Knowing the neighborhood where the call originated, I went down the alley with my lights out. I knew the address given would mean the house would be in the middle of the block. Since I didn't know for sure which was the right house, I stopped in the middle of the alley and quietly got out of my police car. Even though it was quite dark, I could see a guy climbing along the back of the house on the roof. The homes in that neighborhood were so close together that you could jump from one roof to the next one. There was a large tree blocking the view from the burglar to my police car. Since he was headed towards a roof to the right, I quietly climbed up the fence and got on the roof he had just jumped from. The roof made a creaking sound as I was trying to catch up to him. He glanced over his shoulder and then took off running. He jumped across to the next roof but must've sprained his ankle because as he continued to run, he was limping badly. I was gaining on him, and I reached out to grab him just as he was jumping onto the next roof. Although I caught him by the shoulder, his momentum carried him to the other roof. I almost made it onto the roof, but I caught a boot on edge and fell on my back, landing on a hard mound of dirt. I was unconscious, and the dispatcher sent another car to check on me because I was not answering my radio. The officer found me and called for an ambulance. When the paramedics started to move me, the pain woke me, so they rushed me to the hospital. I had suffered a broken back and was out of commission for quite a while. The back surgery went very well, and after recovering, I returned to work.

I was working with my partner on the night shift assigned to downtown Denver. The radio came alive with the three loud buzzing alarm sounds quickly followed by "We have two officers calling for help! cars to cover?"

Since the call came from a downtown high-rise apartment building that was in our area, we quickly responded going with red light and siren. We spotted their police cars in the parking lot and came to a screeching halt right next to them. They were hunkered down with their guns drawn behind the front of their vehicle. We bailed out of our car and got behind the front where the engine would give us some protection. A man was shooting a high-powered rifle at the officers. I always hoped that the oncoming shift which would be notified of how things were left and would go in and get the guy. I could not believe that no officers ever went into the building to get the shooter.

We found out from an informant that a wanted guy was hiding out in a house in our area. Since we couldn't get a search warrant without another informant verifying the information, we just tried knocking on the door to see what would happen. A young girl answered the door and told us there was no one else in the house. Very politely we asked if we could have a look around and she reluctantly agreed. We looked everywhere and came up empty. We were standing in the kitchen, and I noticed the girl quickly glance up at the top cabinets. It was a very old house, and the upper cabinets went all the way to the ceiling and were very small. Just on a hunch I went over and used a chair so I could open doors on the upper cabinets. After I opened the first two or three, I could not imagine anyone could climb into such a small space. When I opened the fourth cabinet door, I could not believe what I was seeing. There were two feet with very bright colored socks on them holding dead still. I skipped a couple of cabinet doors, and when I opened it, there was someone's waist and bare stomach. I opened the cabinet door further to the right, and there was our suspects head staring at me. We tried for a while to get him out and finally called the fire department to assist us. I was amazed that he was able to climb into such a small space without any help other than the young girl that we arrested for aiding and abetting a known fugitive.

We got a call at a loud party and went to the apartment to check it out. We got to the door, and we could smell marijuana and could hear a lot of loud voices and commotion inside. We decided to wait for a backup car and then knocked on the door. The guy who opened the door was so stoned on drugs he didn't even know we were cops. It was a large apartment, and there were stoned people everywhere. The bizarre scene we witnessed next was like stepping into another world. There was a whole bunch of people forming a circle around someone in the middle. The people were cheering and screaming, "Go, go go!"

We pushed our way into the crowd and were horrified at the sickening sight. A guy was doing a push-up with a sword through his stomach coming out his back! Everyone was so stoned they didn't even seem to react to police in the room. We called for more backup and then heard screaming coming from the bathroom. We ran into the bathroom, and we're more horrified by the scene in the tub. A crazy stoned guy was pounding a broken beer bottle into the chest of the little baby.

Arresting everyone was a lot easier than not throwing up at the hideous blood and gore and idiocy of what we witnessed. Even our veteran homicide detectives and the corner were sickened by such blood and gore. The DA's office was not even sure how they were going to prosecute all the people involved. We confiscated several pounds of the purest marijuana the narcotics bureau had ever tested. I feel very blessed that the sight of all this has been completely wiped out of my mind. Even as I am writing this awful story, my mind cannot picture what I saw years ago. The average good citizen cannot comprehend what police officers experience during their service. There is not a night that goes by that I don't pray for our policeman, fireman, paramedics, doctors, nurses, teachers, and counselors.

Cops: 27. Bad guys: 2. (One sniper and one burglar going to or already in hell; one beautiful baby girl gone to heaven; and one injured cop recovered and doing great.)

49

STICK-UP RUNS INTO OFFICER'S BASEBALL GAME

WE WERE ON A BASEBALL field playing a game and of course, none of us were wearing police uniforms. We all had on T-shirts that said PPA which stands for Policeman's Protective Association. About the middle of the game, we saw a man running across the field being chased way behind by a uniformed police officer.

We stopped playing the game and formed a long line of police officers. The guy ran right up in front of us and looked around and realized he was surrounded by police officers playing a baseball game. The police officer chasing him walked up to him, and the man put his hands behind his back so he could be handcuffed. I said to him "you picked the wrong park to run through!" He looked bewildered and frustrated then said out loud "what dumb luck for me!" We all had a good laugh about it.

I had so many close calls with death that my wife could not sleep at night worrying about me. I asked for a leave of absence to have time to think about my future. The civil service talked to my captain and lieutenant and sergeant and because of the numerous official police commendations for outstanding arrest, they granted me a one-year leave of absence with a guarantee I could return without losing any seniority and my pay would go up according to the current pay rate. Lieutenant Brittoon, who was my favorite commanding officer told me he sure hoped I would come back to the department. The civil service said they had never granted a leave of absence like the one they granted for me. At the time I asked for the one-year leave of absence I sent a letter to the chief of police telling him how much I loved the job and hoped I would be returning. I was assigned to the SCAT unit at that time and I so loved all the action. They threw a party in my honor when I was getting ready to leave.

During the party, one of the officers who didn't particularly like me grabbed me and pushed me down on the floor on my stomach with one arm behind me and applied so much pressure it was very painful. He said he would let go of my arm only if I would say a few swear words. He knew that I hated profanity and I would never ever use any bad language. He was hurting me so badly that tears were running down my face when some of the other officers grabbed him and pulled him off of me and said, "What do you think you're doing?"

Even if he would've broken my arm there was no way that I was going to use any bad language he was begging me to do. After I got up and stretched my arm and pulled myself together, he walked up to me and apologized for his ridiculous action. I accepted his apology and we shook hands. All the other officers raised a cheer calling out my name. After that, I left the job under the best of circumstances.

My partner and I were patrolling in our area in District one when we saw the guy walking on the sidewalk that I immediately knew had just got out of prison. He was doing the Buena Vista prison shuffle. The very second my partner stopped the car he took off on a dead run and I chased him down and tackled him and after a few minutes struggle got him handcuffed. When we patted him down for weapons or contraband we found a .38 snub-nose pistol in his waistband underneath his jacket. He also had a couple of baggies full of cocaine in his right pants pocket. I recognized him and when we ran an ID check found out he was on parole and one more violation would put him back in prison. I told him he'd have to turn us on to something really big or he was going back in the joint. It took a while to question him until he finally told us his source was a gang in Colorado Springs. He told us the dealer was flying in the drugs from Mexico and gave us a description of the plane and the approximate time it would be arriving at the airport. I gave the information to the narcotics bureau and they said they had heard a rumor about such an operation but had no real hard evidence. I wanted to go with them on the drug bust but they said they had enough detectives that we're going to meet the plane when it landed. As soon as the plane touched down at the time the snitch had provided, they had several police cars surrounding it. Because the party that I had arrested had a history of providing good information they were able to obtain a search warrant for the airplane. The search revealed over a million dollars in narcotics, all packages ready for sale. I was disappointed that I couldn't have been in on the bust, but I was happy things turned out so well. That's definitely one official accommodation which I should've got but I didn't.

We got a call about a shoplifter that was arrested by a store security officer and went to pick him up. There was just something about him that made me think he was more than just a shoplifter. I ran an ID check on him and he came back wanted for several felonies. He had a wallet full of stolen credit cards. When we started to handcuff him, he started to resist quite violently. Because we did not want to make a scene in the department store, we held each of his hands in such a way that we could easily increase the pain to the level that would've caused him to start crying. As we were walking him out of the store, we would increase the pain and told him to smile really big and act like everything was fine, to which he quickly responded. His arrest cleared up dozens of stolen credit card cases and thefts.

PPA NEWS

READY ON THE FIRING LINE

By DICK BARBER

Smith and Wesson Armorer School was recently the proud recipient of two distinguished Denver area visitors, A.K.A. "Students", Bill Seiwald, Adams County Sheriff's Department, and Gene "Knuckle Draggin" Brunick, DPD Pistol Range. They travelled to Springfiled, Mass. by air, bus and right thumb to study under the great masters at S. and W.

"Knuckle Draggin'" assures us that weapons will now be almost repaired using only the most advanced and recent (as well as acceptable) methods. The two-week course at Smith and Wesson will help bring a higher degree of credibility to the performance of the range personnel.

* * *

Speaking of Credibility?!!! The Pistol Range now has a SERGEANT. After these many years, there is now a supervisor to whom you may take your troubles. Sgt. Don Imes comes to us direct from either Las Vegas or the Traffic Bureau. We are looking forward to good things.

* * *

If you qualified for a shooting award pin last year, the P.P.A. has purchased it for you. Pick yours up at the Range. Minimum Scores for awards

Marksman 75.00%
Sharpshooter 86.00%
Expert 93.00%
Distinguised Expert 97.00%

The Distinguished Expert pins will arrive soon.

* * *

Start sharpening your combat shooting skills now, should you desire to try for a place on the Pistol Team. All you have to do is outshoot someone who is on the team now. Tryouts for next year will be held late this summer.

Will the real Rin Tin Tin please stand!

TOO EFFICIENT
Pot-Sniffing Dogs Evidence Ruled Out

LOS ANGELES – (UPI) – A Federal judge has ruled that the U.S. customs bureau's drug-sniffing dogs can be too efficient, detecting narcotics so unerringly that they constitute an illegal invasion of privacy.

U.S. Dist. Judge Harry Pregerson ruled that the discovery of 1,525 pounds of marijuana in a truck parked at a Santa Ana gas station was an illegal seizure.

Customs agents said they received an anonymous call Oct. 10 that a truck and trailer parked at the gas station were loaded with marijuana. They brought two of the dogs, used to sniff cars at the border with Mexico, to investigate.

The dogs, Blue and Baron, indicated there was marijuana in the truck and trailer, a search warrant was obtained, and John Solis, 29, of Santa Ana was arrested.

Pregerson ruled late Monday that while the dogs may legally be used to examine autos and luggage at border-crossing points and airports where citizens expect such things, bringing them onto private property without probable cause is an unconstitutional invasion of privacy, especially since they are so efficient at detecting hidden substances.

The government was expected to drop charges against Solis, who has more serious problems to worry about. While out on bail following the marijuana arrest, he was rearrested on two counts of murder.

WHAT'S A POLICEMAN FOR?

by R. F. "Doc" Bernhardt

*Lots of things some say
Whether it be night or day*

*He'll deliver your baby,
He'll help the fallen little old lady.*

*He'll chauffeur the drunk
He'll tolerate the punk*

*He'll race to a fight
And He'd better be right*

*And when he's walking proud and tall
He's just a target for a Hollow point ball.*

FIREMEN BACK DRIVE BY POLICE

Denver Fire Fighters Local No. 858 has announced support for the drive by Denver police for individual protective equipment.

"We understand the frustration of the police in trying to get the proper protective equipment, the local said. "For many years we have been fighting a similar battle to insure the safety of our members, and only in recent times have we started making inroads in this area."

**Reprint Denver Post
February 10, 1975**

919 - 249 - 6615

019 · 55 A · 60V

50

DENVER BRONCO'S OFF-DUTY OFFICERS

THE DENVER BRONCO FOOTBALL TEAM paid off-duty Denver Police Officers for security during their home games. Back in those days ten dollars an hour was thought to be great pay. A few years ago, it came out on the news that two top-ranking police personnel in management that were in charge of security for every Denver Broncos home game were charging twenty-five dollars per hour and kept the extra fifteen dollars per hour for themselves. I'm not going to mention their names, but to keep it simple, there was no personnel above these two. This illegal activity had gone on for many years and whether these two are in prison where they should be, I have no idea. It is so disgusting thinking about these two that were being paid more than anyone else in the department. For them not passing on that fifteen dollars per hour to the officers who really needed the extra money was totally criminal. Honesty integrity and obeying every single law is something we all assume would be at the top of any police department.

Anytime I made a large drug bust where there were tons of cash the idea of keeping even a dollar of it never crossed my mind. In my opinion, every police officer should stand out as an exemplary person when it comes to doing what's right. Every single police officer in the country should be going the extra mile to avoid even the very appearance of wrong.

I remember very well flying back to our home in Utah from Ankara turkey in 1961 the headlines of the Denver Post newspaper. Over 50 police personnel were arrested and found guilty of numerous crimes including felonies. It is very hard to imagine the impact this would have on all law-abiding citizens. Even active criminals, i.e., armed robbers, burglars, drug dealers, and other felons, would think, "What the heck. Everybody's doing it, so why can't we?"

In the years I served as a Denver police officer, I always was so happy when I would come across people who are just absolutely honest no matter what. More than a few times, I would be flagged down by a citizen with a wallet containing a lot of cash, and they had just found it. Their only thought was returning it to the rightful owner.

Every time I stopped someone for a traffic violation, if they told me the truth of what they had just done, I would rarely give them a ticket unless they were criminals that I knew. William Shakespeare once said, "To be honest is to be one man in ten thousand!"

Personally, I have lost my cell phone and wallet full of cash more than a few times and had them returned. That kind of honesty is nothing short of a win-win for both people. The super great feeling you have inside is hard to explain when you do the right thing.

I will never forget a few years back when I was a Boy Scout master, and I left the camp to make a phone call. It was several miles to a payphone and I was dressed in my scout uniform including a very well-known campaign hat like Ranger's wear. I put in about six quarters in the pay phone and called my wife. After only talking for a couple of minutes the operator came on the line and said please deposit one more quarter which I did. Just as I put a quarter in the payphone the lower change container started filling up with more quarters. I started to explain to the operator what just happened. "You're not complaining about having to pay more money but you're saying there's extra money in there that you want to report!"

I asked her if I could just start inserting all the money back into the machine and she said, "Yes, that would be great. I've never ever had this happen before."

People just call to complain and want some money back. For a minute or two I felt like I was in Las Vegas winning money from a slot machine the way it was pouring out of the payphone, landing all over the floor. Finally, on my third attempt, all the quarters I put in the machine finally stayed in it. I thanked the operator and she said how good it made her feel to have dealt with such an honest person. I have to admit that for a minute or two, I thought of times that I had been overcharged in a payphone and that this would make up for it, but then I decided that that was a bad excuse. Just as I started to leave the phone booth, I noticed several people standing in front of me, watching what had just happened. Since I was in my scoutmaster uniform, I was so happy I had done the right thing! The group of people started to clap their hands and commended me for doing the right thing.

Cops (two bad ones): 0. Former cop and scoutmaster: 1.

51

BIG DRUG BUST
1201 DECATUR

My partner—Officer CD Burton, also known as "Mad Dog" Burton— and I heard rumors that there was a drug dealer working out of 1201 Decatur St. We spent a lot of time trying to get a confidential informant to fill us in on the information so that we could get a search warrant signed by a judge. One Beautiful fall day we saw a very suspicious-looking guy walking down the sidewalk in a very nice neighborhood. We could tell by the way he walked that he was recently released from Buena Vista prison. We did our trick where we pulled up alongside the curb and drove the car right next to him. The second my partner hit the brakes the guy took off running and I quickly caught up and just as I tackled him a .38 handgun went shooting down the sidewalk. We searched him and found some balloons of heroin in his pockets and placed him under arrest for carrying a concealed weapon as a felon and also illegal narcotics. He has been a confidential informant for some past drug bust we had gone on so we were able to get him to tell us about the activities at 1201 Decatur St.

Since he would be facing going back to prison, he was very quick to give us all the information about the quantities and the parties involved in this big drug dealing place. We took him downtown and booked him and said we'd put in a good word with the DA. We then went to the 1201 Decatur St. address and set a block away with binoculars and watched the numerous cars pulling up running up to the house and coming back down the steps with packages that were obviously making drug deals. We got a judge to sign our search warrant and took some officers to the 1201 Decatur St. house.

We knocked on the door and it was immediately opened, and we went inside with our search warrant and found three parties we arrested for illegal possession for sale of drugs. We were very pleased when we received two official accommodations for our fine police work.

Cops: 3. Bad guys: 0.

DENVER POLICE DEPARTMENT

OFFICIAL COMMENDATION

TO: Office of the Chief of Police

Date   October 30, 1974

FROM: Vice/Drug Control
        Division — District — Bureau

I wish to commend Officer   John Haroldsen   , Serial No.   72-33   ,

who is presently assigned to   District One

for the following:

OFFICIAL COMMENDATION
- [ ] Class Two Award
- [ ] Class Three Award
- [ ] Class Four Award

WHEREAS it is realized that the great bulk of police work is done routinely by good policemen, let it be known that the above-named officer displayed initiative and alertness decidedly in excess of the norm in this particular instance.

Fact Situation: Acting on confidential information, Officers C. Burton and J. Haroldsen executed a narcotic search warrant at the address 1201 Decatur St. which led to the recovery of 850 grams of marijuana and $1,030.00 in cash and the filing of Felony Possession of Narcotics for Sale. These charges were filed against Christopher M. Brown and Geraldine Trujillo. These officers are to be commended for a superior performance of their duties.

Commending Officer   J. A. McCormick, Sergeant   50-40

Command Officer's Approval   C. J. Kennedy, Captain

Read and Approved   T. E. Rowe   Division Chief

Arthur G. Dill   Chief of Police

DISTRIBUTION:
Original and one copy to Commendations Board

(Separate set for each officer mentioned)

– DO NOT FOLD –

DPD 139 (Rev. 6/70)

DENVER POLICE DEPARTMENT

OFFICIAL COMMENDATION

TO: Office of the Chief of Police

Date October 23, 1974

FROM: Patrol - District One
_____
Division — District — Bureau

I wish to commend Officer   J.S. Haroldsen   , Serial No. 72-33   ,

who is presently assigned to   District One - Detail Two

for the following:

COMMENDATORY LETTER
- [ ] Class Two Award
- [ ] Class Three Award
- [ ] Class Four Award

WHEREAS it is realized that the great bulk of police work is done routinely by good policemen, let it be known that the above-named officer displayed initiative and alertness decidedly in excess of the norm in this particular instance.

Fact Situation: On Oct. 22, 1974 Officers Haroldsen and Burton executed a Search Warrant at 1201 Decatur St., based on information they received from an informant. The search resulted in the arrest of Christopher M. Brown, Geraldine Trujillo and Ramona E. Rumley on Ill. Possession of Narcotics for Sale. The officers seized 26 lids of Marijuana and $1030.00 in cash. The officers showed initiative by developing reliable informants and making an exceptionally good arrest.

Commending Officer _____
Sergeant J. Sipos, #58-23

Command Officer's Approval _____
Lt J J Britton 56-25

Read and Approved _____
9/c Paul A. Montoya 50-10
Division Chief

_____
Chief of Police

DISTRIBUTION:
Original and one copy to Commendations Board

(Separate set for each officer mentioned)
— DO NOT FOLD —

DPD 139 (Rev. 6/70)

52

DRUG DEALER AT JUNIOR HIGH

My partner and I were receiving information that Leonard Vigile was giving narcotics to junior high kids to get them hooked so he could sell them. One day we were driving by the junior high school when we saw a car that we knew belong to him stopped by the school talking to a group of young men. We observed from a distance far enough away that he did not notice us. We saw him handing out packages of drugs to all the young men in the group. We turned on our overhead lights and pulled up behind his car. Before he could make a move, we jumped out of the car and pulled him out. We handcuffed him and placed him under arrest. On the way to our district one station, my partner got in the backseat and started yelling at him for all the horrible things that he was doing. I started hearing numerous blows he was receiving from my partner for all the horrific things that he was doing with these young men. What made the situation even better is when we came flying up behind his car with our overhead lights on all the young men threw the drugs on the sidewalk and ran into the school. Since none of the blows he received to his stomach and side were visible, he did not require going to the hospital. Normally, I would not have liked what had taken place but in this case, I was totally in agreement with the blows that he received. It made our day even better when we placed him on the elevator downtown, run by the sheriff's department. When the elevator doors closed, we could hear lots of screaming and blows taking place.

If I would've been the judge of this case, I would've put him in prison for life with no chance of parole ever! Just imagine if you had kids in junior high school that were given drugs so they could get hooked on them and then start buying them from the drug dealer, how you would feel inside? Most kids are good and don't ever want to mess with drugs. The super bad influence that one drug dealer could have on countless good kids is sickening. The new marijuana laws are going to be one of the worst can of worms ever started. Good law-abiding kids that would never use marijuana when it was illegal will probably start trying it out and will end up being hooked on worse drugs. I put thousands of bad guys in prison for heroin, cocaine, and other drugs. Almost all of them started out using marijuana.

Cops: 1. Really bad guy: 0.

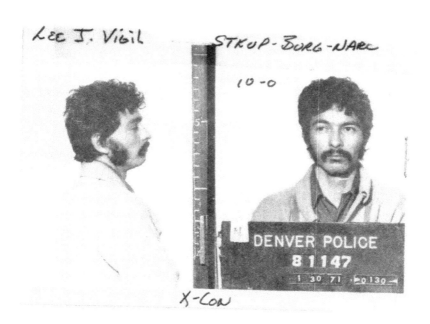

POLICE DEPARTMENT—DENVER, COLORADO		MONTHLY ASSN		PERMANENT HISTORY CARD
LAST NAME: Haroldsen,	FIRST NAME: Jon S.		PHONE NO: 755-4359	
ADDRESS: 3365 So. Wabash Ct. - 80232				
DATE OF BIRTH: 12-29-45	IN WHAT COUNTRY:	DATE OF NATURALIZATION:		DATE DENVER RESIDENCE:

PERSONAL		HOME LIFE		PHYSICAL CHARACTERISTICS	
SINGLE		OWNS HOME		HEIGHT	5'10=1/2"
MARRIED	X	RENTS		WEIGHT	155
WIDOW		DEPENDENTS		AGE	26
WIDOWER		NO. OF CHILDREN		COLOR	W
DIVORCED		NO. OF DEP. RELATIVES		PHYSICAL DEFECTS	
SEPARATED		NO. OF DEP. PARENTS		DOCTORS RATING	

HABITS		FINANCIAL		EDUCATION	
USES ALCOHOL		CRED. RATING		GRAMMAR SCHOOL	
USES OTHER STIMULANT		FINANCIAL REPUTATION		HIGH SCHOOL	X
GAMBLES				COLLEGE OR UNIVERSITY	X

Ricks College - 53½ cr. hrs. in Pre-Law.
Brigham Young Univ. - 75 cr.h. in Pre-Law

CIVIL SERVICE RECORD					
POSITION	EXAM	DATE FROM	DATE TO	SALARY	
Prob. Pat.	77.0	6/16/72		704.00	
Pat 2nd Grade		6/16/74		978.00	

DENVER POLICE DEPARTMENT

OFFICER'S PERFORMANCE REPORT

Officer's Name: JON (First) S (Initial) HAROLDSEN (Last) PAT. (Rank) 72-33 (Serial No.)

Unit Reporting: DISTRICT. 1 Assignment: Detail #3

Reporting Period: From 6-1-73 To 6-30-73 Grade 83 ✓

CHECK SUB-FACTOR RATINGS: + Strong, ✓ Standard, — Weak

RATE EACH FACTOR: For Below Standard / Somewhat Below Standard / Standard / Above Standard / Outstanding

1. QUANTITY — ✓ Standard
   - ✓ Amount of work performed.
   - ✓ Completion of work on schedule.
2. QUALITY — ✓ Standard
   - ✓ Accuracy.
   - + Neatness of work product.
   - ✓ Thoroughness.
   - ✓ Oral communication.
   - ✓ Written communication.
3. REPORTING HABITS — ✓ Standard
   - ✓ Punctuality.
   - ✓ Attendance.
4. FOLLOWING DIRECTIONS — ✓ Above Standard
   - + Observance of rules and regulations.
   - + Observance of safety rules.
   - ✓ Care and use of equipment.
   - ✓ Compliance with work instructions.
5. ABILITY TO COPE WITH WORK SITUATION — ✓ Standard
   - ✓ Use of initiative.
   - ✓ Use of judgment.
   - ✓ Performance in adapting to new situations, unusual demands or emergencies.
6. PERSONAL RELATIONS — ✓ Above Standard
   - + Getting along with other employes.
   - ✓ Meeting and handling the public.
   - + Attention to personal appearance, neatness, cleanliness, hygienic measures.
7. SUPERVISORY ABILITY (ONLY FOR SUPERVISORY PERSONNEL)
   - Planning, organizing and controlling the work.
   - Training and instructing subordinates.
   - Evaluating performance of subordinates.
   - Making decisions.
   - Disciplinary control.

Use COMMENTS space below to describe officer's strengths and weaknesses. Give examples of work well done and plans for improving performance. Explain all ratings which are Far Below Standard or Outstanding.

JON HAS PROGRESSED AS hoped by this COMMAND - He MADE the TRANSformation FROM PROBATIONARY to PERMANENT status with EASE. Future Ratings will Rest upon his Ability to PROGRESS AS well AS A PERMANENT PATROLMAN AS he did ON PROBATION.

(Continue comments on attached sheet, if necessary.)

OVER-ALL EVALUATION

Far Below Standard	Somewhat Below Standard	Standard	Above Standard	Outstanding
		✓		

Prepared by: [signature] 55-23

Rank: Sgt Date: 6-30-73

Approved: (Second Level Supervisor)

Unit Commander: Capt. J. Lakey

Form 360 (Rev. 2/64) DPD White - Personnel Bureau Pink - Unit File

PPA NEWS

Scott Haroldsen	Editor
Russ Mathews	Publisher
Steve Barrett	Assistant Editor
Jon Benrud	General Manager

FOR ADVERTISING INFORMATION: 321-5881
DENVER PPA: 297-2930

Published Monthly by Midwestern Publishing Co., Inc., 2801 East Colfax, Denver, Colorado 80206

This publication goes to all members of the Denver Police Protective Association, the Denver Police Pension Association and widows of both associations, and to all Denver policemen, all Denver Honorary Police, Junior Police and Auxiliary Police. In addition, it goes to a number of other law enforcement agencies in Colorado.

---

city, state, and federal level, using all our resources to improve all matters of concern to police officers.

It will be among the responsibilities of its council to fill the communication gap in our own department as well as with other departments.

LAW ENFORCEMENT OFFICERS KILLED

According to information collected through the FBI's Uniform Crime Reporting Program, five law enforcement officers were killed due to criminal action in September 1974.

During the first 9 months of 1974, 95 local, county, State, and Federal law enforcement officers were killed due to criminal action. In the same period in 1973, 101 officers were slain.

Forty-two officers were killed in the Southern States, 26 in the North Central States, 14 in the Western States, 9 in the Northeastern States, and 4 in Puerto Rico. Twenty-eight officers were slain handling disturbance calls, 18 while attempting arrests for crimes other than robbery or burglary, 17 in connection with robbery matters, 11 while investigating suspicious persons, 6 in connection with burglary matters, 5 while making traffic stops, 6 in unprovoked or premeditated ambush-type attacks, and 4 while handling prisoners.

All but two of the officers were killed by firearms. Handguns were used in 65 of the killings.

DID YOU KNOW

The miranda warning only applies to felonies

There were 20,518 murders in the U.S. in 1974.

DPD is not going to lay off any policeman.

IN THE UP COMING ISSUE:

Cop of the month

Who's retiring

Who bit the bullet

Mystery cop contest: $10.00 to first police officer who identifies the officer in the photograph.

Want to sell something? Put an ad in the PPA paper.

---

time or work period as we will still use the new

May I suggest with o we put forth changes in Charter to meet not needs of the citizen bu the *police officer* as we change requires the F

The F

An Editorial Comment by Scott Haroldsen

Funk and Wagnalls minority as a part of a tion differing from other characteristics and oft jected to differential tre Be it Black, Spanish A Jew, Oriental, Indian criminal (I hope they a minority)--how do they They stick together, th care of their own. The the minority, the closer as a group. There are mately 350 thousand the U.S., out of 200 mil people, and about 135 in Denver out of a popu approximately 1 millio that's what I call a mino

We get shot at, spit a at, sued, slandered and to as being akin to a legged fat beast with snout who eats garbage our single worst enemy other. "As a person I l but he's a lousy cop", gotten more police wo that dummy will ever "Oh no, I don't like hir he pads his log sheet minutes before quitting that _____ dispatch me a three car accident more listing or cleara I'M giving that car a quitting time."

If there ever was a that needed a feeling of hood and unity its CC

Meeting of the minds

Editorial comment by Scott Haroldsen

The first day in the police academy, representatives of the union and PPA explained the benefits of joining their respective organizations. At that time there seemed to be a great deal of confusion as to any benefit in joining both organizations. Many members of the new recruit class felt they would be duplicating protection by joining both.

The same confusion that existed three years ago still seems to be around. With the addition of The Brotherhood and Platopp, we now have four employe organizations. Why four instead of just one?

Some officers look at it from a protection point of view. They feel if they're sued and a union attorney doesn't produce, they'll try the PPA; if the PPA falls short, they go to The Brotherhood and if they're black, they may feel better represented by Platopp. At the current dues rate, the four would cost $20 per month.

Some officers assert all the organizations should be combined into one. Practically speaking, three of the four are not going to dissolve and give their support to the fourth.

Assuming the four will remain, what can we do to make these organizations more beneficial for all of us?

Assuming the four exist for the benefit of each individual officer, why haven't they been able to give us all the benefits we need? Shotguns, better cars, bullet-proof vests, protective shields, guaranteed cost of living raise, better ammunition, 20-year retirement — all things could have been easily obtained if the Union, PPA, Brotherhood and Platopp were pulling together. Our own organizations are defeating each other's proposals, which if passed, would be beneficial to all of us.

The administration and city council delight in the fact that the whole department is always split on everything. Who was really against a good 20-year retirement? Very few. Yet because the Union and the PPA seem to be on oposite sides, their combined confusion seems to be defeating what basically could have been beneficial to all. How could we expect an uninformed citizen to vote in a 20-year retirement plan that half the police department didn't fully understand or fully agree on? Whether it's twenty-year retirement, a civilian review board or pay increases, they affect all of us.

It's time for a meeting of the minds. Once a month representatives of each organization should meet together in an effort to reach a consensus on issues that affect every individual officer. These organizations should be a means to obtain an end, not the end in itself. Is it possible that the pettiness between these organizations can be overcome for the good of all?

Our good, our benefits, our job should come first above all else. If we unite the organizations to fight together for our best interest, we could have the best police department in the country.

Saluting the Denver Police Dept.

C E C

399-6931

4425 Grape

Denver, Colorado

The snitch is under attack

Editorial comment by Scott Haroldsen

Where would Law Enforcement be today without informants? Historically speaking, from the earliest days of cops and robbers most major crimes, whether it be a homicide, stick-up or a big narcotics deal, have been solved through some type of informant. In 1966 Chief Justice Warren said, "It has long been acknowledged by the decisions of this court . . . that, in the detection of many types of crime, the government is entitled to use decoys and to conceal the identity of its agents."

It has been estimated that 95 percent of all federal narcotics cases are made by use of informants. The papers are full of police related articles that read something like: "Acting on a tip, narcotics officers . . ."; "An unrevealed source told police . . ."; "An anonymous phone call lead police to . . ."

However, there seems to be a continuing trend towards curtailing police power. Starting with the vagrancy law being thrown out, police are being put on trial for search and seizure, and now the courts are trying to reveal the identity of confidential informants.

The courts argue that a defendant in some cases cannot get a fair trial without revealing who the informant is. If the informant acts as a tipster and merely points the finger of suspicion at someone, the courts generally don't require disclosure. In cases where the informant is present during a crime, acts as a go-between or actually is a participant in a crime, the courts are beginning more and more to demand his identity be revealed.

The "in camera" or "in chambers" hearings are becoming more prevalent. This type of hearing allows the judge to question the informer in private to discover the nature of his possible testimony. If the judge feels the informant's testimony is necessary to insure the defendant a fair trial, disclosure will be ordered. A written record is usually kept of this hearing in case of a later appeal.

As it stands now, good informants are hard to come by. Every good police officer has at least one or more informants, but if the courts get their way, none of us will be able to buy, borrow or steal a snitch. No would-be confidential informant is going to give police information if they think they might have to testify on the stand, answer questions in a judge's chambers or have their identity revealed in court. A good cop-informant relationship is built on trust. If that trust is jeopardized, our whole informant system will collapse. If the courts destroy that system, the criminal element will solidify as never before.

With the fear of ratting on each other gone, the old saying, "No honor among thieves," will no longer exist.

Retired Capt. Bill Wiley to run for city council

counselor for Denver County Court. While council elections are classified as non-partisan, all three men are recognized as Democrats.

Wiley, who lives at 1060 S. Vallejo St., said he had the opportunity to become familiar with council operations and practices while serving as a police captain.

Remarking on the controversy over hollow-point bullets, Wiley said he thought it had been "blown far out of proportion" by those showing very little emotional stability to the subject.

He noted, however, that if a man is going to steal, rob or rape, he should realize he is taking a calculated risk, "and this risk could involve being shot with a hollow-point bullet."

Dear Chief

I would like to express my appreciation for one of your men - Policeman Haroldson.

On Tuesday evening, Dec. 9 my children called the emergency number 911 to get help for me as I'm an epileptic and was having seizures.

Policeman Haroldson arrived and helped immensely. My two older children especially the oldest one were very upset. He got them calmed down, and even went the extra mile. He stayed with us until someone arrived, to stay until my husband got home. He put the two older ones to bed, reassuring them that I was O.K. as this was the first time they remember seeing me have seizures.

Before this happened someone had scared my children about policeman now even my toddler knows that all policeman are friends and help people.

Policeman Haroldson even came by

the next day to see how things were.

My children still talk about the "policeman who helped the fireman when Mommy got sick".

My husband and I both wish to thank Policeman Haroldson for his help in a situation that could have had a very traumatic affect on our children. With policeman like Policeman Haroldson we know we are in safe hands.

Sincerely

Beverly Mutzabler

380 Cleveland

Dec. 11, 1975

Dear Officer Haroldson,

There are not enough words to thank you for returning my daughter, Stacie Estes, safe and sound. By the time I realized something was wrong, I had visualized many horrible events. Although Stacie had walked those 3 blocks on many occasions, she will never walk alone again.
I am very grateful to you and the citizens of this fine city.

Thankyou

Mrs. C. Michael Estes
725 K St., Apt 11

State Mutual Life Assurance Company of America

James H. Thompson, C.L.U., C.P.C.U.
Associate General Agent

The Colorado Agency
252 Clayton Street
Denver, Colorado 80206
Business Telephone: 388-5911
Home Telephone: 333-6736

Feb. 11, 1975

Chief Arthur Dill
Denver Police Department
13th & Champa Street
Denver, Colorado 80202

Dear Chief Dill:

It seems to be the right of all of us to comment on the police and their actions.

Three of your men were at our building recently, I assume, on their off-duty time. They spent much time going over our building, analyzing its' security.

I was most impressed with their dedication, intelligence, and over all attitude. I'm sure we will be most pleased to review their suggestions and act on them.

It is our privilege and honor to have such men on our Denver Police force as Officers Robert B. Steely, Badge No. 64-1; H. Eckard, Badge No. 69-81 and J. Haroldsen, Badge No. 72-33.

Yours very truly,

JAMES H. THOMPSON, CLU, CPCU
JHT:rj

CC: Councilman Don Wyman

Home Office: Worcester, Massachusetts 01605

THE
AMERICA
GROUP

THE UNIVERSITY OF DENVER
CONFERENCE AND INSTITUTE DIVISION
DEPARTMENT OF SPEECH COMMUNICATION

in cooperation with

THE DENVER DEPARTMENT OF POLICE

awards this certificate to

JON HAROLDSEN - 72-033

for successfully completing a course
ADVANCED POLICE OPERATIONS AND TECHNIQUES
conducted at the University of Denver
February 24 -- February 28, 1975

Arthur G. Dill, Chief of Police, Denver, Colorado

University of Denver

CERTIFICATE OF
SPECIAL ACHIEVEMENT
to

SCOTT HAROLDSEN

FOR OUTSTANDING

INITIATIVE, DEDICATION TO DUTY,

TEAM SPIRIT AND HARD WORK

Assistant Secretary for Housing-
FHA Commissioner

Regional Administrator (Acting)

August 16, 1976
Date

BOOK II

MY LIFE WHEN I WAS NOT A POLICE OFFICER

THESE STORIES ARE ABOUT ME when I was no longer a police officer. They do show how I was still living on the edge, and in fact, I died several times and was saved by first responders in most cases. My life has been greatly blessed by a loving Heavenly Father. Some people would say that I was darn lucky, but luck had nothing to do with dodging my many encounters with death. I could not have loved my job more as a police officer and missed the wonderful action and opportunities to help people in trouble. I felt great putting thousands of bad guys in prison. It is my very fervent prayer that the really bad ones are still in prison and hope many of the worst ones never get out!

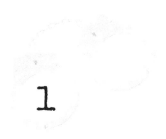

1

RUSSIAN EMBASSY, ASBESTOSIS, LARGE WAVE BREAKS RIBS, SCAFFOLD FALLS

WHEN I WAS 13 YEARS old, I was living in Ankara, Turkey, when my dad worked for the state department. We lived there for two years, and I just loved it. When we first arrived there, they had all the young people go to the American Embassy and give us a rundown of things that we needed to be aware of. One thing they told us about was a couple of young American kids that were walking along at Atatürk Boulevard in front of the Russian embassy. The two boys wrote some silly note slamming the Russians and folded them up and threw them over the Russian embassy wall. Some Turkish police officers saw what they did and immediately arrested them. They were immediately convicted of supplying information to the Russians. In downtown Ankara Turkey they do public hangings every few weeks.

These two young boys had their lives ended very quickly over the stupidest thing. One day, I was curious to see what a public hanging was like. I got within a few blocks of where a hanging was taking place when my parents picked me up. To this very day, I was very thankful that I didn't witness such a gruesome scene. About a year later, a friend of mine and I were walking down the sidewalk in front of the different embassies, including the Russian embassy. We wanted to have a little excitement because we were bored. We took a couple of pieces of paper and folded them up and looked around for any policeman watching and threw the notes over the embassy wall. We heard a policeman's whistle and heard him yelling, and we took off running like our lives depended on it, which I think they did. I am sure that our adrenaline kicked in, and we were flying down the sidewalk, and it seemed like our feet were not even touching the ground. We reached the American Embassy and slowed down, acting like everything was okay, and went inside. As I am writing this, I can't believe I was so stupid to do such a dangerous, dumb thing.

For several years, I worked for a contractor in Rockford, Illinois, that insulated pipes with asbestos. One job that we did was at a Chiclet Gum factory. I remember very well the very sweet smell of the gum that was being made in huge stainless-steel vats. We were wrapping all the pipes with asbestos insulation. At the end of every day, I would go home and take a shower and wash the tiny bits of white airborne itching particles out of my nose, and eyes, and mouth. At that time, nobody knew how dangerous asbestos was. When I started a construction company, I remember one of the first jobs we had was putting cutting out holes in the siding to put new windows in. The siding was made of asbestos, and at the end of each day, my nose would be stuffed with fine airborne white particles. I would stay in the shower for at least half an hour, trying to get it all rinsed out of my nose and eyes and itching all over my body. Later, in my career as a contractor, I was working at the Idaho Nuclear Engineering lab. We were doing a remodeling job on the north end of the nuclear site, drilling into a wall that started white airborne particles flying in the air. It turned out that it was asbestos, and the government contracted with an asbestos removal company to take care of the problem. The name of the company at that time was Waters Asbestos. Not very long after that work, two of the people in the company died of asbestosis.

Very soon after that, I developed a horrible cough that would last for months. I went to a pulmonologist who had x-rays done on my lungs. I remember a technician that did the x-ray when he looked at the results; he said, "so you have been smoking three or four packs of cigarettes a day all your life, right?" I told him I had never smoked, and he said you have major scarring in your lungs and asked me if I'd ever worked around asbestos. A couple of days later, I met with the pulmonologist, and he said, "your lungs are just filled with asbestos particles, and you have major scarring all over your lungs!" I also remember very well his next comment was, "I am currently treating seven workers on the island with asbestosis, and for some reason, your body seems to be handling it like it's not even there!" Over the next several years, just like clockwork, I would develop a horrific cough that no amount of cough medicine could help. I went on Google to read up on asbestosis. There has never been a confirmed case of asbestosis where the person ever survived more than three or four years. The article also said it takes up to 30 years or more before symptoms can be diagnosed. My pulmonologist told me to be sure and get pneumonia shot every year because if I ever got pneumonia, I would be dead. About two years ago, I stopped having this horrible cough every year. The doctor did some more x-rays, and when I met with him, he told me that my lungs were completely clear and had never witnessed anything like that in his life. He further stated that he was not one who believed in miracles, but he could not come up with any other explanation. Immediately, I knew and have always known from then on, that the Lord blessed me with an amazing miracle, and that's the only reason I'm still alive.

About twenty years ago I was trying to surf on the island of Kauai at our favorite beach called Kelawaii. I wasn't having any success, so I decided to use a boogie board instead. I caught a wave about six feet high and thought I was going to do just great, but instead of dropping down into the front of the wave, I fell over the top, and my chest landed on the sand below, and I broke several ribs and my glasses and almost drowned. Every time I would try to get up out of the water, another wave would pound me back down under it. Anyone familiar with the ocean knows (you never turn your back on it!). I started to be able to make my way a little further towards the beach when a huge rogue wave slammed me down and sucked me back out into deep water.

I quit looking at the waves because I was concentrating on the beach, or I wouldn't have got knocked down without any warning. With the help of my family, they finally pulled me out of the big breaking waves. The one positive thing about getting tumbled and rolled in the ocean saltwater is it sure does a good job clearing your nasal cavities. If you ever have a bad cold, jump in the water and get tumbled, and you'll feel much better if you don't drown. We have often seen spinner dolphins, turtles, and even sharks at the beach. There's a river that you can kayak up and end up at a beautiful waterfall while passing through a truly amazing jungle.

I took my crew of guys to Wichita Kansas to do a facelift, including painting on a seven-story high building. The only way that we could have access to the outside of the building was to rent a 30-foot-long aluminum rolling scaffold. Setting this thing up on the roof was quite a challenge since I've never done it before. There are two large beams that you cantilever out over the roof with massive counterweights on the other end, so the scaffold hangs from the cables. The cables go through two electric motors that both must be operated at the same speed, so that the scaffolding remains level as you go up and down the side of the building. Since there was an OSHA approval stamp on the motors and the equipment, I felt we were going to be safe. We had a power washer on the scaffold and a total of four guys, including myself working on it. We raised the scaffolding to the very top and started power washing and scraping the paint that was coming off in large chunks and paint chips. The building was 90 ft high, and our rolling scaffolding had a total working height available of 100 ft. A couple of days into the job, the wind was blowing kind of hard, and paint chips and chunks were flying all over. We had the building manager move all the cars around the other side where we weren't working so everything was going to be okay. What we didn't know was on the opposite side of the building where the paint chips were blowing around outside were several brand-new unmarked police cars. When I went down to the parking area to check out where all the paint chips were going, I was sick when I saw all these paint chips stuck to these brand-new police cars. I immediately brought our power washer down and started power washing the paint chips off the new police cars. A police detective came out and saw what I was doing and what he said was quite surprising. He told me, "Hey, you don't need to worry about these new police cars, they are owned by the city, and they'll be just fine!" I felt very relieved but continue to wash off most of the big chunks of paint that were stuck to the cars like glue. I went back to the scaffolding that was down at the bottom and got on it and started to go up. I think my guys appreciate a few minutes' break, and when we got up about 70 ft suddenly, the scaffold started to fall for some unknown reason, the cables were slipping through the motors. Amazingly the whole scaffolding suddenly stopped. My guys were all very angry and scared and refused to stay on the scaffolding in order to work. Since we were very close to the top, we slowly when up until they could all climb off. I tried to assure them that since it was an OSHA-approved rig that I was sure it would continue to work without any problems. I lowered it several feet and started jumping up and down as hard as I could. After a few minutes of demonstration one by one, they finally agreed to get on it, and we never had another problem. As an added safety measure, we all put on a repelling harness. Each had a rope that went up to the very top and tied into a very secure steel beam. By that extra measure, if the scaffold were to fall out of control, our repelling rope would stop us. One day I wanted to show off a little bit, and I was 40 ft above the ground, and I told my guys that I could repel down with only one jump into the building and back out. I got into position, jumped way out from the building, and let the rope zip through my figure eight so fast that it was burning hot.

Instead of slowing way down on my one jump with my feet going into the building and pushing back out, I hardly slowed down.

When I hit the ground, I felt like my legs were broken, and I was six inches shorter. Luckily, I didn't break anything, but my feet hurt and burned for two or three hours. No matter how good of a mountain climber you are and good at repelling, never show off because that could kill you.

2

BEAR ATTACK, ALMOST SHOT BY TURKISH MILITARY

My wife and I were on her honeymoon driving up through Yellowstone park when we came upon some bears in the road. We waited for them to move out of the way and were ready to drive on, and my wife saw one with its head buried in the garbage can. She asked me if I would take a picture of the bear. Her dad had let us borrow his car because we didn't have one to drive on our honeymoon. I pushed the power window button and down several inches so I could take a picture. She said she wanted me to get a close-up of the bear. I got out of the car and got about 10 ft away from the bear, ready to take a picture when it pulled its head out of the garbage can and stood up sniffing the air. It turned around standing on its back legs, and when it saw me, it dropped down to all four legs and charged at me. I had shut the car door, so I ran around the car with the bear close behind. He was so fast that I could tell that another three or four laps around the car that he would have me. I tried changing directions, but he was too fast and actually got closer to me. My wife reached over and threw the car door open, and I dived in and slammed the door shut. He brought his mouth up to the partially open window breathing heavily, and I could even smelt his weird breath.

My wife had a loaf of bread on her tap to make sandwiches and took a slice out, and threw it towards the open window. The bread hit the window and fell on my tap. The bear reached his paw through the window, and as he started to pick it up, he extended his claws out, which were at least three inches long. I knew he was going to take a chunk of my leg with the bread. Much to my surprise, his claws grabbed just the bread, and he started to pull his paw out the partially open window. I quickly reached down to roll the power window closed, and it caught his paw. The bear tried pulling it free and started the car rocking back and forth. I hurriedly lowered the window just enough to let his paw get free. During the whole time, I just knew he was going to reach through the window and grab me. He then stood up and started to push the car violently back and forth. When he stepped back away from the car, I opened the window just enough to be able to throw a handful of bread at him. Even though he scared me to death, we had a good laugh over our very close and encounter.

We were headed to Mount Rushmore, and it was very dark on a steep winding road. I was driving pretty fast considering the road conditions when all of a sudden, the headlights went out. I tried to remember how much the road was curving as I brought the car quickly to a stop. It was so dark that we could not see anything, including the road or how close we were to the edge. I asked my wife to open the door and see how many feet away we were from the very steep edge. She opened the door and started to get out of the car when she realized that we were exactly at the edge of the cliff. There was nothing for her feet to touch when she tried to step out onto the road. We said a quick prayer, and amazingly our headlight came on. It was not until then we realized that our car was on the very edge of the enormous cliff. Another 1 ft and we would've gone over the cliff. I pulled the car away from the cliff and drove the rest of the night very slowly and carefully. We had the electrical checked in the car, and the mechanic said there was nothing wrong and had no idea why the lights went out. I always felt very sure that the Lord was giving us a clear warning to drive slower. Sometimes you can get perspiration confused with inspiration, but in this case, we knew exactly why we were alive.

Another near-death experience happened to me when I was doing a roof at Ricks College on the old Spori building. I believe the building has been torn down since that time. The school is now called BYU Idaho. A professor saw us working on the roof and complained that we should be tied off to work safely. I had done many jobs similar to this in the past without a problem. But since they insisted, I got a rope and tied it around me and had my son Josh hold the end of the rope up on the peak of the roof and wrapped it around the chimney.

I had been spraying for about half an hour when some excess oil dripped from my gun, and I stepped in it and quickly slipped down the roof. I went so fast on the slick oil and graphite that if I had not had that rope tied around me, I would've gone flying off, and 40 ft down to the cement below would've killed me for sure. My son Josh yelled, "Hold on, Dad!" as he held tightly on the rope that was around the chimney, which gave it enough friction that he was able to stop me.

My legs had gone all the way over the edge just above my knees when he stopped me. It took him several minutes to carefully pull me up since I was not able to help. When I finally reached the peak and sat down holding on to the chimney. I was so shaken it took me an hour before I could go back to work. I wish I knew the name of the professor who complained about us not working safely. He was my lifeline to cheat death. My son Josh was a big part of saving my life. Even though I had sprayed graphite and linseed oil on numerous steep roofs in the past without a problem, there's no doubt in my mind that the Lord inspired the man who complained about us not working safely that day.

When I was thirteen years old, my dad was working for the state department, and we were living in Ankara, Turkey, for a couple of years. We took a trip to drive throughout the holy land in parts of the Middle East. There was a war going on between Syria and Jordan at the time. I remember very well that we came to the border between the two countries, and some border guards searched our car and asked us a lot of questions. Tensions were very high at that time, and one of the guards found a box with my sister Sue's play dough in it. The Border guard immediately thought that it was C4 explosives. My dad had my sister start rolling it and breaking pieces off and making a snake and a horse and other animals. She also took it up to her nose to smell it and let them smell it. The border guards immediately realized that it was something to play with, not an explosive. They waived us on, and we drove across no man's land headed to Syria when we heard a massive explosion behind us. My dad stopped the car, and we looked back at the border station we have just left, and it was burning. I remember that night that we stayed in a motel in Syria that was right on the edge of no man's land. You could hear machine gunfire throughout the night and could see the flashes coming from the guns shooting towards Jordan. I always loved adventure and thought it was great that I got to witness all this. The noise that a tank makes going down a road is something most people will never experience.

We lived in an apartment on the third floor that had a beautiful network of steel designs going from the top to the bottom and handrails across the balconies. I woke up hearing the sound of the tank going down the road and a loudspeaker warning all Americans and Turks to stay inside their home because of a coup d'etat that had started that morning. They told us it would not be safe on the streets and to remain inside until further notice. Machine gunfire and explosions could be heard off in the distance. My adventuresome spirit overcame my good sense, and I carefully climbed down the metalwork on the building and headed downtown to Ataturk Boulevard, where all the action was. The closer I got to the Russian embassy, the louder the machine-gun fire became. I finally got across the Boulevard from where the Russian embassy was, and there were numerous military personnel and equipment in front of it. The Turkish military was shooting the Russians as they ran out of the embassy. I remember very well seeing some of the rounds hitting the building and leaving holes everywhere. Chunks of the building and

COP LIVING ON THE EDGE

dust were flying everywhere all over the building. I was just thinking of crossing the street to get a closer look when I was about to be shot. A jeep came to a screeching halt right in front of me with a machine gun mounted on the back. The soldier quickly turned the machine gun aimed at me and pulled back on the magazine, ready to fire. I heard the officer tell him, "durdurmak ates etme," which is Turkish for "stop, don't shoot."

Thankfully, the officer riding shotgun spoke some English. He said in a loud commanding voice, "You foolish American boy, better get your butt home right now!"

He then yelled, "daha cabuk acele et," which is Turkish for "faster, and hurry up."

Just at that point, some more people came out of the Russian embassy, and the machine-gun fire continued, and I couldn't help but watch totally mesmerized. The officer stood up and pointed at the machine gun and yelled, "cabuk -cabuk."

In my whole life, I am sure that I never ran as fast as I did towards our apartment. Later in the day, the tank went by announcing that we were free to leave our studio. We learned that the top politician in turkey named Menderes was in the act of selling the whole country out lock stock and barrel to the Russians. A top military man named General Gursel found out about the treason and had his military killing the Russians that were involved and any Turkish politicians that were involved. We drove our station wagon downtown to Ataturk Boulevard, where there was a parade going on. Every block or so armed military guys would search our car and then wave us on. They were trying to find Menderes, who had tried to sell his country out to the Russians. There was a cool chant that everybody was singing, including Americans, which was, "yah yah yah sha sha sha ordu ordu ordu cok yasha!" Translated, it was a chant saying how good their army was.

Two or three days later, Menderes was caught trying to leave the country and was executed.

Anayasayı hazırlıyacak olan Ord. Prof. S. Onar "Hayatımın en güzel işidir,, dec

MİLLİ Birlik Komite Başkanı Orgeneral Cemal Gürsel'in radyolarda, kendi sesinden yayınlanan, millete beyanatı:

«Aziz Türk milleti.

Bir aydan beri memlekette cereyan eden ve memleketi süratle korkunç buhranlara sürükleyen hâdiseleri biliyorsunuz. Bu gidişin memleketi kanlı bir kardeş kavgasına da götürmekte olduğunu her aklı başında vatandaşın takdir ettiğine kaniim. Dünya ahvali her gün biraz daha kötüye doğru giderken hususi politika ihtirası yüzünden vatanımızın maddeten ve mânen perişanlığa sürüklenmesi vicdan sahibi bütün vatandaşları dilhun etmektedir. Bu hal nereye kadar gidecek?

Bu feci âkibete, hissiz ve alâkasız seyirci mi kalmak lâzım? İşte vatandaşlarım, bu ahvali ıstırap içinde aylardan beri düşündüm. Ve bu zevata çıkar yolları gösterdim. Fakat onlar kapıldıkları politika

(Devamı sa. 5, sü. 3 de)

★

Tuğgeneral Tulga'nın basın toplantısı

İstanbul Askeri Vali ve Belediye Reisi Tuğgeneral Refik Tulga dün saat 16.30 da yerli ve yabancı gazetecilerle bir basın toplantısı yapmış ve yazılı olarak şu beyanatı vermiştir:

«— Sayın arkadaşlar, Silâhlı Kuvvetlerimizin yayınladığı tebliğlerin ifade ettiği mânaya yeni birşey ilâve edecek değilim. Sayın İstanbul halkının Silâhlı kuvvetlerimizin, h hareket tarzına güvenerek huzur ve emniyet içinde bulunmalarını temenni ederim. Şimdilik daha fazla malûmat veremeyeceğim için beni mazur göreceğinizi ümit ederim. Hepimiz ve herşeyimizle Vatanımızın hizmetindeyiz.

Sizlerin de Türk Basını olarak her zamanki vakarınızla bu dâvaya yardımcı olmanızı rica ederim.»

★

27 Mayıs 1960

Yeni bir sabah. Sabaha karşı saat 02. İstanbula dört yönden uzanan yarı aydınlık yollarda, sayısız tank ve bindirilmiş motorize askeri birlikler hareket halinde...

Saat 02. 30 Askeri birliklerin harekâtı devam ediyor. İki milyonluk İstanbul şehri büyük bir sessizlik içinde uyuyor.

Saat 03. 00 Askeri birlikler ve zırhlı kuvvetler

Orgeneral Cemal Gürsel kimdir?

MİLLİ BİRLİK Komitesi Başkanı, Silâhlı Kuvvetler Başkumandanı Orgeneral Cemal Gürsel, 65 yaşındadır ve evlidir. Bir erkek çocuğu vardır. Aslen Erzurum'lu olan Orgeneral Cemal Gürsel, Birinci Dünya Harbi sırasında 19 yaşında genç bir subay olarak Çanakkale muharebelerine katılmış, daha sonra da Filistin cephesinde çarpışmıştır.

(Devamı Sa: 5, Sü: 4 da)

3 Mayıs ve Orgeneral Gürsel'in veda yazısı

K.K.K. ANKARA   Konu: VEDA   3 Mayıs 1960

1 — K.K.K. dan izinli olarak ayrılıyorum. Bütün silâh arkadaşlarıma veda ederim.

2 — Sizlere son sözlerim şunlar olacaktır:

Her şeye rağmen ordunun ve taşıdığınız üniformanın şerefini daima yüksek tutunuz. Şu sıralarda memlekette esen hırslı politika havasının zararlı tesirlerinden kendinizi korumasını biliniz. Ne pahasına olursa olsun, politikadan katiyen uzak kalınız. Bu sözlerim, şerefli ordunun kudreti ve memleketin kaderi için hayatî ehemmiyeti haizdir. Bütün gayretinizi memleket müdafaası için lâzım olan kudretinizi arttırmaya ve onu en yüksek derecede çıkarmaya hasrediniz. Sizlere inanıyor, son erden en büyük kumandana kadar cümlenizi derin saygı ve sevgi hissi ile selâmlıyorum.

Bu yazımın en küçük birliklere kadar ulaştırılmasını rica ederim.

Cemal Gürsel
Orgeneral
K.K.K.

Dağıtım: Kara Kuvvetleri birliklerine telsizle bildirilmiştir.

🔊 TURKISH ✕

bir aydan beri melekette cereyan eden memleketi suratle korkunc buhranlara surukleyen hadiseleri biliyorsunuz. Bu gidisin memleketi kanli bir kardes kavgasina da goturmekte oldugunu her akli basinda vatandasin takdir ettigine kaniim. Dunya ahvali her gun biraz daha kotuye dogru giderken hususi politika ihtirasi yuzunden vatanimizin maddeten ve manen perisanliga suruklenmesi vicdan sahibi butun vatandasiari dilhun etmektedir. Bu hai nereve kadar gidecek?

Camera Handwriting Conversation Voice

"Bir şikâyet vâki olursa MENDERES adalete verilecek"

Saat 03.05. Bütün idari mekanizma beş dakika içinde Türk Silâhlı Kuvvetleri Birlikleri tarafından ele geçirilmiş ve bütün yurtta olduğu gibi İstanbulda da muvakkat bir Askeri İdare duruma hâkim olmuştur.

İSTANBUL RADYOSU YAYINA BAŞLIYOR

İstanbul radyosu her günkü programından çok önce saat 04.05 de yayına başlamış ve çalınan İstiklâl Marşını müteakıp silâhlı kuvvetlerimize mensup bir subay Türk Silâhlı Kuvvetlerinin saat 03.00 den itibaren bütün Türkiye'de kan dökülmeden yapılan bir hareket sonunda idareyi ele aldığını millete bildirmiştir.

İstanbul radyosunun bu yayını aralıksız devam etmiş ve Türk Si-
(Devamı sa. 5, sü. 2 de)

Basın toplantısında M. Birlik Komitesi sözcüsü 1 soruyu böyle cevaplandırdı

Ankara, Hususi, Cuma

Millî Birlik Komitesinin basın işleri ile vazifelendirdiği Kurmay Albay Ener, bugün saat 15 de Genel Kurmay Başkanlığının büyük Brifing salonunda yerli ve yabancı gazetecilerin katıldığı bir basın toplantısı yaparak izahlarda bulunmuş ve gazetecilerin sorularını cevaplandırmıştır.

Albay Ener, iç ve dış basının en kısa zamanda serbest bırakılacağını ve dış memleketlere doğru ve serbest haber vermenin bugün sağlanacağını bildirdikten sonra, soruları cevaplandırmaya geçmiştir.

Sorulan sorular ve Albay Ener'in cevapları şöyledir:

Soru: Bu sabahki hareketi nasıl tafsil edebilirsiniz? Bir darbei hükümet mi olmuştur, yoksa anayasaya dönüş mü, bahis konusudur?

Cevap: Yürürlükteki anayasa, idare tarafından çiğnenirse o idarenin meşruiyeti şüpheye düşer. Onun için biz birkaç senedenberi memlekette anayasanın ihlâl edildiğine şahit olduk. Fakat sabırla bekledik ve içten temenni ettik ki, bu yol parlamenter nizam
(Devamı sa. 5, sü. 3 te)

Diğer fotoğraflar altıncı sayfada

Yeni Anayasayı hazırlayacak komiteden:
Prof. TUNAYA — Ord. Prof. ONAR — Prof. KUBALI

🔊 TURKISH ✕

Bir sikayet vaki olursa Menderes adalete verilecek,,
Basin toplantisinda M. Birlik Kamitesi sozcusu boyle cevaplananau.   Ankara Hususi Cuma.
Milli Birlik Komitesinin basin isleri ile vazifelendirdigi Kurmay Albay Ener, bugun saat 15 de Genei Kurmay Baskanliginin buyuk Brifing salonunda verli ve yabanci gacetecilerin katildigi bir basin toplantisi yaparak izahlarda bulunmus ve gazetecilerin sorularini cevaplandirmistir.

Camera   Handwriting   Conversation   Voice

◀) TURKISH ✕

Milli Birlik Komitesi Baskani, Silahli Kuvvetler Baskumandani Orgeneral Cemal Gursel, 65 yasindadir ve evlidir. Bir erkek cocugu vardir. Aslen Erzurum'lu olan Ogeneral Cemal Gursel. Birinci Dunya Harbi sirasmda 19 yasinda genc bir subay olarak Canakkale muharebelerine katilmis, daha sonra da Filistin cephesinde carpismistir.

Camera   Handwriting   Conversation   Voice

3

DEAD ON THE GRAND TETON

AFTER I LEFT THE DENVER Police Department, I moved to Idaho Falls, Idaho, and was a scoutmaster for fourteen years. I had always wanted to climb the Grand Teton and finally decided I would take a group of scouts up there. We had a great leader John Walker who is a fireman paramedic and has climbed the Grand many times. We had a meeting with him and the boys to discuss the dos and don'ts and important information about climbing a mountain like the Grand Teton. He stressed the importance of being in top shape and so I worked out every day climbing up and down that huge staircase in the old Shelton church that we lived in. My granddaughter Kameha was my cheerleader coach and made it fun going up and down the stairs to the music of the Beach Boys. He also stressed that there was a thing called "Summit Fever" that we have to be very aware of. He said it would be a long, long, arduous hike and climb and so when you get close to the top if you start feeling sick you let everyone know and we will all turn around and go back down. I even remember telling the boys to remember what he said not having any clue what was to come. I was in such great shape that I was always at the very front of the group. When it got steeper, I would sometimes climb up on top of a rock and wave my arms back and forth and yell, "Are you really going to let this old man beat you to the top?"

Feeling so invincible, I just knew I could run circles around all of them! We finally made it to base camp and set up our tents and got our equipment all ready for tomorrow morning. We ate dinner early and retired to our sleeping bags because we are going to be leaving at four in the morning. Half-past three came early, and we had a quick bite to eat, got our gear on, and started hiking up the trail. We wore headlamps so that our arms would be free for the arduous climb up the mountain. It was pitch black outside when we started up the very steep part of the mountain when we saw a very surreal sight down below. There was another group of climbers down below, and the only thing we saw was what looked like lights floating in the air moving up-and down back-and-forth in the pitch-dark blackness. We quickly figured out that it was the headlamps of a group of climbers coming up the trail well below us. Some of the areas were at most totally vertical rock which required roping up and using our other climbing gear. One area we came to was about 10 ft across, and there was no trail, and there was no way to rope up. It meant crossing an area with about a 2000-foot vertical drop. It required great finger strength because the ledge above was only two or three inches wide. The ledge below for our feet was no more than three or four inches wide. I got about halfway across and was afraid I couldn't hold on. John Walker extended his foot out on one of the ledges so I could put my foot on his foot and that helped me get across. The young scouts in the group got very excited when they saw what they were going to get to cross. They said things like "seriously we get to go across here where it's over 2000 ft straight down the cliff, and we're not even going to rope up with our equipment!" I think a lot of prayers got everybody across that hazardous exposure. We reached an area about fifteen minutes from the top that was fairly flat with solid rock. Even though it was in August, the weather was looking very threatening for some type of storm.

John Walker said he would be back in a few minutes and walked around a very narrow ledge of rock and disappeared for a while. When he returned from that very scary narrow ledge, he said we had to hurry to get to the top because a terrible-looking snow storm was coming. We were all sitting down hugging up against the

COP LIVING ON THE EDGE

vertical rock that leads to the top on a ledge about five feet wide. I hurried and put on my waterproof bottoms and top preparing for the winter storm that was only minutes away. Suddenly I felt so sick that I thought I was going to die right there on the mountain. Even though I remembered what he had said about "Summit Fever!", since we were so close to the top, I didn't want to deprive all these young men the opportunity to reach the very top of the Grand.

We climbed quickly over these gigantic boulders that were the last obstacle to reach the peak. Because the storm was coming in so fast and hard, we only stayed on the top a couple of minutes and headed down to the 5-foot ledge just minutes below us. Even though I was trying very hard to not look or act sick, I could barely move and started to throw up like I never had in my life. The food and drink I was throwing up shot out of my mouth like a cannon going way out over the steep cliff. Since it was daylight now, I could see the cliff right at the edge where we were standing was several. thousand feet straight down. I felt like I would be dead within a very few minutes.

The snow started pounding at us, whipped by winds 30 or 40 miles an hour. John Walker was distraught with me since I had not let him know that I had started feeling very sick almost an hour earlier. My body quickly became totally immobile, and I could not stand anymore. Just as he was trying to figure out how to get me down the cliffs, some professional climbers came along and were very willing to assist with my rescue. The only thing I can remember about the descent down the cliff was telling them that I knew how to use the rope to slow down and stop rappelling down the cliff. John said he was afraid I might pass out at any second and I would fall to my death. Remembering about the descent down, I was totally out of control, and had it not been for the safety rope attached to me I surely would've plunged to my death. Briefly, I regained consciousness when we got to the saddle. There was a rope with many knots in it which was used to climb up and down that straight-up and-down area. I was able to stand up for just a minute, and I told John that I was dying and totally collapsed in his arms.

At that very second, I saw my dad right in front of me dressed in white, and he whispered to me, "It's not your time, Scotty!" My dad had died earlier, and I realized I had just seen a brief glimpse of heaven. The guys wrapped me up like a mummy with a rope so they could let me slide down the glacier. Darin Bateman was one of the boys that I could faintly hear yelling things like "You're going to make it! You'll be all right!" as they ran down along the side of the glacier. I really don't know how John Walker was able to let me slide down that giant glacier without losing control of me.

By this time the storm was like, a whiteout blowing so hard and furious you could not see or hear anything but the wind was so far gone at this point that I have no recollection of how I got into the tent at the base camp. Because the blizzard was very life-threatening, the leaders helped the boys down off the mountain. I was left in the tent with Bishop Larry Stucki. Many hours later some search and rescue Park Rangers called my wife. She never answers her phone in the middle of the night, but because she did, I am alive today. She had no idea that there was any problem with me climbing the Grande.

One of the park Rangers named Goldie told my wife that they had been looking for me in a whiteout blizzard for over five hours and could not find me. He said to her that he was sure that I had not survived and wanted permission to give up the search. She asked him some questions about what happened, and he knew very little. She pleaded with him to please keep looking because she was sure that they could find me. They continued searching for me and after several more hours came across our tent. They could not get any pulse or heartbeat and were sure I was dead. Bishop Stucki asked them to please keep trying. It took them over half an hour to finally get an IV into my collapsed veins. The IV fluids they had were so close to freezing that it jump-started me, bringing me back alive when it hit my heart. The whole time, they were in my tent working on me I could faintly hear them talking. I can very well remember when they said, "He's gone! There's nothing we can do!"

I wanted to say "I'm here, I'm alive, please don't give up!" But I could not as much as twitch or blink or say a word. After the IV got me hydrated, I woke up just enough to throw up a few times and went back into a deep sleep. That next morning, I woke up feeling terrible but much better than the night before. The two rangers and larry's Stucki somehow managed to help me down the mountain. I can faintly remember getting into a car and being taken home.

My wife took me to the Doctor who examined me and told me he was sure that I had HACE (high altitude cerebral edema). He told me I needed to get to the hospital immediately and have an MRI of my brain. That test showed swelling in my brain which caused me to be so severely sick. I don't even remember how long I was in the hospital before I was able to come home. For about a year I could not talk or walk or eat by myself. My daughter Tamara through hours on the Internet found a doctor in Telluride Colorado named Peter Hackett who is a world-renowned expert on HACE. He has personally climbed Mount Everest. She got hold of him, and he told her that I needed to go to a psychologist and have tests done to determine what part of my brain was damaged. The doctor had me do a series of straightforward tests.

One of the tests was a wooden jigsaw puzzle that had a circle, a rectangle, a square, a diamond, and a couple of other simple shapes that he told me to put together. I tried very hard to put the puzzle pieces in the correct place, but I could not get even one of them to fit. I got furious at the doctor and told him that he was trying to torture me because I knew none of the puzzle pieces worked. He explained that even a five-year-old kid could do this and try a little more. No matter how long I tried, I could not get one single piece to go in the correct place. He had me do some other tests that I failed just as badly. I recently contacted Dr. Peter Hackett who was very interested in helping me. He said I needed to get the test results that I had done years ago at the psychologist's office. I then found out that the psychologist had died and his records had been destroyed. One very cool thing happened when I went back to church for the first time in about one year. One of the boy's dads said to me when I went and sat down by his family, "I did not know that there was any kryptonite on the Grand!"

It did not hit me for a minute what he was talking about. When it did, I said, "I did feel like Superman for part of the climb!"

To this very day, I have symptoms of terrible balance, falling down, passing out, terrible headaches, and horrific shooting pains, and no doctor has been able to determine the cause of these problems. I started going to the University of Utah's neurological department where they performed numerous tests with no known diagnosis. Because of the multiple times I passed out, often in public places, I have been transported by ambulance to several different hospitals. I was at my brother's house and had an episode started with a seizure, and I passed out on the couch.

Thankfully for me, he was having a massage given by a registered nurse. Because of my history of passing out my brother and sister were not too worried about me until the nurse checked on me. She told them to call 911 immediately because I was not breathing and I had no heartbeat. The firemen and paramedics arrived and could not do CPR on me because I was lying on every soft couch. I had no signs of life and time was of the essence. Right next to the sofa was a large 3-inch-thick marble coffee table top that weighed about 600 pounds. They yelled at my brother to move it out of the way so they could get to me. He started to pull it out of the way but the legs underneath collapsed. There was a blanket under me, and just as the paramedics began to lift me, the marble slab crashed to the floor, and they dropped me. The shock to my body dropping me to the floor started my heart going. No! That was not a coincidence. The man upstairs is in charge, and it was not my time to leave this world once more. Thank you, Lord, for another blessing and miracle in my life!

Cleaning up our yard around our house and an additional three and a half acres is one big job. There was a pile of dead branches and other wood debris that I had been piling up for a couple of months and wanted to get rid of it. I lit it on fire. I found a box of matches and had a gallon of gasoline to make it easier to start. The pile of wood was probably 7 ft high and 15 ft in diameter. I poured the gas all around on the wood and set the gas can quite far away. I reached in my pocket for the box of matches, but I couldn't find them. I did have a clicker type of lighter, so I poured the last bit of gas, forming enough wick out away from the wood about 2 ft long, and bent down and clicked the lighter. Because I had not waited long enough for the gas fumes to dissipate, the fumes and the gas caused a massive fireball explosion that sent me flying 25 ft in the air.

My next-door neighbor saw the explosion and saw me flying in the air. As he was looking out the window, it appeared that I was in the center of the fireball and most likely burning to death. His wife ran over and told my wife, and they called 911. My wife told me later that she could not decide in her prayer to ask that my life might be spared, although I would be burned beyond recognition, or that I would just quickly die without any pain.

Amazingly, the explosion sent me so far in the air away from the fire that I barely had burns on my arm and foot. At some point during the blast, I once again was gone with no sign of life. I don't know if it was a fireman or the paramedics that brought me back, but once again my life was spared.

4

MOUNT TIMPANOGOS RESCUE

A KNOCK CAME ON OUR door at our apartment at the married student housing at BYU in Provo, Utah. A student who had been climbing Mount Timpanogos the day before turned up missing, and everyone available was asked to go on a search and rescue mission. Since I was finished with my classes for the day, I went with our next-door neighbor up to the bottom of Mount Timpanogos, where sheriffs, deputies, and rescue rangers were gathered. Everyone was assigned in pairs. We were told to go up to the left side of the glacier and come down to the right side of the glacier. We were told they would sound in air horn when we're supposed to return to the temporary headquarters. I had climbed to the top of the mountain the year before and was familiar with the terrain, but I was amazed at how gigantic the glacier was this year. It took us a couple of hours to make it up to the very top of the enormous glacier. There were boulders and tree branches and tree stumps and all sorts of heavy debris along the edge of the glacier. It was a very rugged terrain we had to climb over around and through to get to the top. Because it had been so rough going up, I suggested that we could slide down the glacier, but my neighbor said that was a terrible idea.

He started going down the other side of the glacier as I carefully walked out to the middle at the top of the packed snow. I sat down and dug my heels in the ice and then let them up and started to slide down. In a matter of only about thirty seconds, I was going too fast; I knew I was in trouble. As the seconds went by, my speed exhilarated to the point that I was totally out of control. No matter how hard I dug my heels in, I didn't seem to slow down a bit, and ice and snow were flying into my face. At this point, I was going so fast, and being blinded by the snow and ice that I couldn't see anything. I tried rolling over onto my stomach and digging my toes and my fingernails into the glacier ice, but nothing I did helped slow me even a little. Because the glacier was so steep and so slick with ice, I must've been doing at least 50 miles an hour or faster. I remembered all the broken trees and boulders and sharp hard large objects that were at the bottom of the glacier and knew I would be dead when I hit there. My whole life passed through my brain in a matter of seconds, and I started to pray for a miracle. By the time I got more than halfway down the glacier, I was going much faster, and I knew when I hit the large boulders at the bottom, I would be a smashed-up bloody blob. I rolled over again on my back and tried digging in my heels even harder. This only increased the snow and ice hitting my face, which was now totally numb, and my eyes were frozen shut. Suddenly, my feet slammed into something so hard and solid it almost broke my legs. I quickly sat up to see what I had hit.

Flabbergasted and scared to death when I saw my feet, we're just hanging over the edge of a massive crevasse about fifteen feet wide. What my feet had to hit, and the object that stopped me was nothing less than a miracle from heaven. My companion had been running down along the side of the glacier, screaming, "Hold on until I get there!" When the situation dawned on me, I started digging a place for my butt and digging my heels in the ice right above the edge of the opening of the crevasse. Since there was nothing visible that was keeping me from falling over the edge into the abyss, I was frantic. There was nothing that I could push my feet against at the edge of the chasm. I kept trying to dig out a place in the glacier to hold me from going over the edge. My partner yelled that he was looking for something that would reach to me to pull me back to safety. He kept screaming, "You're on the edge of an enormous crevasse that I cannot see anything but blackness towards the bottom!"

He finally found a long tree branch that he reached out to me, but it was a couple of feet too short. He kept looking for something longer but could not find anything and kept yelling at me to hold on for dear life. He finally got a little footing with some rock debris on the edge of the glacier and was able to get the tree branch almost to me. The big problem I had then was I just pictured if I grabbed the branch; I might swing like a pendulum and go crashing hundreds and hundreds of feet to the bottom of the abyss. It took me a lot more praying and trying to build up more faith, and I finally grabbed the branch and told him to pull me fast, or I would be dead. It was another miracle because when he pulled me with the tree branch, I didn't slide down over the edge of the crevasse. We both took some rocks and tossed them out in the middle to listen to how long it took before we heard them hit bottom. It took several seconds, so we knew it was very deep, I had to sit down on a rock at the edge of the glacier for about half an hour before I could pull myself together enough to go down to the bottom of the glacier carefully. At that very moment, the air horn went off, telling us all to return to the temporary search and rescue headquarters. We were all hoping that someone had found the missing hiker, but no one had.

The next day the search and rescue people sent two professional climbers down the crevasses on the glacier that I almost fell into. The next day they notified us that the missing hiker was found dead at the bottom of the crevasse. Only a few feet away from his body, they found another hiker who had been missing for three years. Their bodies were well preserved because of the year-round ice. I have never stopped thanking the Lord for that amazing miracle that saved my life.

Rescuers: 2—for finding those men. Blessings from the Lord: 1 (me!).

5

BIG HUNT

WHEN I WAS ATTENDING BYU Provo, I was working part-time but not making very much money. We hadn't eaten meat four a couple of months. A friend and I decided to go deer hunting to put some meat on the table. I borrowed a rifle from my uncle, and we headed up into the mountains. It was in late October, and there was no snow, so we knew we had to go up high to find any deer. We picked a large canyon, and I went up on the right ridge, and my buddy went up on the left. We left early enough in the morning that it was still dark as we moved up the mountain. We were getting near the top when we could hear a lot of movement down below in the canyon. It was still very dark, and I lay down with my gun aimed in the direction of the sound. The movement was getting louder and closer, and then I could smell the deer.

The sun would not be coming up for quite a while, so I got comfortable and laid there patiently excited as the smell got stronger and their movement got closer down below. There's smell quickly went away as an extreme wind started whipping down the mountainside. Suddenly I felt chilled to the bone and realized that a massive snowstorm, more like a blizzard, was coming down on us. Because the snow was heavy and wet, within only a few minutes I was getting buried lying there on the ridge. Even though I could not smell the deer, they were making a lot more noise moving much faster down the canyon. The blizzard was driving them further and further towards the bottom of the canyon. When I started to stand up, I could not believe how deep the snow was and how heavy it was on my back. We had not dressed for this kind of weather, and I realized I was getting soaking wet. I yelled as loud as I could across the canyon that we should move down quickly towards the bottom ahead of the deer. The blizzard was blowing the heavy snow so fast that I couldn't see and before I had run 50 ft, the snow was up to my waist.

It started to get just light enough that I thought I might pick out one of the deer and have a good shot. Since the snow was so deep, I crouched down and steadied my gun. The next sound I heard was very surprising and also disappointing. What we thought was a herd of deer started to go baa! baa! Nothing but a bunch of smelly stupid sheep were below in the canyon. The wave of disappointment over my body quickly changed to the realization that I was going to freeze to death if I didn't get moving. I yelled over and over at my partner, but the blizzard drowned out my voice.

I headed down the bottom of the canyon, hoping to find him. In all my many years of winter camping with the scouts, I had never witnessed such heavy snowfall. Instead of hiking down the canyon, I ended up sliding and falling until I hit the bottom. I yelled again for my buddy and was thrilled when I heard him answer just up towards the ridge. He kept yelling something, but I could not make out the words. I started up towards the ridge and luckily came across what felt like a zigzag pattern of a deer trail. The heavy snow made it nearly impossible to stay on the trail, but I pushed forward, falling down many times on the way up. I found my partner leaning up against a huge fir tree that was keeping the snow off of him. We were both soaking wet and shivering almost uncontrollably. We gathered together some dead pine cones right above us and used some of the tree sap to light a fire.

When the fire got going, fanned by the wind, we took off our jackets and used them along with our guns to make a windbreak. We added some branches so that our windbreak would stay up while we stripped off our clothes to dry them in front of the fire. Since our feet were freezing, we took off our boots and started drying our socks on sticks next to the fire. We kept feeding the fire with dead branches right above us on the tree. We debated taking off our underwear since we were soaking wet to our skin. With our underwear off we held it up by the fire, I could feel the heat drying them even though we were shivering from our bare skin. The heat from the fire not only started to warm our bodies and clothes but also helped calm our anxious minds. There is something very magical and mesmerizing as you stare at a fire! Suddenly and without any warning, what happened next reminded me of the book by Jack London, "How to Light a Fire."

The heat from the fire warmed up the snow-laden tree's branches, and a huge pile of snow came down in one big mass and put out our fire. Here we were one minute getting warm and getting our clothes dry, and then our hopes of survival were shattered when our toasty warm, beautiful fire was doused. I told my partner that it was essentials that we did not panic. At the time, the words made sense, but the snow started blowing sideways, hitting our naked bodies. Pulling on partially wet clothes on wet bare skin was very difficult and almost impossible. The last thing we put on with great difficulty was our cold—nearly frozen—boots. For a couple of minutes, we thought if we stayed on the other side of the trunk of this big pine tree which was partially blocking that blizzard blowing sideways that we might be able to survive.

Because we were both shaking uncontrollably, we knew that we had to get off this mountain or we would be found frozen to death. We started down the mountain as fast as we could maneuver in the deep cold and slippery snow. Many times, I would fall down on my back, completely covered in the snow and I used my rifle like a paddle to try to keep me headed straight down the mountainside. After about an hour of the strength-sapping ordeal, I slammed into a large pine tree. The branches were so laden with snow that they were almost touching the ground ten feet out from the trunk. It was almost like they had formed a snow cave protecting the area around the trunk from the wind. The ground I was laying on was soft because of the many pinecones that had fallen through the years. I rolled over on my side and brought my knees up to my chest in the pre-natal position. Amazingly, I started to feel warm and toasty and started to fall asleep. Just as I was almost in a deep sleep, I suddenly awakened remembering teaching the scouts about hypothermia. The idea flashed through my mind that when someone freezes to death, they often have a feeling of warmth and comfort but end up freezing to death. I hated leaving my little shelter, but it dawned on me that I almost signed my own death certificate, thinking I was safe and warm and could take a nap. With great effort, I stood up and with my adrenaline no doubt pumping, I started back down the mountain.

There is absolutely no doubt in my mind that the Lord directed both of us to end up coming to the road right where his truck was parked. Our hands and feet were totally numb, and we could not even move our fingers to unlock the truck. I took off my gloves, and my partner slid the key between my nearly frozen fingers. By pushing the key in and twisting my wrist, I unlocked the door. We climbed into the truck, and the cold key was still frozen between my fingers. I pushed it into the ignition and turned my wrist, and the truck started right up. It probably only took about ten or fifteen minutes before the heat started, but it seemed like it was an hour, and we were both shaking uncontrollably and could not even talk. We didn't dare sit in the nice warm truck very long because the road was totally covered with snow and was only getting deeper by the minute. Even with a four-wheel drive, we couldn't move the truck.

Thankfully, he brought a couple of shovels, and we started digging in front of the tires far enough ahead to get the truck going. We had no idea how we would know where the road was but started going ahead anyway. Our GPS that took us back down to the main road was definitely our Heavenly Father. We had to go fast enough not to get stuck but relied totally on what we thought was instinct but really was the Lord above. We didn't have meat on the table, but we both were alive and well and felt so blessed.

6

ALMOST BEATEN TO DEATH

I TOOK A GIRL FROM a town a few miles out of Ames Iowa to the drive-in movie theater one night. Some of the kids from her high school found out about me taking her on a date. About halfway through the movie, several guys walked over to my car, pulled me out, and started beating me up. I was able to handle one or two guys, but the rest of them would jump on top, and I didn't have a chance. I don't remember how many stitches I got, but I was a real bloody mess. After two or three weeks of recovering, I went to Iowa State University and enrolled in a judo and karate class. Since my dad was a professor there, I didn't have to pay anything for the class. Several months later, I was exceptionally good at both martial arts. I won every match that I entered, and a couple of years later, I got my black belt. I became so proficient that I could take on five guys at once and beat every one of them. While I was attending Ricks College in Rexburg, Idaho, I started judo and karate classes, and I was paid very handsomely.

Most of the students I was teaching became so good that we put on exhibitions. We used the room with mats on the floor that the wrestling team also used. I scheduled my classes, so there was no conflict with the wrestling team. Once in a while, one of the wrestlers would come into the room and give us a hard time. My reputation on the campus had made me well-known.

284

I had a roommate that was from Korea who was very expert in martial arts. One day we were in front of the apartment throwing a football around when a car stopped, and five huge football players from the school got out and wanted a fight with me. My roommate, Bum Sick Hong, asked them to wait a minute while he went into the apartment to get something. I thought he was going to get some type of weapon, but instead, he walked over to the football players with a piece of paper on a clipboard. He said to the big, tough-looking football players, "as soon as you sign this, I will do my best not to injure any of you too seriously!" They all laughed at him, thinking and acting like they could squash him in a second. The biggest guy in front took the clipboard and read it out loud to the others. It read, "I understand that Mr. Bum Sick Hong is so expert in the martial arts that he will likely cause me serious bodily harm. By signing my name on this document, I agree that I will not hold him liable for any injuries, hospital expenses, surgeries, or any other medical expenses. I will allow any of the undersigned to make the first aggressive move. If this becomes a police matter, the parties agree that they were the ones that instigated this confrontation!" When he had finished reading the document, all the guys started laughing but then quickly stopped and had a very serious look on their faces. The big guy in front handed the clipboard back to my roommate, and in a split second, he did a high sweeping kick and barely tapped the guy's nose. He told the big guy he could have easily knocked him out or killed him if he wanted to. It happened so quickly that the big tough guy didn't even know how to respond. I said to my roommate, "since there are five of them, I think I should help you!" He replied to me, "these guys be no problem for me; it only takes me about a minute!" I moved over closer to him as a gesture that I am going to be part of this. Much to my amazement, the big tough football players loaded up in their car swearing at us is as they drove off.

Later on in my life, I was a scoutmaster and took our scout troop up to Island Park Scout Camp. We had a great time on the lake canoeing and trying out the sailboats. later in the day, we are getting ready to do some swimming when a horrible thunderstorm hit. We quickly had dinner, and after a few police stories around the campfire, we got in our tents and settled in for a good night's sleep. Very horrific rain started coming at our tents sideways, being driven by unbelievable wind. Our campsite was right in the middle of a lot of the very tall pine trees and some quaking Aspens. The thunder was so loud there was no way we could sleep for the first couple of hours. The wind was so fierce I was afraid our tents would get blown over. What happened next seemed so surreal and almost impossible. Massive trees were uprooted, and we're falling around the campsite. Some of the trees were so big when they hit the ground, it felt like we were having an earthquake.

When I unzipped my tent door and looked out at the fallen trees, many of them had landed only a couple of feet from the boy's tents. I thought I should wake them all up and find a safer place. Just as that thought crossed my mind, several trees came crashing down. One of them landed only a foot in front of my tent where I was looking out. The trees were crisscrossed all around the campground, just barely missing all of the tents. It was like a giant game of pick-up sticks. I felt a powerful impression that I should kneel and pray for protection from our Lord. It was a challenging prayer as the falling trees kept interrupting my inspiration.

When I started the prayer, I thought that I should get the boys out of the tents and move somewhere else. As I finished praying, I felt much calm and knew the best thing was to let everyone stay where they were, and we would be saved. Before I knew it, I was waking up as the Sun's rays made my tent glow. I hurriedly unzipped the tent and stood outside, looking around at boys' tents. Not a single tree had hit any of the tents. They did make a wall of tree trunks around each tent. As I got all the boys up and we looked around, they were astonished the same as I was.

I told them about my prayer, and every boy said they were also praying. They all were so afraid that they were going to be crushed as they were lying in their sleeping bags. Every couple of years, I always spray the roof of our house and our two-story garage with an apartment above with graphite and linseed oil.

It keeps the shingles looking new and prevents them from warping and makes the roof more waterproof. Since the roof is so steep, you could barely stand upon it. I use the hose to my spray gun as a way to keep myself from slipping and falling off the roof. Usually, I have somebody down on the ground by the sprayer holding the hose tight to keep me from falling or slipping. Since I didn't have any help, I pulled the hose tight and let out slack when I needed to go down to the edge. I was moving up towards the peak, keeping the slack tight when I stepped on the hose and fell sliding quickly down on the very slippery graphite and oil. My feet had just got to the edge of the roof when out of nowhere, my neighbor Heath pulled the hose tight. Because I had the spray gun in my hand, I was able to stop myself from falling to the concrete driveway below. OSHA says that a thirty-foot fall onto a hard surface is fatal in about fifty percent of cases, and the other fifty percent end up in a wheelchair for the rest of their life. I do not attribute this too good luck but to our loving Heavenly Father up above. The only injury I received was a couple of slivers and the sure knowledge that I should never do the spraying myself again.

I was building a commercial building in Kauai, working with vertical rebar for a footing. Two of the rebar were in the wrong place, so I cut them off. I then drilled a hole in the concrete and was pounding the rebar into the holes with a sledgehammer. The rebar was such a tight fit in the hole that I had a tough time getting it even started. I had a two-foot-long piece of rebar that I set over the hole and tried to keep it balanced for a second.

Just as I hit it with a sledgehammer, it tipped over, and the end went into my leg, making a large hole hitting my bone. It severed a couple of major blood veins, and blood was spurting out of the hole all over the place. I yelled to my son Jon to bring me a clean rag to try to stop the bleeding. I could not put enough pressure on it to stop the bleeding. Hey quickly grabbed the role of surveyor's pink ribbon and started rapping it tightly over the rag. He got the bleeding stopped good enough and got me to the hospital. The doctors told me that the hole was so big that they could not pull the skin together to stitch me up. The doctor said to me that he could not believe that the rebar didn't shatter my bone. He also said that if I hadn't gotten that bright surveyor's ribbon so tightly wound around my leg over the clean rag, I could've quickly bled to death. They got me bandaged up, and he said that the hole would heal, and eventually, the blood vein would repair themselves over time.

I was working in my shop building cabinets and had just put on a brand-new carbide-tipped twelve-inch blade on my table saw. I had probably made a couple of dozen cuts on the hardwood for the face frame of the cabinets. I was tired and sore and, for a few seconds, not paying attention to what I was doing. I was wearing leather gloves, and I bent over, reaching for another piece of wood. I was not thinking clearly when I braced myself by putting my hand directly on top of the running saw blade. The brand-new blade cut through my thick leather gloves, and because I had pushed down so hard, I knew all my fingers would all be gone when I pulled out of my glove. When I tried pulling the glove off with my other hand, I was amazed that blood was not spurting out the ripped open glove. I thought maybe I should leave the glove on to help stop the bleeding.

I grabbed onto the fingers that I knew had to be severed. There was absolutely no feeling in those fingers, so I knew they were cut off. I decided to pull the glove off because I had a brand-new bag of rags on the assembly table. My whole hand felt numb as I pulled off the ripped-through glove. Before I go to glove off, I was thinking as long as I could stop the bleeding and get my fingers taken to the hospital, maybe they could stitch them back on. I was dumbfounded when I pulled the glove off and saw a bright red line across the palm of my hand, and the skin had not even been cut. Both sides of the red line on my hand looked a little bruised but not a drop of blood anywhere. Once again, this was not luck, but a loving Heavenly Father was giving me a miracle.

7

BLOOD POISONING

DURING MY SENIOR YEAR IN high school, I was a part-time meat cutter. Each meat cutter had an individual 3x3' butcher block with slots along the side where all of their different-sized butcher knives went in. One day I was sharing a butcher block with a meat cutter when I reached across the block to withdraw a knife. The other meat cutter was not looking when he went to stick the knife in the slot, and he pinned my hand to the block. I let out a scream, and he looked at the knife he had stuck into my hand. When he pulled it out, it hurt even more and started squirting blood out of the severed vein. I went to the back room where my bose cleaned up and bandaged the wound. He said because we were shorthanded, he would appreciate it if I could work the rest of the day.

A couple of hours later, I noticed a bright streak of blood moving up my arm. I remember in first aid training in Boy Scouts that that could be a sign of blood poisoning. The knife that stabbed my hand to the block had been used trimming pork that day. I showed my arm to my boss, and he said you need to get to the hospital right now. Since I had a fever and was feeling very sick, he had one of the other guys drive me. When I arrived at the emergency room, I showed the problem to a nurse who quickly called and the ER doctor into the room. They got an IV going with antibiotics and applied pressure right above the red streak moving up the arm. The doctor told me that if that blood poison went into my heart that it could have easily killed me. Score one for Boy Scout first aid training.

In my last year in high school, I bought a beautiful silver, black and white Honda 305 Super Hawk. I always have enjoyed going fast, and so the motorcycle helped me fulfill my love of speed. I would take my motorcycle to a local park in Ames, Iowa, and see how fast I could go from one end of the park to the other. One day when I was riding my motorcycle there, I saw two missionaries I knew sitting over on the park bench and went over to talk to them. I would've let them ride my motorcycle, but I knew that was against the rules, so I thought I would show off for them. I went down to the one end of the park and took off like a bullet. By watching my tachometer and waiting to hit the redline before shifting gears, I knew I could go a lot faster. I got carried away watching the tachometer and speedometer, and before I knew it, I was at the other end of the park just coming up to the tennis court curb. I tried to put the motorcycle on its side, but when I hit the curb, I went flying in the air, slid across the tennis court, and hit the fence on the far side. Someone had removed the nets on the court, or I would've only gone halfway across. I was wearing shorts and a T-shirt, and all the skin on my legs and arms and stomach and part of my face were gone, and I was bleeding all over.

I had no idea why the missionaries took me home instead of the hospital. My sister put some hot water in the tub and poured the whole container of Morton salt in it and told me to get in. I put a toothbrush between my teeth because I knew it would hurt like crazy. As soon as I laid in the tub, I bit the toothbrush in half because the pain was more than I would've guessed. For the next three days, I got in the tub and did the same thing. I was so crazy then I didn't even wear a helmet.

We used to heat our house with a large wood stove. Every fall before the snow came, we would go up into the mountains and cut firewood. Since my children were young, I always kept them back from me while I ran the chainsaw. I was busy cutting short logs from the large trees that I had just cut down. Some guy startled me when he came up behind me to ask a question. When he touched me on my back to get my attention, the chainsaw hit my leg and ripped through my pants. Knowing that I was going to probably bleed to death because of the way the chain would've cut through my leg, I panicked and dropped the saw. I quickly pulled my pants down and couldn't believe what I saw. The jagged teeth on the chainsaw ripped through my pants, and my leg was bright red. The chain saw teeth had not even cut through my skin. As hard as that chain hit my leg, it was a miracle that I was not also injured. I had just put on a brand-new chain on the saw when I started cutting down the tree. I was working in downtown Chicago at a law firm called Sidley in Austin. There were 76 attorneys and 150 secretaries and the firm.

I was working as a law clerk with the idea I was going to go to law school eventually. I always walked down La Salle Street on the way to work. When I got halfway down the block, for some unknown reason, I ran across the road to walk on the other side of the street. Within only a few seconds later, I heard horrible screaming coming from way up above. Two construction workers, we're falling from a rolling scaffold because one of the cables had snapped. At about the same time, they hit the sidewalk, so did several large scaffold planks. One of the planks hit a small car where two older ladies were sitting. The edge of the plank hit the top of the car and went all the way down between the two passenger seats. Neither of the two women was seriously injured. The car looked like some huge giant had karate chopped it almost in half. If I had not crossed the street, then I would've been right there on the sidewalk where the two guys were splattered along with the planks crashing down everywhere.

My job mainly consisted of taking legal documents to the Cook County Courthouse every day. There was a man at a desk on the main courthouse floor that I got to know quite well through the year I was working there. He was amiable and always notarized the documents I had free of charge. He kept meticulous records of every notarized transaction. About 20 years later, I heard on the national news that he was threatening a lawsuit against Cook County. He had claimed that his job description did not include notarizing documents, and wanted to be compensated for the extra work. Cook County reached a settlement agreement that paid him well over a million dollars.

Now, I understood why he was so friendly. He must've been seeing dollar signs in his brain after every document he's notarized with his stamp. His retirement plan was quite creative! Cabinetmaking was something I always enjoyed doing in my shop. When I would use my table saw cutting 4 x 8 sheets of plywood, I always remove my construction belt. This particular day I had put on a large cowboy belt with the big buckle in front and added another big belt to hold up my baggy pants. Since I was assembling some of the cabinets, I needed to wear my carpenter apron to hold all the screws. When I went over to the table, saw to cut a sheet of plywood, I never thought of removing my carpenter apron. The plywood I was trying to rip in half was solid oak and very heavy. The table saw motor was mighty powerful and was working extra hard cutting through this oak wood. Suddenly the plywood got a little crooked, and it came shooting back at me, slamming me against the wall. I felt like I had been cut in half at my waist. As I pushed the plywood back, I realized that the three heavy leather belts had saved me from severe injury. Why did I put on all those belts? Only the Good Lord above knew!

Through the many years of working in construction, I did a lot of painting. There was a huge beautiful barn I was working on just west of Idaho Falls. The gable ends of the barn were 50 feet high, and the soffits at that point went out almost eight feet. I had a 40-foot ladder that I had been using as I spray painted the barn bright red. I usually would never spray paint on a windy day, but I was under a tight schedule, and the barn was isolated from other buildings that I didn't have to worry about overspray. I moved the ladder over to do one of the gable's ends of the big barn. I hoisted the 40-foot ladder to the very highest position. With the sprayer in one hand, I used my left hand to climb up the rungs.

I realized to paint the very top of the barn and reach out to do the overhang; I would have to go to the very top ladder rung. I carefully went to the very top so that I could reach the highest point. Everything was working out well on the vertical surface of the barn, but reaching behind me straight up to do the overhang was very tricky. Since I was on the top rung, there was nothing to hold onto, so I tried my best to keep my body tight against the barn wall. Just as I reached up and out, spraying the overhang, a big gust of wind pulled me backward away from the barn. I was defying gravity as I was leaning way back from the ladder. Falling 40 feet was almost always fatal to anyone falling that far. I was violently swinging my arms and teetering back and forth with my mind baffled that I hadn't fallen yet. It seems that I had been up there for at least a minute but probably only a few seconds. A gust of wind that had pulled me backward was gone, and I was slammed up against the barn from a different wind gust. I carefully climbed down the ladder and sat down against the barn. Trying to comprehend what had just happened was mind-boggling. Before very long, I found myself saying out loud, "Thank you, Lord! Thank you, Lord!"

Being a scoutmaster for fourteen years was a beautiful and fantastic experience. I always liked rock climbing and climbing mountains and had all the gear I needed. I took a group of scouts up to Heise, where there was a perfect rock to climb up and go repelling down. I was demonstrating how to back down over the cliff wearing a harness with the rope going through my figure 8 hardware. I showed them the position of your hands holding the rope out away from your body to go down faster and then positioning the rope around your side tight against the middle of your back to slow down or stop. Starting down the vertical cliff, I demonstrated the positions of going down and how to stop. I showed how they could jump out away from the cliff and go down fast and then slow down and stop as their feet come back hitting the cliff. I glanced up at the boys at the wrong second and smashed hard against the cliff and broke several ribs, and because the pain was so bad, I let go of the rope. I could barely breathe. To this day, I don't know why I didn't fall. None of the scouts were experienced, but somehow, they managed to pull me back up to the top. I still don't even remember what happened after that as I woke up in the hospital.

Sometime later, after recovering, I asked the boys what happened. They all agreed that they don't know how they were able to pull me up. Once again, the only thing that makes any sense at all is a kind loving Heavenly Father was there for me.

8

DEATH AT
FORTY THOUSAND FEET

For the past couple of years, I've been having medical problems no doctor could diagnose. A cardiologist wanted to eliminate my heart as a possible factor in my health problems. I was having seizures for no known reason and would pass out for several hours at a time. After leaving the Denver Police Department, I started working in Kauai, Hawaii, as a building contractor. On October 12, 2017, I boarded a Delta Airlines in LAX bound for Kauai. I happened to mention my wire loop recorder to one of the flight attendants and said that I knew I would be just fine and not to worry about it. A few minutes later, the pilot came back to inform me that I could not be on that flight, and I had to leave the airplane. Delta was courteous enough to give me a free hotel that night and a couple of free meals.

The next day I boarded the plane and did not say anything about my health problems. The flight was almost halfway to Kauai when I had a seizure and passed out. This time, however, my heart stopped, and I quit breathing. The pilot turned the plane around heading back to LAX. I was told later that he requested any doctors or nurses on board to help with a patient who had stopped breathing and had no signs of life. Amazingly, there were two doctors and a nurse who were on vacation who came to try and get me back. They did CPR and hooked me up to oxygen and finally brought me back. I know it was not a coincidence that these medical people happened to be on the same flight that I would've died on it if they had not been there. I was barely conscious when some paramedics and firemen put me on a gurney and took me off the plane. I remember thinking when I heard them talking, and I had no idea the aircraft had landed and thought how in the world did they get on a plane in mid flight. They rushed me to the hospital in record time as I keep going from alive to dead several times. I have no memory of that night I spent in the hospital. I finally came fully conscious and was able to talk and walk and said I needed to go back to the airport. They recommended that I stay to be observed for a few days, but I said I was going to be just fine. I took a taxi back to the airport and went to the counter to check-in for my flight. The red coat lady whose name was Gainor called Delta corporate office and also talked to their Doctor, and they said that I could not ever fly again on their airlines. When she told me that I couldn't fly on their airlines, I told her I had lots of Hawaiian air miles and would go on their airlines. She then informed me that my name would be sent to all the airlines, and none of them would let me fly.

The red coat lady really went to bat for me and asked what can we do to make it possible for him to fly on Delta. The medical doctor for the airlines told her that I could only fly if I got a written note from the Doctor at the hospital stating that I was on medication that would prevent me from any further seizures or near-death problems. During these last two days, my balance was so bad I could not walk and had to be transported in a wheelchair. I took a taxi back to the hospital, and after waiting a couple of hours, I got the paperwork that was requested. The very helpful red coat lady called the Delta Airlines medical Doctor and read the information I had given her. The Doctor then told her he needed to know the name of the medication I was on and the name of the Doctor who prescribed it because she could not read his signature. I then got another taxi cab and went back to the hospital and waited another couple of hours to get the requested information. After taking another taxi cab back to the airport, I gave her the information which she passed on to the corporate office, and they reluctantly approved me to fly to Kauai. Through that many years, I have been flying back and forth to Hawaii, I always insist on an aisle seat. However, with these circumstances, I wanted to be seated by the window so that if I had a problem, the flight attendants would not notice. There was a very friendly, nice young couple sitting next to me. I briefly explained to them my medical problems and asked them to please not say anything to the flight attendant unless I stopped breathing. I put a pillow against the window and pulled the blanket up over my head and went to sleep. I was delighted when I felt the plane touch down at the Lihue airport in Kauai.

Just over a month later, I was driving a car that I had just purchased, along the main highway in Lihue when the engine caught on fire. I was only stalled in traffic for less than a minute when a friendly Hawaiian man pushed the car hard enough that I coasted into a gas station next to two gas pumps. I got out of the car and was going to try to put out the fire in the engine compartment when the vehicle exploded. Several fire engines quickly arrived at the scene fearing the burning car would catch the gas pumps on fire. I ended up about 20 feet away when I had another seizure and quit breathing and was totally gone. An off-duty paramedic headed to the ocean to go surfing saw me laying there totally lifeless and started CPR. I started to come back the very second the ambulance attendants were putting the charged-up paddles to my chest. Once again, my life was saved by some wonderful medical people.

9

HANGING IN THE AIR

WE WERE BUILDING A TORPEDO testing site for the government. Back in those days, they didn't have concrete pump trucks, so we had a crane that would lift a sizeable concrete bucket with a large big metal handle that you would pull down to release the concrete to fill up formed walls. My job was to pull the bar down when it was centered over the formed wall. I was standing on the top of the wall that we are working on, which was 35 feet high when the crane lifted the first tub of concrete. The wind started blowing pretty hard, and we had and scary time getting the concrete bucket stopped in place over the wall. I grabbed the steel bar and pulled down on it, releasing the concrete into the wall. A hand signal directed the crane operator to lower the tub down for the next load. The concrete truck filled up the bucket, and the crane started lifting the bucket of concrete to the top of the wall. Just as the concrete bucket got a little above the wall, a big gust of wind made the concrete bucket swing way out of reach. Just as it was swinging back to the wall, I reached out to try to stop it. The weight and the force of the movement started to knock me off the wall. As I was starting to fall, I reached out, grabbing at the handles on the bucket but grabbed the release bar instead. The concrete started pouring out down below, hitting some of the workers. With the bucket now empty, the wind was whipping it much harder back-and-forth as I was hanging on for dear life. My hands were starting to lose their grip on the release handle.

I knew if I let go, falling that far my body would be skewered on the vertical rebar below. The wind did not let up as the bucket kept swinging back and forth above the top of the wall. The crane operator was helpless because the bucket was swinging so far out from the wall if he started to lower it that would send it crashing into the wall. Not only would that send me falling to my death, but it could also easily knock the other guys off the top of the wall. He started raising the crane, which would shorten the amount of swinging of the bucket. My hands were starting to slip off the handle, and there was nothing I could do about it. The crane operator realized this was only going to make my fall a lot further. The other guys on top of the wall signaled and yelled for me to let go just as the bucket came swinging across the top. I knew this was a do-or-die situation, and so I let go as they reached out and grabbed me. The force almost sent all of us flying off the wall. The crane operator had them unhook the concrete bucket and put a heavy steel headache ball on the end of the cable. He then lowered each of us one by one from the top of the wall down to the ground riding on the ball.

A few days later, we were stripping the steel forms off of the wall. You always start at the very top taking the forms off one by one and using a crane to lower the big ones down to the ground. I was working down on the ground, removing some of the concrete dried on the edges of the concrete forms. I didn't realize that the guys working above had moved so fast along the top that they were now directly above me. One of the two-foot-wide by eight-foot-long steel forms came loose so fast that they couldn't hold onto it. The form hit me right on the top of my hard hat and knocked me out. My hard hat had a large V-shaped crease all along the top. Although the aluminum hardhat saved my life, they are no longer accepted by OSHA because of how they can so easily be crushed. If I had been bending over when the form hit me, I would've definitely been killed. A few years later, I was working just south of Salt Lake City, Utah, by the point of the mountain as a flagman. My job was to stop traffic coming down the highway whenever a dump truck had to cross the road. It was the middle of July and was about 100°, and the air was very calm without the slightest breeze. That time of day, there was very little traffic coming down the highway. I had a jug of ice water that I went over to get a drink. Since I didn't have a cup, I had to hold the jug up in the air and catch the water as it came out of the spout. As I was drinking, I heard the sound of a semi coming down the highway going very fast. I looked behind me and saw that a large belly dump truck was going across the highway. I grabbed my handheld stop sign and ran over to the road and held it high above my head and waved it in the air. This semi driver locked up his brakes, and it came screeching tires headed right at me. The edge of the highway was only about three feet wide where I was standing.

Since the tires were all locked up and burning rubber down the highway caused the truck to start pulling to the right and was headed right at me. My only option to stay alive was to dive way over the embankment where the highway was presently being built up. I barely had time to take a couple of running steps as I dived over the dirt, landing over 20 ft down below. Miraculously, the semi coming down the hill with the brakes locked up stopped only a few feet short of hitting the middle of the dump truck as it crossed the highway. This semi driver was very shaken up over a near-death accident. Both drivers and myself could have easily been killed.

My next construction job was at Northwestern University, building a forty-story building. Back in those days, we never even heard of OSHA. I was working as a laborer on the thirtieth floor of the building. Every morning the crane operator would let me sit on the headache ball, and he would lift me to the thirtieth floor and give the cable a little swing, and I would jump off the ball onto the floor. One day at the end of my shift, I walked over to the edge of the floor, which did not have any handrail for safety concerns. Once again, the wind was a factor even with just a headache ball and the cable. I reached out to grab the cable so that I could get a ride down on the ball, and

I missed the cable and was teetering on edge and almost fell. It was like there was a giant magnet pulling me over the edge. I finally caught my balance just enough to fall to the floor with my head and shoulders hanging over the edge. The crane operator carefully got the ball right at the edge of the floor so I could climb on it and ride down. The ride down was my favorite thing I got to do every day. The crane operator would let me free fall about twenty-five stories and then would slowly lower me to the ground. If OSHA came to a project where that was going on, the company probably would shut down forever. This will be my idea of "back in the good all days!"

10

PONTIAC FRONT END GONE

I WAS DRIVING OUR PONTIAC Grand Prix one day, talking on my cell phone as I approached Telford Road at Highway 20. Suddenly the thought came to me, throw my phone down and pay attention at this intersection. I sensed something terrible was about to happen, and I stopped my car several feet back from the white line at the stop sign. There was quite a bit of traffic on the highway when a vehicle from the opposite direction coming from Telford Road tried to cross both double lanes of traffic each going in a different direction. A truck traveling north on 20 hit the front end of the car trying to make it across the two double lanes of traffic. After the truck collided with the car, it shot right at the front end of my car and I braced for impact. The next thing I saw was the truck doing many rolls high in the air, above the bar pit with tools and equipment flying everywhere. I was so relieved that it had missed the front end of my car.

I grabbed my cell phone and started to get out of the car to check on the truck driver when I saw the front end of my car was gone, and I collapsed totally unable to walk. I don't ever remember feeling hearing or seeing the truck hit my car and ripping off the whole front end. I was taken to the hospital where the doctors said my only injury was a concussion. For the next two weeks, I could not walk, talk or think clearly at all. One night at the dinner table when I felt like I was doing a little better, I tried eating. I took a forkful of food, and halfway to my mouth, I froze and could not move the tiniest bit.

I tried eating dinner with the family several times, which turned out to be pretty hilarious. I was having trouble talking, and I would point at the milk carton and say something like, "Pass me the telephone pole."

One day, I looked at the vacuum cleaner and asked my wife if she wanted me to go get the Whirley curl. For months I could not use the correct word for something I was pointing at or wanted. I knew the name of the object in my mind, but my mouth would say something totally different. The whole thing became a kind of a family joke on dad! I often would leave a space in a sentence I was writing and left out some words. Since I had my own business as a building contractor, I was doing a lot of math, and l would always use a calculator. I remember one time showing my wife that I was going to make six hundred thousand dollars on a paint job in Hawaii. She asked me if I was sure of the numbers, so I did them in front of her on my calculator. I entered six thousand dollars per building times ten buildings equals six hundred thousand dollars. She quickly said, "No, that is sixty thousand dollars."

I remember I put in the numbers again and told her to see the calculator even shows it's six hundred thousand dollars. It took her a few minutes with that calculator before I realized I was off by five hundred forty thousand dollars. I had to quit bidding jobs for a while until my brain started to function correctly. To this very day I still sometimes make unbelievable mistakes with math describing objects, stuttering, and sometimes not been able to talk at all.

Two years ago in June, I was building a carwash, a Chevron station, and a Circle K store. I went to Home Depot to buy some material and walked up to the contractor's counter to pay for some material. I took out my credit card and handed it to the cashier and suddenly collapsed to the floor. The next thing I knew five hours later I was waking up in the ER. They did every test imaginable to try to determine what had happened. The doctors told me that they had no idea what was going on and what caused me to pass out as I did. During the next several months the same thing happened every few days. Sometimes I would be out for five or six hours and sometimes only two or three hours before I would come around. That happened so often that the ambulance drivers and firemen started to remember me from my numerous trips to the hospital. I was at church one Sunday when the meeting ended, I got up to leave with my family, and I collapsed and brother Gonzales our stake president caught me before I hit my head. My doctors in Kauai finally said that my case was too complicated for them to figure out and I needed to go to the mainland to the Mayo Clinic. I made an appointment with the Mayo Clinic and was just getting ready to go there when I found out they don't take Medicare. I was able to get into the University of Utah Medical Center at the Neurological department. After several weeks of extensive testing, the head of the department told me that they learned a lot in medical school, but they learned a lot more from their patients. He stopped and paused for a minute and then he said to me, "I think, in your case, we may end up naming a disease after you!"

The other doctor in the room said to him, "You know we wouldn't do that; we would name the disease after us!"

I really wondered if they thought that would make me feel better, which of course, it didn't. I even told the doctor that I had a wealthy brother and I was sure he would give me a chunk of cash if they would make my case a priority. The doctor only responded, "Things don't work that way!"

The doctor suggested that I go to the ear nose and throat specialist and see if they can figure out what is going on in my inner ear that can cause havoc with balance problems. Well, I was waiting for my upcoming appointment with the ear specialist. I was burning some weeds out in the pasture. So that I wouldn't burn any part of our fence, I spent quite a while raking the weeds towards the middle of the field. I took the weed burner and went all the way around the pasture, getting the weeds burning.

Everything was going well until I collapsed in the middle of the field. Totally unconscious at the time, the fire had surrounded me, and when it was within a few feet of burning me, a car stopped and called an ambulance and the fire department. Whoever had called 911 said I was in imminent danger of death, so the emergency responders were there before I got burned. Once again, I was at the hospital where they performed more tests but could not diagnose the cause of my collapse.

Thanks to a concerned citizen driving by, my life was spared once again. I did not have a doubt that they must have been inspired to notice me and called for help. My doctor's appointment was still coming up, so I started working out in the field to finish burning the weeds. Being extra careful this time, I had a water hose near the fire. My weed burner was working very well and much safer than using gasoline. Without any warning at all the wind started to blow with huge gusts causing the fire to burn out of control. Not wanting to have to call the fire department since they had been there so recently, I tried my best to put the fire out since it was moving towards a 30-gallon propane tank. Because the wind was pushing the fire faster than I could control it, I finally called 911. One of the firemen in charge turned out to be John Walker, the guy who helped save me on the Grand Teton. He wisely advised me to never burn weeds when there's any wind blowing. I remembered several years earlier I was burning weeds when it got out of control and burned my barn down and a big stack of hay.

I went to an ear doctor, and their technician did all sorts of tests for my inner ear. One test they did made me scream as I thought the room was spinning around so fast that I was sure I was going die right there on the table. After he performed some other tests, he said he had never seen anyone with such horrible balance problems. He told me "I am amazed that you could even walk at all!" I started to ask him some questions about what he thought was causing it and he said the doctor will go over all that with you. A few days later I had an appointment with the doctor, and he walked in with a clipboard and read through my medical report. It was very apparent that he had not looked at it before my appointment. He said, "Well, there's no surgery, and there's no medication to help you. Sorry!" And he walked out of the room. Some doctors have a poor bedside manner; others have an excellent bedside manner. This quack had no bedside manner at all!

I have always thought that my medical problems stem from my climbing the Grand Teton and getting HACE. I was driving my four-wheelers around our property cleaning things up and went out by the road to get the mail. I saw a large semi coming down the road towards me so I put it in reverse and backed up too fast into the driveway and flipped the four wheeler over and it threw me out by the road. The tires of the 18-wheeler just barely missed hitting my head. My daughter told me she was coming to the house and saw the accident happen and at least ten or more cars stopped to help. One of the firemen remembered who I was and told the paramedic he passes out like this a lot and he will okay. I couldn't talk, but my leg hurt so bad I knew it was broken. When they started to move me away from the road the pain in my leg caused me to scream. They took me to the hospital, and the x-rays showed my femur was totally broken in half. The doctor said it was such a straight dean break; it was almost like it was cut in half with a saw. They gave me a ton of morphine, but it didn't even come close to helping the pain. Because my pain was so terrible, the doctor stayed late into the night performing the surgery where they put three eight-inch titanium screws in the femur to hold it together. I went to physical therapy for a while and got well enough that I started to bike every day to have it heal better. As I was biking on a path along the ocean it began to rain. I ran into a curb and flew in the air, landing on my other hip. Some neighbors nearby called an ambulance, and they took me to the hospital where I had a total hip replacement.

11

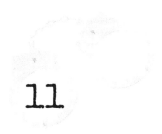

BACKHOE FLIPS OVER ON ME

I HAULED MY TRAILER WITH my backhoe on it to Salt Lake City, Utah, to build a house on the mountainside. The owner had me start by grading the area flat so we can layout the swimming pool tennis court and residence. About six feet of dirt had to be cut down on the upper side of the lot. I was in the process of cutting six feet from the upper part of the slope when the teeth on my bucket hit something metal and very solid. Suddenly two county vehicles came tearing in slamming on their brakes and bailed out of the car like I was about to hit some buried explosives or something. They came running towards my backhoe, screaming at the top of their lungs, "Stop, stop!"

I turned off the machine so I could understand what they were yelling about. They informed me that approximately 5 feet below the area I was digging was a 60-inch diameter high-pressure main waterline. They told me if I would've made a crack in the pipe, the pressure could've cut me in half and would've shut water off in Salt Lake, Ogden, Provo, and other cities hundreds of miles away. I called the owner and told him the lot would not be available for construction. The backhoe I had is one of the largest made and required a super heavy-duty trailer and my dump truck to haul it. With the motor cranked up, I started driving it carefully onto the trailer when suddenly the worst thing possible happened.

The throttle stuck in the wide-open position as the front bucket slammed into the front rail of the trailer. The second I hit the brakes, the backhoe pivoted and tipped off the trailer. I knew that if I did not brace myself and stay inside the cab, I would be thrown out of the open cab and crushed by this gigantic machine. The machine teetered on its edge for a second or two and then tipped over off of the trailer. I had locked it in 4-wheel drive, so with the throttle stuck wide-open, the tires were all digging in, and the machine was flying all over on its side. Somehow, I managed to hold onto the framework when it landed so that I didn't get crushed by the machine. I couldn't risk trying to reach the key to turn the machine off as it whipped around, stirring up dust and dirt so thick I couldn't see. It hit a large boulder and sent me flying to the ground just in front of the large spinning back tires. For whatever reason, I will never know, the engine died just as the spinning tire rubbed against my leg. In a little less than 30 minutes, twice, I cheated death and had my life spared. I kept thinking that with my near-death experiences, surely someone had seen me and would come to give me a hand. After a little while, I gained my composure. I used a heavy chain to pull the backhoe backup with my dump truck. I never did figure out why the throttle stuck. After a little while, and I got the nerve to drive the machine onto the trailer. I was so upset and distracted that when I was driving back to Idaho, I drove right past the weigh station, and I got chewed out by a state policeman. After I told him about the too near-death experiences, he said he understood and didn't give me a ticket. When I got back home, I put my dump truck, trailer, and backhoe for sale, and I was happy as can be when I got them sold. From that time on, I've always used a subcontractor to do my dirty work.

When I was working back in Illinois, building a high-rise building at Northwestern University, I had another near-death experience. Back that many years ago, OSHA was not even up and running. We had scaffolding built up to the 30th floor on this building, and it was not quite completed. I thought all of the scaffold planks had been put in place. I went walking along the scaffold, which at that time also did not have any handrail. One of the large cranes was lifting a load up to the building in front of me, and I was distracted. I slowed down a little bit but kept walking as I watched the crane in front of me when suddenly I stepped down, and there were no scaffold planks under my foot. I frantically grabbed out for something to hold onto, but there was nothing. I stood on one foot teetering on edge, but the entirety of my momentum was pushing me forward to my sure death thirty stories below. I finally fel forward-thinking I would die of a heart attack as I went falling through the air.

Miraculously, someone had placed one single scaffold plank that I crashed onto on my stomach and face. When I hit the plank, it felt like it was going to snap in two from my weight and rapid dissent. Although I was shaking violently, I was not dead. It took a while before I was rescued from my near-death plunge. I don't even remember to this very day how they rescued me.

A few winters ago, we had a camp out planned in January for the Boy Scout troop. There's a special recognition for a scout troop that goes camping every month throughout the year regardless of the weather. The weather on this particular Friday and Saturday was like 33 below zero plus the wind was blowing 30 and 40 mph. The wind chill factor would've been just too dangerous to take the boys out camping. Since we didn't want to miss getting our year-round camping award, we decided to go to the 17-mile cave. The cave is 17 miles west of Idaho Falls which has a small hole going straight down in the ground and then finally curves horizontally into a regular type of cave. Since it was snowing really hard, we had a hard time finding it.

The entrance is tiny even without snow. About 100 yards back in the small part of the cave opens up into a great big open area. We set up our tents in that area and then the boys had a lot of fun playing laser tag. We stayed up kinda late having a lot of 'fun and then we all hit the sack. Early the next morning I woke up having a hard time breathing and started choking. When I turned on my bright flashlight. I saw heavy smoke hanging just below the top of the tents.

I was sure that no one would be stupid enough to start a fire inside the cave. I couldn't think of what else could be causing this. I ran towards the entrance of the cave trying to discover where the smoke was coming from. Just a little before I went to the cave opening, I saw a bonfire going with a leader and some scouts around it. I ran up to the leader and told him to douse the fire immediately, or he was going to kill a whole bunch of boys back in the cave because of the smoke. He told me he thought all the smoke was going up out of the entrance. I aimed my flashlight towards the back of the cave where he could see the thick smoke was going up along the ceiling. I ran back to where all the boys were, and we hurriedly took down our tents, grabbed our gear, and ran back towards the entrance to the cave.

I've had to bend down low to keep from breathing in the smoke that was getting thicker and lower in the cave. One very unwise scout leader almost killed seven Boy Scouts and their scout leader. We went from having a hard time getting through thick smoke to a blizzard blowing ferociously as we came up out of the cave entrance. The wind chill factor was quickly 50 below zero outside. The electrical in our home built in 1929 had never been updated, so I installed all new wiring in the house including a new 200-amp meter on the outside. I put a meter base above their 200-amp panel where the power would go down through. The power company sent out a man with a truck that is a boom lift. He looked at the way I had run wires into the meter base and told me I had done it wrong. I had two wires running all the way through from the top through the middle and down to the bottom. He told me by doing it that way that the meter would not work because I was bypassing going through the center. He told me to cut the wires out in the center where the meter would read the usage and send the power into the house. Because the cables were so big around, I had to separate each strand then cut them one at a time. He was in the boom lift above bringing the power line from the electrical pole over to the mast running up above the panel and meter base, attached to the house. He was wearing some enormous heavy-duty leather gloves that reached all the way up to his elbows.

As I was working down below on the meter base, I glanced up and saw he was bringing the large for 440 Volt wire to run down through the three-inch conduit into the meter base. A good friend of mine who is an electrician told me earlier that whenever you are working on electrical always leave one hand in your pocket. That way if there is electrical power you didn't know was on, the energy goes into your arm, straight down your side, and out your leg. if you had both hands doing electrical work and power came through, it would go in one arm across your chest through your heart and out your other arm and kill you. Because I was doing as he told me it was challenging to cut the wire with only one hand. Since I knew there was no power coming down the conduit yet. I reached in with the other hand to cut the wire. Suddenly, the meter base flashed like it had been struck by lightning, and the explosion sent me flying backward.

The man from the power company up in the bucket lost his grip on the 440 Volt line, and it touched the mast, welding it to the conduit and sending all that power down to the meter base. Since I had just reached in with my other hand. The 440 Volts ran through my body and should've killed me. The guy in the bucket gasped and then finally started laughing uncontrollably. I think he did it to cover up the fact that it scared him that he almost killed me. It took him a while to get the wire that was welded to the conduit free. I told him that I would not finish cutting the wires unless he moved totally out of the way. He agreed and carefully took the 440-volt wire back away from the house. I could not believe that he had actually tried working above me with a live wire. Why that voltage didn't go in my one arm across to my heart killing me, I'll never know! Actually, I do know that it had to be a very loving Heavenly Father.

For many years we've had a mama and papa hawk living in a pine tree right next to our big two-story house. Every spring we are always excited to see the new baby hawks born and through the summer learning to fly. One summer in July the Blue Angels jet fighter team came out on their show at the Idaho Falls, Idaho Airport. Our kids and grandkids came to be in our yard to watch them flying practice runs just over the treetops around our house. I wanted to be able to see them landing on the runway, so I climbed up on top of our home. By standing on the very peak, I could see them touch down on the runway. I did not notice the mama and papa hawk circling high above me probably upset because I was close to the tree where their babies were in the nest. Hawks like to attack their prey by being high in the sky with the sun directly behind them as they come diving down. My grandson Sam was watching the mama hawk as it flew straight up towards the Sun and then he lost sight of it. I was very glad that I was wearing a very heavy-duty hat that day because the hawk came straight down out of the sun, hitting me with its extended claws. It hit me so hard that I started to fall off the peak of our house. The roof of the first story below was not as steep, and was able to stop from falling the rest of the way. If I had not been wearing a perfect hat, those claws would've torn into my head so deep; I would've been bleeding everywhere.

My grandson Sam is the one who saw the hawk just before it hit my head coming directly from the bright shining Sun. For the rest of the summer every time I would walk out the back porch that mama or a papa hawk would come swooping down at me and I would often duck my head a couple of seconds before they would've hit me. I talked to some fish and game officers about the attack, and they told me that this year has been the craziest year ever for that kind of thing to happen. He told me just outside of Boise a man was heading back to his vehicle from the rest stop when an eagle attacked him. His injuries were so severe they had to take him to the hospital where he got seventy stitches on his head.

I was with my son in Kauai body surfing in a place called Shipwreck. When we started to walk down the beach to the water, I told him the waves were way bigger than I wanted to go in. He told me I would be okay if we would just dive under them. It took some doing, but I worked my way through several big ones. I tried riding one big wave in but only ended up getting tossed all over the place and I came up choking from swallowing some water.

Another big wave hit me before I could get a good breath of air. When I came up out of that wave, I barely got my mouth open to gasp for some air when another big wave hit me and rolled me over and over. The same thing happened several times to the point I thought I was going to be drowned any second. One more big wave hit me, but this time it pushed me towards the shallower water where I was able to stand up. Although I got knocked down a few more times trying to work my way up the beach, I finally made it far enough up the beach I fell down, gasping for air. One more big wave ten feet out would've done me in for good.

12

STOPPED BREATHING

On January 17, 2019, I was in bed just getting ready to go to sleep, and I couldn't breathe. Thanks to my brother Mark I had a small canister of 95% pure oxygen, which I had by my bedside. I felt I would not be able to make it waiting for an ambulance. I held the oxygen tank up to my face, and as I drove exceedingly fast at least 100mph to the hospital.

The tank that I was breathing from quit working just as I almost got to the emergency doors, and I collapsed on the ground. A couple of paramedics, a nurse, and a doctor rushed me into the emergency room, where they saved my life, putting an oxygen mask over my face. They kept me for a few hours until, for unknown reasons, I was able to breathe on my own. The very same thing happened about a month earlier, where I went through an entire oxygen tank and then started to breathe on my own. What is really bizarre is a few years ago, I was diagnosed with asbestosis. My Pulmonologist said that my lungs were horribly scarred and had numerous little pockets of asbestos. He said that it could quickly turn into mesothelioma. I had worked in construction around asbestos for several years. Two guys I worked with both died of mesothelioma. My Pulmonologist x-rayed my lungs again and was absolutely stunned when he saw the results. He said my lungs were clean with no scarring and no signs at all of asbestos or mesothelioma. He told me that he was treating seven other guys, with lungs about the same as mine, who were also dying.

He told me that after thirty-three years of practicing medicine as a pulmonologist, he had never seen such bad lungs all of a sudden look totally normal.

The horrible balance problem that I've had for two years with numerous times I've been taken to the hospital is still going on. I've been going to the University of Utah neurological center, and they don't have a clue what could be causing me to blackout and four times actually to be totally gone. They have done numerous tests that have not indicated what is causing my problems. One test they do is called a tilt table. They strap you to a table lying down, and then it stands you up, and both times they did it on me, I passed out. They also do a test where they have a strobe light go on every two or three seconds while you're lying on a bed. As soon as they had it gone really fast, I totally passed out. I couldn't even guess how many times I've gone down, but I've broken both hips.

Almost every time I go into a store that has fluorescent lights for more than 30 minutes, it's almost a given that I'm going to pass out. Most of the paramedics with the ambulances have come to get me so many times that they know if they wait a little bit, I'll come around. If I quit breathing or my heart stops, then, of course, they take me to the hospital.

13

MY BLOOD PRESSURE DROPS

On November 13, 2018, I was sitting on the couch in the living room when I started feeling very lightheaded even though I was not standing up. I was very unstable and shaking uncontrollably. I got my blood pressure machines and started to check my blood pressure. The first reading was 110/67, and my heart rate was 60. I waited a couple of minutes and retook it, and it was 99/58. The next reading was 80/53. I was feeling weaker by the minute, and then it dropped to 74/48 and my heart rate was 51. I was so weak I thought I would be passing out. I called the doctor's office, but I was put on hold for over 10 minutes. I called the emergency room at the hospital and a nurse I talked to said call 911 immediately because if I passed out and my blood pressure kept going down, I would probably die. I just barely had enough strength to bring the phone up and dial 911. I could barely talk, and finally, the operator understood the address and said an ambulance is on its way. The paramedics and the fireman knocked on the door, but I couldn't say anything. They finally came into the house, yelling very loud, "Paramedics, firemen, where are you?"

My wife was so sound asleep in the bedroom she never heard a word. When they checked my blood pressure, it continued to go down to the point they said I would be referred to as the walking dead! Even though it took a lot of effort, they finally got an IV started in my collapsed blood veins. They rushed me to the hospital where a doctor and two nurses were waiting. After five or six hours of some special IV solution, I started coming around. The doctor told me if I wouldn't have got to the hospital, the way my blood pressure kept dropping, I would've been dead in a couple of hours. Being so far gone, I could not talk. One of the paramedics placed my phone in my hand, and I dropped it because I had no strength at all. I am so thankful for the 911 operator who stuck with me until the firemen and paramedics arrived at the house. They got to me so fast I'm sure they saved my life. Five times in the last year, I have been gone with no sign of life. The fact that I am still alive on this planet earth is because of many answered prayers and miracles from heaven. My grandkids often say, "You know what, grandpa, cats have nine lives, but you must have 999!"

They are so right!

I was working as a building contractor at The Idaho National Engineer site about 45 miles west of Idaho Falls. Early one morning, when it was very dark, in late December, I was driving to the site in my van. I came over a little hill, and as I went down on the other side, I hit two large deer standing right in the middle of the road. I didn't even have time to hit my brakes, and I went from 65 miles an hour down to about 3 miles an hour and rolled to a stop in total darkness. The two large deer totaled the front of my van. I didn't have any lights, and a couple of minutes later, a truck came flying over the same hill and stopped about 3 feet short of hitting the back of my van. They told me that they would help me get the van off the road before I got killed by some other vehicle coming over the hill. To my utter amazement, when I got in to start the van, just for the heck of it, I turned the key, and the motor started right up. Within a few minutes, the sun came up so I could drive slowly down the road without any lights. Even though the radiator was smashed into the engine, I was able to drive it to the job site. There was tons of blood and guts even on the very back end of the van. It seemed to me impossible that there would be blood splattered all over the very back windows. The collision with the two large buck deer turned them into bloody hamburgers.

I was driving north on Interstate 15, headed to Salt Lake to take my daughter and her husband and our grandkids to the airport. The roads were snow-packed, and it was snowing very hard. We were running a little late, so I was going about 70 miles an hour, despite the bad weather and bad roads. We were riding in my brand-new Pontiac Grand Prix, which was the first front-wheel-drive vehicle I ever drove. It was handling amazingly well on the snow-packed road. I suddenly got a very overpowering feeling that I should immediately slow down. Just as I let off the gas, a van traveling on interstate 15 going south slid off the road, bouncing across the wide area between the highways, and shot right past the front of our car missing us by only inches. It flipped over and rolled several times into a field off the highway. Several of the cars behind us stopped to help, so I kept going. If I would've hesitated even a second longer, we would've hit the van and probably all been killed. When you feel some inspiration, do not hesitate even a second.

A similar experience happened to me when I was driving my motor scooter in the dark through a dip in the road across a bridge in a jungle area in Kauai.

I was going about 50 miles an hour going down the hill towards a bridge when I suddenly felt inspired to stop immediately. I skidded to a stop only a few inches from a transmission that was lying across the road. I tried to move it, but it was so heavy, it wouldn't budge, so I called 911. That near miss accident may not have killed me, but it would've broken every bone in my body. I firmly believe that when you are living a good honest life, the spirit of the Lord is always there if you will pay attention. I will never forget the day that I felt inspired to stop my truck and trailer and check the load. I was hauling some large steel canopies bolted to the wooden trailer bed. Each of the four legs on the canopies had four holes for anchor bolts. I had just put two lag bolts in each of the legs thinking that would be sufficient. I received inspiration that I should pull over and check the load just as I was passing the Bank of Commerce.

The bank was closed, the parking lot was empty, and there was an outdoor electrical outlet on the side of the building. I thought to myself that this would be a perfect place to check everything out. I ignored the warning and continued driving out to the nuclear construction site. I was going about 65 miles an hour and heard a terrible sound and looked in the rearview mirror and saw all the canopies go flying off the trailer, bouncing across the road nearly hitting several cars. A couple of guys in a truck that was behind me stopped and helped me load up the mangled canopies onto the trailer. By not following that inspiration from the Lord, I almost killed some people, and it cost me a lot of money to rebuild them.

14

MY HEAD ON FIRE, TRAIN JUST ABOUT KILLS MY FAMILY

I WAS ON MY WAY home from a college class and saw a car at the side of the road with the hood up and stopped to see if I could help. The guy had run out of gas and had put two gallons of gas in the gas tank, but the car wouldn't start. I said if we took the air filter over the carburetor off, we could pour a little gas left in the gas can into the carburetor and start it. I told him not to turn it over until I said I was ready. As I was pouring the gas into the carburetor, I realized there was a lot more gas in the can than I had thought, and I said, "Hold on!"

He heard the word "on," so he turned the engine over. It backfired shooting gas in my face and all over my upper body. When I jumped back away from the engine, a spark from somewhere set me ablaze. I could smell my hair burning, and my face and bare arms and chest were on fire. I remembered to stop drop and roll, but the only place I could do that was either on the asphalt road or the gravel to the side of the road. The pain was excruciating as I tried slapping at my head and ears and face to try to get the flames out. My arms were also on fire, and I burned my hands every time I tried to get the fire out. The guy jumped out of his car with a blanket and covered me up and smothered the flames out.

When he got me to the hospital, amazingly, my arms, head, and hands only received second-degree burns. My ears and the top of my arms were the only parts that took a long time to heal and hurt for several days. Even though I could hear the hair on my head crackling and smell it burning, the top of my head was burned.

I was driving my truck with my little kids in it during a snowstorm with the roads covered in snow and ice when I came to the railroad crossing. I had the radio up, and we were all singing when at the last second, I heard a train whistle. Suddenly, a train was going by right in front of us. I hit the brakes but quickly realized I was going to slide right into it. I let off the brakes and slowly turned the steering wheel, and at the same time, I slammed it into 4 wheel dr. and hit the gas. The truck slid sideways toward the train but also started to go forward in the same direction as the train. The side of the truck was only about a foot away from the train moving parallel with it. As the truck came to a stop, it became apparent how fast the train was going, since the truck's side windows that we were looking through were only a foot away from the train zooming by. We could hear the screeching sound of these steel tires looked up, sliding down the rails. The train finally stopped a very long distance from us. The engineer came running alongside the train from the locomotive, thinking that we had all probably been shredded into thousands of pieces. He could barely squeeze between the train and my truck as he approached my window. Although he was relieved to see we were not hurt, he screamed at me, "Didn't you hear the whistle?"

I told him that I did not until the train was zooming right by in front of us. He told me that he saw the trucks sliding on the road as he went very fast past the intersection. He assumed that I was not able to stop and that the truck and whoever was in it would've been shredded like cheese. His concern for our well-being was mixed with a lot of anger, probably scaring him thinking the train had killed us. I forgot until that moment that I had yelled at the kids to get down on the floor just before I thought for sure we would be smashed to pieces by the train. Sometime later, I was driving my truck approaching the intersection of Iona Road and Yellowstone.

I was slowing down for the stop sign and had the distinct impression to stop way back from the white line. Not more than two or three seconds after I came to a stop at least 25 feet behind the stop sign, a huge truck came screaming around the corner, missing the front left corner of my vehicle by no more than a couple feet.

15

HIT STEEL POST WATERSKIING, STUCK ON CLIFF

My friend Mark McVicker and I used to go water skiing every week. During the school year, we would always go on Monday, so the teachers wouldn't think that we are skipping school. We were skiing one day on the lake, which was right next to the highway when it started to snow like a massive winter blizzard was blowing in. We always started from the dock with three or four loops in the tow rope so that we wouldn't get wet. I put on a sweatshirt and went over to the pier, and Mark got me a good fast start, so I didn't get wet above the ankles. I remember going along even with the highway.

    A semi driver was looking at me and blew his horn over and over again and shaking his head like you guys are crazy! We had water skied on this lake numerous times, and just as I was coming into the dock fast so that I wouldn't get wet, my ski hit something and sent me flying into the ice-cold water. When I swam over to get my ski, I found a steel fence post about a three-inch diameter, a couple of inches below the waterline. I thought about how many times we had come within inches of hitting that post. The worst of all, if we had fallen on top of that post, it would've been fatal. We rigged a flag attached to the post sticking up so that other skiers would know something was there. I could picture very quickly in my mind landing on that post and have it going right through my stomach and out my back.

One winter, when I was attending Ricks College in Rexburg, Idaho, my roommates and I decided to have some fun hooky bobbing behind the car. One roommate Barry Whittaker had a speedy Chevy with a big engine, so we decided to see how fast we could hang on the bumper sliding down the ice and snow-packed roads. We drove a little out of town where there was a beautiful stretch of ice and snow-packed straight highway. Two of us grabbed the back bumper as Barry took off. He got up to about 65 miles an hour when we started seeing some dry patches of road zipping by our feet. We tried screaming at him to stop, but he couldn't hear us. Fearing we would hit a massive dry patch of road, and our boots would no longer be sliding on the ice, and we would have been dragged to death on the road, so we let go of the bumper. We were gliding along on the ice and snow-packed highway going 65 miles an hour with nothing to hold to maintain our balance. We saw dry patches of road zip by our feet. We both hit a big one and went tumbling down the road at breakneck speed. As Barry was driving the car, he saw us let go and pulled over a little to the side as we both went tumbling past him. Amazingly neither of us had broken a single bone. We decided to do it in town on the solid snow-packed and icy roads. We were only going probably 25miles an hour when I saw the reflection of police overhead lights on the bumper of the car. My roommate let go and slid off to the side and disappeared. I waited too long to let go and got busted by the cops and got a ticket. At least I lived to tell the tale!

I always loved rock climbing, but in my earlier years, I didn't have any equipment. My friend and I found a beautiful cliff up at Logan, Canyon. I felt confident I could make it to the top, which was about 125 ft. One mistake we made was we started too late in the day. I never knew until that day that going up was way more comfortable than going down. When you're climbing up, you can see what's above you and reach with your hands and pull yourself up. You can also see good small ledges for your feet. Although I was making excellent progress, the sun was starting to set, and I realized very soon I would be stuck on a cliff in total darkness. I was about halfway up the cliff when my friend yelled. I needed to come back down because it was almost dark. He had a better sense than me and had returned down before it got so dark. I was terrified at this point because I could not see any good handholds or places for my feet above me, and of course, it was impossible to see what was below me. I realized my only chance of getting off the cliff alive would be for him to go for help. My legs started to shake, and my arms were aching, and it seemed like it was several hours before rescuers arrived to save me.

The darker it got, the more certain I was that I would be falling to my death at any minute. To this day, I do not remember who had rescued me and how they got me down off that cliff in total darkness.

CPSIA information can be obtained
at www.ICGtesting.com
Printed in the USA
BVHW072313101121
621198BV00007B/713